D1398155

Visual Basic 6

PROGRAMMER'S REFERENCE
Second Edition

Dan Rahmel

Osborne/**McGraw-Hill**

Berkeley ▪ New York ▪ St. Louis ▪ San Francisco
Auckland ▪ Bogotá ▪ Hamburg ▪ London
Madrid ▪ Mexico City ▪ Milan ▪ Montreal
New Delhi ▪ Panama City ▪ Paris ▪ São Paulo
Singapore ▪ Sydney ▪ Tokyo ▪ Toronto

Osborne/**McGraw-Hill**
2600 Tenth Street
Berkeley, California 94710
U.S.A.

For information on translations or book distributors outside the U.S.A.,
or to arrange bulk purchase discounts for sales promotions, premiums, or
fund-raisers, please contact Osborne/**McGraw-Hill** at the above address.

Visual Basic 6 Programmer's Reference
Second Edition

Publisher   Brandon A. Nordin
Editor-in-Chief   Scott Rogers
Acquisitions Editor   Megg Bonar
Project Editor   Betsy Manini
Editorial Assistant   Stephane Thomas
Technical Editor   David Rahmel
Copy Editor   Jan Jue
Proofreader   Joe Sadusky
Indexer   Dan Rahmel
Computer Designer   Michelle Galicia, Peter F. Hancik
Illustrator   Sue Albert, Brian Wells, Beth Young
Series Design   Peter F. Hancik

12131415 DOC / DOC 019876543

ISBN 0-07-882576-8

I would like to dedicate this book to the unsung heroes at Microsoft who, though much maligned, have produced an Insanely Great family of programming products.

About the Author

Dan Rahmel is a Visual Basic programmer with over 13 years of experience designing and implementing information systems and deploying mid-sized client/server systems using Visual Basic and Visual FoxPro. He has authored several books including *Teach Yourself Database Programming with Visual Basic in 24 Hours*, *Developing Client-Server Applications with Visual Basic*, and *Server Scripts with Visual JavaScript*, and is a regular contributor to *DBMS*, *Internet Advisor*, and *American Programmer* magazines.

CONTENTS

viii   Contents

x Contents

ACKNOWLEDGMENTS

Writing this book has been extremely enjoyable due to the contents of the book itself and the people I had the pleasure of working with. I often have wanted just this book, organized with quick examples and powerful index. Because of the amazing sales of the previous edition, I was able to take the extra time to make substantial new additions such as the How-To sections that I thought would make the book even more useful.

Combining the creation of the book with the superior Osborne staff often made the difficult seem easy. I'd like to thank the people on the Osborne staff with whom I often interacted (Megg Bonar, Betsy Manini, Jan Jue, and Stephane Thomas) and all the others who had to work tirelessly in production and editing to produce the book.

I'd like to thank my parents (Ron and Marie), siblings (David and Darlene), and friends (David Rahmel, Greg Mickey, Ted Ehr, Don Murphy, Ed Gildred, Juan Leonffu, Weld O'Connor, Thomas Rommell) for their unconditional support. To David Rahmel, who made fantastic suggestions on how to improve the book and actively took part in shaping the new edition, my many thanks.

Most of all, I'd like to thank the reader. By buying this book, you make it possible for all of us in the book industry to labor to produce good work. When pulling the long hours to complete a book, knowing that every little improvement will help your audience is what really makes the difference. Thanks.

INTRODUCTION

Welcome to the new edition of the *Visual Basic 6 Programmer's Reference*. This book contains reference information for the Visual Basic/VBA/VB Script family of products. The book generally assumes some programming experience, but if you're new to programming, you will most likely find this book invaluable. I have tried to provide extensive cross-references within the book.

If you know the general type of functionality you need, following the **See Also references** or other aids in the text will lead you to your exact topic. For any reference book, an introduction is crucially important because this is typically the only place in the book where a reader will actually sit and read. The rest of the time spent with a reference book is usually for quick lookup. The **Introduction** sets the tone for how the book can be used. I have written this book with the idea of making it extremely usable for programming projects.

The most unique feature of this book is the **Immediate Window examples** provided with each reference command. Seldom does a programmer want to know about a Visual Basic command for random curiosity. I want to know how to use the command, so I constructed the book with this philosophy in mind. With each term is an example that can be entered and executed immediately.

This concept has been expanded in the new edition with the **How-To sections** you'll find in Part II. These show step-by-step examples of common operations that you always seem to perform, but can't quite remember the exact method of implementation. Now you can just jump to the proper section and see the framework.

Another great feature of the book is the inclusion of **Object Diagrams** in Part IV. Object diagrams provided by Microsoft and replicated in most other books show a jumble of objects and collections. It is often difficult to tell which shape in the diagram denotes a single object versus a collection. Not so in my diagrams. Each diagram shows only a single level of the object model. Collections are obvious both by their appearance (like a deck of stacked cards) and the listing of the plural collection name followed by the singular object name shown below in parentheses.

I hope that you find these object models an invaluable reference when creating Visual Basic/VBA projects. Object models are becoming almost more important to a project than the actual programming language. For this reason, any improvements that can be made in understanding and referencing the object model (whether it's for Excel, PowerPoint, or any system) should be embraced.

Everyone looks up topics in a different way. If you don't find something listed under the heading you expected, please make a note of it and send us the information. That way, the next revision of the book can be even better.

I hope you find this book as useful as the people at Coherent Data (www.coherentdata.com/cscentral) and Hobby Planet (www.hobbyplanet.com) already have. I also hope you'll provide feedback with any suggestions you have or mistakes you find. We have a page on our Web site dedicated to taking your suggestions. Please stop by.

Part I
Overview of VB, VBA, and VB Script

The Basic language has been evolving for almost 30 years. Much of the code that was written on earlier versions of Basic (such as MS-Basic, AppleSoft, Qbasic, QuickBasic, and so on) will execute with very little modification. Line numbers and GoTo statements of the past have been mostly discarded for the subroutine/function model that is currently in use.

There are approximately 250 commands and functions available in the Visual Basic (VB) language. The language also supports object-oriented programming access through the use of dot (.) commands to navigate the object hierarchy. Visual Basic, for good reason, does not support multiple inheritance as do other languages such as C++. Because Visual Basic does not support this programming construct, its object programs are far easier to understand and debug.

In the near future, the Visual Basic language will probably expand little, if at all. Microsoft has been increasing the functionality available on the Visual Basic systems primarily through their increasingly robust object models (see Part IV). In fact, some functions that used to be included in the language itself have been moved into a particular object (such as the Err object).

New Visual Basic 6 Elements

The most recent update to Visual Basic, Version 6, has added a number of features that make it more powerful. Among these new features are the numerous enhancements to the development system and 22 new language commands. Most of the new technology is simply a refinement of features included in Visual Basic 5. However, each new feature will save programmers numerous hours of development.

New Features

The development environment for VB 6 includes a number of new features. Primary among them are the new integration of a comprehensive, reusable Data Environment and the Data Report generator. While the Data Access Objects (DAO) model is still included in VB 6, Microsoft is making ActiveX Data Objects (ADO) the common way of accessing data sources on the Windows platform. ADO is already the standard method of database access from Active Server Pages.

Visual Basic 6 adds new technology including

- **Data Environment**   This design-time environment allows the creation of shareable and reusable data objects. Data environments are saved in a separate file (with a DSR file extension). A data environment can hold Connection and Command objects that can be used with ADO or bound to ADO controls.

- **Data Report**   This report generator is similar to the report generator included with Microsoft Access that allows drag-and-drop creation of reports from any data source including hierarchical recordsets. Reports can be printed or exported as HTML documents.

- **ActiveX Data Objects (ADO)**   This new data objects replacement for DAO and Remote Data Objects (RDO) is also supported in Visual Studio 6.0 and Active Server Pages. See the ADO section in Part IV.

- **ADO Data Control**   This new data control can be bound to ADO data-aware controls (including text boxes, list boxes, combo boxes, and so on).

- **Query Designer and Database Designer**   These database development tools enable simplified visual wizard creation of queries and databases. Note that the Query Designer and Database Designer are only available in the Enterprise Edition of VB 6.

- **Hierarchical data grid control**   The new FlexGrid can display data from recordset data sources including hierarchical recordsets in a grid format. Data displayed in the control cannot be edited like the traditional DataGrid control.

- **Data View editor**   This global data source library allows browsing of data sources for tables, views, and stored procedures. It features drag-and-drop support for data environments.

- **Data Object Wizard**   This automates the creation and management of ActiveX objects for multitier deployment that provide custom access to data sources.

- **Data Repeater control**   This control acts like a repeating frame for data-aware controls and can display multiple records within a form.

- **File System Objects**   File objects provide complete access to files much like traditional VB commands. Objects are streamlined and provide a standardized way for accessing files that is available from VB, Visual Basic for Applications (VBA), or VB Script.

- **Format objects**   Conversion objects that can sit between a data set and bound controls that allow two-way conversion.

- **Ability to pass arrays**   VB 6 finally allows a complete array to be passed or received by a function.

- **Public passing of User-defined Types**   Variable types (defined with the Type...End Type keywords) can now be passed between Public methods.

- **CreateObject remote enhancements**   The CreateObject function accepts new parameters that allow the object to be instantiated on a remote machine.

The primary new objects, such as the ActiveX Data Objects (ADO) and File System Objects, are detailed in Part IV.

New Language Commands

Microsoft has further refined the Visual Basic language by adding new commands to allow for precision Type setting, formatting, event manipulation, and other functions. Most of these new commands will be included in the new version of VBA that will ship with the next edition of Microsoft Office.

The new commands include

AddressOf	FormatDateTime	MonthName
CallByName	FormatNumber	Option Private
DefDate	FormatPercent	RaiseEvent
DefDec	Friend	Replace
Enum	IMEStatus	Round
Filter	InStrRev	Split
FormatCurrency	Join	StrReverse
		WeekdayName

Differences Among the Languages

Visual Basic and VBA use the same central language engine. The differences between the two languages are extremely minor, such as the lack of a LoadPicture command in VBA. The only commands missing between the two implementations are those based on the environment that they run within.

VB Script differs greatly from the other Visual Basic programming languages. The VB Script language was created as a subset of the Visual Basic language with the intention of making the VB Script language engine small, simple, and easy to port to various machine implementations and microprocessors. Because the VB Script language needed to download in real time across a network, whether on a web page or within an Outlook/Exchange form, security was another primary factor to take into account.

VB Script, therefore, lacks some commands that might be difficult to implement in various environments (such as the Timer command), functions that could be accomplished using other means (trimming the number of string functions, for example), and leaving out all disk access capabilities. For a complete list of commands that are missing from the VB Script language, see the "VB Script Missing Commands" section later in this part of the book.

Three Development Systems

Visual Basic is now available across a broad range of development systems and applications. The standardization of the Visual Basic engine has done a great deal to make the various Visual Basic and Visual Basic for Applications (VBA) implementations provide the same general features, look, and feel.

Visual Basic Environment

The Visual Basic environment is a complete development environment with form designer, tool palettes, debugger, and project management capabilities. If you are unfamiliar with the Visual Basic environment, it is recommended that you purchase one of the many fine books on learning Visual Basic. Microsoft did as much as possible to make both the Visual Basic and VBA environments in their current implementations look and feel as alike as possible.

Visual Basic and VBA differ most not in their language implementations, which are nearly identical, but in the controls included with the system. Figure I-1 shows all of the controls that are included by default in the Visual Basic Control palette. These are only the components that are on the simplified palette. This palette does not have other controls included with the VB system, such as the Windows Custom Controls (tab strips, toolbars, clocks, and so on), data access controls (data-aware grid control, data-aware list box, and so on), and extra user interface components.

You might notice that the two most prominent inclusions in this palette that are missing from the VBA palette are the DataControl and the Timer items. Graphical data access in VBA applications must be done with direct coding to the Data Access Objects (DAO), Remote Data Objects (RDO), and ActiveX Data Objects (ADO)—see the appropriate section in Part IV—or through Microsoft Access. Time-based applications must use the Timer function to manually monitor time progression.

It is usually much easier to use the keyboard to access key commands. For this reason, a table of the most frequently used keycodes is included. Most operations in the Visual Basic

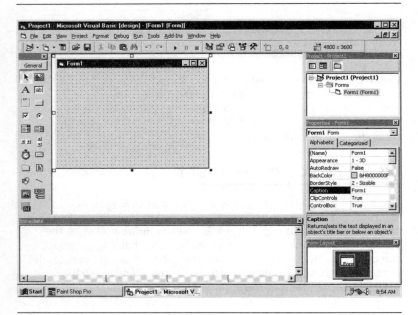

Figure I-1.   Visual Basic Control palette

environment have a keyboard equivalent. Table 1-1 shows the keyboard shortcuts for particular operations that are often needed repeatedly.

Visual Basic for Applications Environment

The Visual Basic for Applications (VBA) environment provides a complete project-based development system for creating VBA applications. Figure I-2 displays the environment that may be accessed by pressing ALT-F11 in Excel, Word, PowerPoint, or Project. It is also available under the Macro menu. Access 97 contains its own specialized environment that mirrors VBA, but includes additional special features for database access.

The left window in the VBA environment shows the current Project window. Within the Project window will be displayed all of the current open documents. Within the documents, objects, modules, user forms, and references may exist. If a macro is recorded, it is either added to the document itself or to a code module. The figure

Key	Description
F2	Object Browser
F4	Show properties
F5	Compile and execute
CTRL-F5	Start with full compile
F8	Step into
SHIFT-F8	Step over
F9	Set breakpoint
SHIFT-F9	Quick watch
CTRL-G	Show Immediate window

Table I-1. Frequently Used Keycodes

Object Browser icon

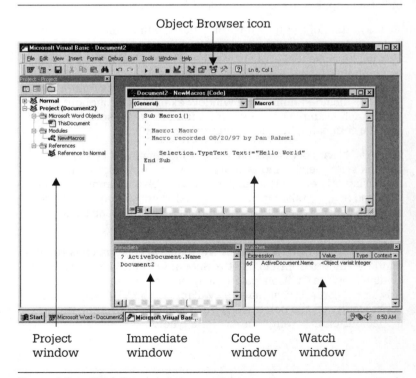

Project window   Immediate window   Code window   Watch window

Figure I-2. VBA Programming environment

shows a single module created in Word automatically by recording a macro.

Double-clicking on a module item will display a Code window. The Code window displays all of the code associated with a module or a user form. The two combo boxes displayed at the top of the window determine what procedure is shown in the window. The left combo box is used to select the current object (forms, control, and so on) or can be set to "(General)" for the general procedures not attached to a specific object. Since a Code module has no objects, the window will always display "(General)" in a module. The right combo box is used to select the procedure or event code to be shown in the actual window.

The gray area on the left of the Code window will show any current breakpoint and the position of the current execution line when VBA is in the debugging mode. Clicking in the gray area that is parallel to a code line will set a breakpoint on that line. A red bullet will appear in the area to identify a set breakpoint.

At the bottom of the screen you'll notice the Immediate window. This window is one of the most powerful aspects of the VBA system, because it allows entry of nearly any Visual Basic command for immediate execution. This enables you to test small parts of code and new commands and see the results right away. We have included Immediate window examples throughout this book. Each example demonstrates a fundamental aspect of the specific command, function, property, or method.

The Watch window is used to display information on particular variables. For debugging purposes, the Watch window can be used to consistently examine a small set of variables. Changes can be watched as they take place. Conditional watches may also be set that will cause a break to occur when the variable reaches a particular value.

Adding a User Form to a project will display the Form construction window and the Controls palette. Shown in Figure I-3, any controls available on the Controls palette may be inserted into the form. Additional controls that may be available to the VBA system but not currently on the palette may be added by clicking the right mouse button in an empty area of the palette.

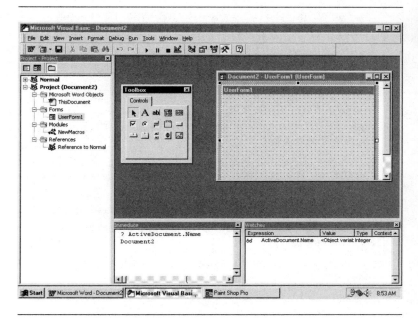

Figure I-3.   VBA Forms and Controls palette

What Can't VBA Do?

With all of the new features in VBA, people often wonder what extra capabilities are provided by the complete Visual Basic environment. Visual Basic offers significant additional features including

- Compilation of an EXE (although there is an Access run time now available)

- Creation of ActiveX DLLs (required for use when creating Active Server components and for use with Microsoft Transaction Server)

- Database tools such as the Data Manager

- Creation of OLE Automation servers

- Production of ActiveX Documents

- Creation of ActiveX Controls

- Fully compiled for faster execution (although you cannot create a stand-alone **EXE**)
- Support for multiple projects
- Source code control through Visual SourceSafe
- Creation of reusable VB components
- Construction of class files
- Data Control and data-aware controls (such as TextBox, Grid, ListBox, ComboBox)
- Numerous additional controls, such as disk access controls (DirListBox, DriveListBox, and so on) and user interface controls (status bar, toolbar, and so on)
- Support of data environments for shared database access
- Data reports (except using the report builder included in Microsoft Access)
- Creation of data-aware controls (data consumers) for data controls
- Call-back procedures for WinAPI calls that require a procedure reentry point

Many users have no need for these additional features. For professional-level development, however, using the full Visual Basic system is essential. Additionally, any VBA applications require the Office application itself to execute. This adds to memory and hard disk space overhead for the deployed system.

VB Script Outlook or Internet Explorer

The VB Script environment is far different from VBA. Rather than being an emerging standard environment, VB Script programming environments are diverging as the language is included in increasingly varied applications. The most dominant VB Script environment is the Outlook groupware application included with Microsoft Office.

The Outlook design environment is shown when an item is placed in Design mode. The normally invisible development tabs are displayed, and controls may be inserted onto the tab form. In the following illustration, the tabs that have titles enclosed in parentheses ( ) are currently invisible to the user. Design mode is the only place from which accessing the VB Script environment is possible. Selecting the View Code option under the Form menu will display the Scripting window.

System   User modifiable
tabbed page   tabbed page

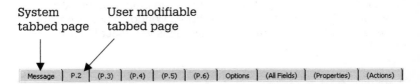

Any code written or any change made in the VB Script environment is stored with the particular form being displayed. This form can be stored in an Exchange server, where all of the code and controls will be kept with it. An Outlook user accessing the groupware server will then receive the form as well as any additions that have been made to it.

The Outlook Scripting window shown in the following inllustration is an extremely rudimentary text-editing window. Code is entered into the window and may be executed in a way similar to the Immediate window by selecting the Run option from the Script menu.

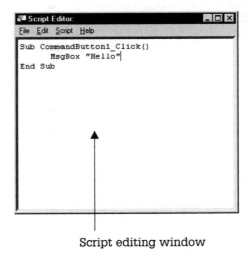

Script editing window

Note that VB Script does not include any of the common Constant values that are so often used in VBA. VB Script can only accept the actual values of the constants. This limitation stems from the intention for VB Script to run anywhere. Bringing along large files of Constants would severely limit its portability.

The other VB Script environments are rapidly evolving. Internet Explorer moved through a dramatic change from Version 3 to Version 4. The newest VB Script edition, Windows Scripting Host, is merely a command line at this time. This will most likely change as it becomes a full-featured tool.

Windows Scripting Host

With the introduction of Windows 98, VB Script will be included in the system itself. Known as Windows Scripting Host (WSH), it is already available for download and installation on Windows 95 and Windows NT. It will also be included as a part of Windows NT 5.0.

WSH uses the actual VB Script engine, so all of the VB Script commands denoted in this manual will be completely functional as part of the operating system (OS). The operating system will have an object model that allows control of network, disk operation, and other processes. Microsoft has decided not to finalize the object model for the OS until more progress has been made on Windows NT 5.0. Check the Microsoft BackOffice web page for the latest information on this technology (http://www.microsoft.com/products/backoffice/).

Object Browser

The Object Browser is provided as part of the Visual Basic and VBA environments. It can be used to examine the object of any OLE object models installed on the Windows system. The Object Browser is not included with the current version of Outlook or Internet Explorer, although their object models can be accessed through the browser.

In Figure I-4, you'll see the Object Browser that is available under the View menu, from an icon on the toolbar, or by pressing F2. The Object Browser contains three panes, the Classes pane, the Members pane, and the Search pane. The Libraries combo box shows what current libraries are being shown in the various panes.

Objects and collections   Methods and properties

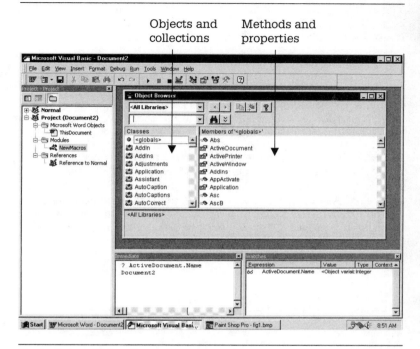

Figure I-4.   Object Browser

The *Classes* pane displays an alphabetical list of all the available objects and collections. In Part IV of this book, you will find the complete Object Model diagrams for all of the Office applications as well as other components. Using these diagrams in conjunction with the Object Browser should enable you to create nearly any object-based solution. Clicking on an object or collection in the Class pane will automatically change the members shown in the Members pane.

The *Members* pane contains all of the properties and methods for an object class (object or collection) shown in the Classes pane. Methods have an icon that looks like a speeding box. Properties have the traditional icon that represents properties. Clicking on a particular member will fill the bottom of the dialog box with the calling conventions of that member. If the member is a property, it will detail the data type held in that property. A method will show any values that it requires to be passed as arguments and any values it will return.

The *Search* pane is hidden until you activate a search. To the right of the Search button (the button with the binoculars icon), the double-down arrow icon expands the Search pane.

All of the objects shown in the Object Browser are the object libraries assigned to the current project. This does not mean that these are the only libraries registered with your system. For example, Excel defaults to adding the Excel object libraries to the project, but doesn't add the Word libraries, because most people will have no use for them in an Excel project.

To add other libraries to the project, select the References menu option. Depending on the application you are using, this will appear on different menus. The References dialog box is shown in Figure I-5. All of the boxes with checks denote the object libraries currently available to your project. By selecting others, you can add them to your project. They will become available in the Libraries combo box of the Object Browser.

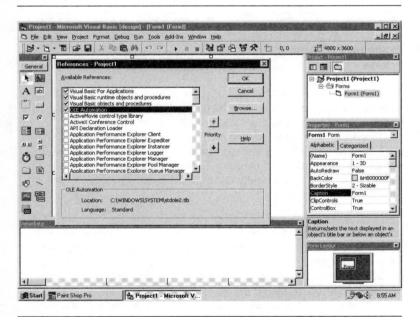

Figure I-5.   Object references available to the project

Error Chart

Visual Basic allows you to identify, through a trap, most of the errors that occur in your program. Writing a comprehensive debugging routine or using a product such as VB/Rig to create error checking routines will save your users a great deal of time and save you debugging. Technical support calls are very difficult to handle without a clear understanding of which problem actually occurred.

The following chart lists all the trappable errors and the descriptions that will be returned by the Error$( ) function. You can use the Error$( ) function within your program to provide a description of the error that occurs.

Error Number	Description
3	Return without GoSub
5	Invalid procedure call or argument
6	Overflow
7	Out of memory
9	Subscript out of range
10	This array is fixed or temporarily locked
11	Division by zero
13	Type mismatch
14	Out of string space
16	Expression too complex
17	Can't perform requested operation
18	User interrupt occurred
20	Resume without error
28	Out of stack space
35	Sub or Function not defined
47	Too many DLL application clients
48	Error in loading DLL
49	Bad DLL calling convention
51	Internal error
52	Bad file name or number
53	File not found
54	Bad file mode
55	File already open
57	Device I/O error

Error Number	Description
58	File already exists
59	Bad record length
61	Disk full
62	Input past end of file
63	Bad record number
67	Too many files
68	Device unavailable
70	Permission denied
71	Disk not ready
74	Can't rename with different drive
75	Path/File access error
76	Path not found
91	Object variable or With block variable not set
92	For loop not initialized
93	Invalid pattern string
94	Invalid use of Null
96	Unable to sink events of object because the object is already firing events to the maximum number of event receivers that it supports
97	Cannot call friend function on object that is not an instance of defining class
321	Invalid file format
322	Can't create necessary temporary file
325	Invalid format in resource file
380	Invalid property value
381	Invalid property array index
382	Set not supported at run time
383	Set not supported (read-only property)
385	Need property array index
387	Set not permitted
393	Get not supported at run time
394	Get not supported (write-only property)
422	Property not found
423	Property or method not found
424	Object required
429	ActiveX component can't create object
430	Class doesn't support Automation

Error Number	Description
432	File name or class name not found during Automation operation
438	Object doesn't support this property or method
440	Automation error
442	Connection to type library or object library for remote process has been lost. Press OK for dialog box to remove reference
443	Automation object does not have a default value
445	Object doesn't support this action
446	Object doesn't support named arguments
447	Object doesn't support current locale setting
448	Named argument not found
449	Argument not optional
450	Wrong number of arguments or invalid property assignment
451	Object not a collection
452	Invalid ordinal
453	Specified DLL function not found
454	Code resource not found
455	Code resource lock error
457	This key is already associated with an element of this collection
458	Variable uses an Automation type not supported in Visual Basic
459	Object or class does not support the set of events
460	Invalid clipboard format
481	Invalid picture
482	Printer error
735	Can't save file to TEMP
744	Search text not found
746	Replacements too long
31001	Out of memory
31004	No object
31018	Class is not set
31027	Unable to activate object
31032	Unable to create embedded object
31036	Error saving to file
31037	Error loading from file

Command Groups

Finding the correct command or group of commands to accomplish a particular task is often very difficult. To aid you in finding the functions that you need, here is a reference that provides groupings into the following common areas: Financial, Disk Access, Mathematical, Date and Time, and Strings. After you have located one of the commands you need, the See Also references included with each command will guide you to similar commands.

Financial

Here are the Visual Basic financial commands:

CCur	FV	NPer	PV
DDB	IPmt	NPV	Rate
DefCur	IRR	PMT	SLN
FormatCurrency*	MIRR	PPmt	SYD

Disk Access

These are the Visual Basic disk-access commands:

ChDir	FreeFile	MkDir
ChDrive	Get	Name
Close	GetAttr	Open
CurDir, CurDir$	Input #	Print #
Dir, Dir$	Input, Input$	Put
Environ, Environ$	InputB, InputB$	Reset
EOF	Kill	RmDir
FileAttr	Line Input #	Seek
FileCopy	Loc	SetAttr
FileDateTime	Lock...Unlock	Spc
FileLen	LOF	Width #
		Write #

(See also SSO in Part IV.)

*New to Visual Basic 6

Mathematical

Here are Visual Basic's mathematical commands:

*	\	DefDbl	FormatNumber*	Mod
+	^	DefDec*		Not
-	And	DefInt	FormatPercentage*	Oct, Oct$
/	CDbl	DefLng		
<=	CDec	DefSng	Hex, Hex$	Or
<>	CInt	Eqv	Imp	Rando mize
=	CLng	Exp	Int	
>	Cos	False	IsNumeric	Rnd
>=	CSng	Fix	Log	Round*
				Sgn

Date and Time

These are the Visual Basic commands related to date and time:

CVDate	DateValue	Month	TimeSerial
Date	Day	MonthName*	TimeValue
Date, Date$	DefDate*	Now	WeekDay
DateAdd	FormatDateTime*	Second	WeekdayName*
DateDiff	Hour	Time	Year
DatePart	IsDate	Time$	
DateSerial	Minute	Timer	

Strings

These are the Visual Basic commands pertaining to strings:

&	Instr	Mid, Mid$	Split*
+	InStrRev*	Option Compare	Str, Str$
Chr, Chr$	Join*		StrComp
ChrB	LCase, LCase$	Replace*	String, String$
ChrW	Left, Left$	Right, Right$	StrReverse*
CStr	Len	RSet	Tab
DefStr	LenB	RTrim, RTrim$	Trim, Trim$
Filter*	LSet		UCase, UCase$
Format, Format$	LTrim, LTrim$	Space, Space$	Val

*New to Visual Basic 6

Display

These are Visual Basic's display commands:

Circle	Line	QBColor
Cls	PaintPicture	PSet
Draw	Print	RGB

VB Script Missing Commands

VB Script is a subset of the entire Visual Basic instruction set. Most of the key Visual Basic commands are included in VB Script. Noticeably excluded are all disk access and financial functions. These commands were removed for security and space reasons.

As VB Script grows in popularity and becomes incorporated into the system, understanding the functions that are missing will be increasingly important before a new programming project is undertaken. Planning around missing capabilities can then be accomplished. Most of the missing functionality can either be created by using a number of the existent commands together or by using a supplemental object that supplies the missing operation.

Active Server Pages, Microsoft's dynamic web server component, uses objects in exactly this way to extend the VB Script included. A Disk Access Object, for example, provides complete file features. In this manner, each VB Script environment can include the necessary custom features without having to rewrite or directly extend the language.

!	Choose
#Const	Close
#if...#else...#endif	Command
AddressOf	CommitTrans
AppActivate	CurDir, CurDir$
Beep	CVar
CallByName	CVDate
CDec	CVErr
ChDir	Date, Date$
ChDrive	DDB

I

Declare
DefBool
DefByte
DefCur
DefDate
DefDbl
DefDec
DefInt
DefLng
DefObj
DefSng
DefStr
DefVar
DeleteSetting
Dir, Dir$
DoEvents
End
Enum
Environ, Environ$
EOF
Err object
Error
Error, Error$
Event
FileAttr
FileCopy
FileDateTime
FileLen
Format, Format$
FreeFile
FreeLocks
Friend
FV
Get
GetAllSettings
GetAttr
GetAutoServerSettings
GetSetting
Global
GoSub...Return
GoTo
IIf

IMEStatus
Implements
Input #
Input, Input$
InputB, InputB$
IPmt
IRR
IsError
IsMissing
Kill
Let
Like
Line Input #
Load
LoadPicture
LoadResData
LoadResPicture
LoadResString
Loc
Lock...Unlock
LOF
LSet
MIRR
MkDir
Name
NPer
NPV
On Error...
On...GoSub
On...GoTo
Open
Option BaseOption Compare
Option Private
Partition
PMT
PPmt
Print #
Property Get
Property Let
Property Set
Put
PV

QBColor

RaiseEvent

Rate

Reset

Resume

Return

RmDir

Rollback

RSet

SavePicture

SaveSetting

Seek

SendKeys

SetAttr

SetDefaultWorkspace

Shell

SLN

Spc

Static

Stop

StrConv

SYD

Tab

Type...End Type

Unload

Val

Width #

With...End With

Write #

Part II
Programming System Information and How-To Examples

II

ASCII Chart

While working on a complex programming project, you will often need to directly access characters in the format in which the computer stores them. ASCII is the standard for the relation

23

between a number value and a character type. Each character consists of a single byte, or 8 bits.

The following ASCII chart shows the values of all the characters between 0 and 255. The chart includes the decimal and hexadecimal values of the characters, as well as a basic character name and title of the character. Some of the characters cannot be displayed as characters, but are instead used as control characters (such as #7, the bell). In these cases the character (Char) column remains empty, and the Title column describes the character used at this value.

Additionally, the values for the characters within the newer Unicode standard are included. Unicode represents each character as two bytes (16 bits) to accommodate the numerous extra characters of various non-English alphabets.

Decimal	Char	Hex	Decimal	Char	Hex
0		/x00	20		/x14
1		/x01	21		/x15
2		/x02	22		/x16
3		/x03	23		/x17
4		/x04	24		/x18
5		/x05	25		/x19
6		/x06	26		/x1A
7		/x07	27		/x1B
8		/x08	28		/x1C
9		/x09	29		/x1D
10		/x0A	30		/x1E
11		/x0B	31		/x1F
12		/x0C	32		/x20
13		/x0D	33	!	/x21
14		/x0E	34	"	/x22
15		/x0F	35	#	/x23
16		/x10	36	$	/x24
17		/x11	37	%	/x25
18		/x12	38	&	/x26
19		/x13	39	'	/x27

Decimal	Char	Hex	Decimal	Char	Hex
40	(	/x28	75	K	/x4B
41	)	/x29	76	L	/x4C
42	*	/x2A	77	M	/x4D
43	+	/x2B	78	N	/x4E
44	,	/x2C	79	O	/x4F
45	-	/x2D	80	P	/x50
46	.	/x2E	81	Q	/x51
47	/	/x2F	82	R	/x52
48	0	/x30	83	S	/x53
49	1	/x31	84	T	/x54
50	2	/x32	85	U	/x55
51	3	/x33	86	V	/x56
52	4	/x34	87	W	/x57
53	5	/x35	88	X	/x58
54	6	/x36	89	Y	/x59
55	7	/x37	90	Z	/x5A
56	8	/x38	91	[	/x5B
57	9	/x39	92	\	/x5C
58	:	/x3A	93	]	/x5D
59	;	/x3B	94	^	/x5E
60	<	/x3C	95	_	/x5F
61	=	/x3D	96	`	/x60
62	>	/x3E	97	a	/x61
63	?	/x3F	98	b	/x62
64	@	/x40	99	c	/x63
65	A	/x41	100	d	/x64
66	B	/x42	101	e	/x65
67	C	/x43	102	f	/x66
68	D	/x44	103	g	/x67
69	E	/x45	104	h	/x68
70	F	/x46	105	i	/x69
71	G	/x47	106	j	/x6A
72	H	/x48	107	k	/x6B
73	I	/x49	108	l	/x6C
74	J	/x4A	109	m	/x6D

II

Decimal	Char	Hex	Decimal	Char	Hex
110	n	/x6E	146	'	/x92
111	o	/x6F	147	"	/x93
112	p	/x70	148	"	/x94
113	q	/x71	149	•	/x95
114	r	/x72	150	–	/x96
115	s	/x73	151	—	/x97
116	t	/x74	152	˜	/x98
117	u	/x75	153	™	/x99
118	v	/x76	154	š	/x9A
119	w	/x77	155	›	/x9B
120	x	/x78	156	œ	/x9C
121	y	/x79	157	•	/x9D
122	z	/x7A	158	•	/x9E
123	{	/x7B	159	Ÿ	/x9F
124	|	/x7C	160		/xA0
125	}	/x7D	161	¡	/xA1
126	~	/x7E	162	¢	/xA2
127	•	/x7F	163	£	/xA3
128	•	/x80	164	¤	/xA4
129	•	/x81	165	¥	/xA5
130	,	/x82	166	¦	/xA6
131	ƒ	/x83	167	§	/xA7
132	„	/x84	168	¨	/xA8
133	…	/x85	169	©	/xA9
134	†	/x86	170	ª	/xAA
135	‡	/x87	171	«	/xAB
136	ˆ	/x88	172	¬	/xAC
137	‰	/x89	173	–	/xAD
138	Š	/x8A	174	®	/xAE
139	‹	/x8B	175	¯	/xAF
140	Œ	/x8C	176	°	/xB0
141	•	/x8D	177	±	/xB1
142	•	/x8E	178	²	/xB2
143	•	/x8F	179	³	/xB3
144	•	/x90	180	´	/xB4
145	'	/x91	181	µ	/xB5

Decimal	Char	Hex	Decimal	Char	Hex
182	¶	/xB6	219	Û	/xDB
183	·	/xB7	220	Ü	/xDC
184	‚	/xB8	221	Ý	/xDD
185	¹	/xB9	222	Þ	/xDE
186	º	/xBA	223	ß	/xDF
187	»	/xBB	224	à	/xE0
188	¼	/xBC	225	á	/xE1
189	½	/xBD	226	â	/xE2
190	¾	/xBE	227	ã	/xE3
191	¿	/xBF	228	ä	/xE4
192	À	/xC0	229	å	/xE5
193	Á	/xC1	230	æ	/xE6
194	Â	/xC2	231	ç	/xE7
195	Ã	/xC3	232	è	/xE8
196	Ä	/xC4	233	é	/xE9
197	Å	/xC5	234	ê	/xEA
198	Æ	/xC6	235	ë	/xEB
199	Ç	/xC7	236	ì	/xEC
200	È	/xC8	237	í	/xED
201	É	/xC9	238	î	/xEE
202	Ê	/xCA	239	ï	/xEF
203	Ë	/xCB	240	ð	/xF0
204	Ì	/xCC	241	ñ	/xF1
205	Í	/xCD	242	ò	/xF2
206	Î	/xCE	243	ó	/xF3
207	Ï	/xCF	244	ô	/xF4
208	Ð	/xD0	245	õ	/xF5
209	Ñ	/xD1	246	ö	/xF6
210	Ò	/xD2	247	÷	/xF7
211	Ó	/xD3	248	ø	/xF8
212	Ô	/xD4	249	ù	/xF9
213	Õ	/xD5	250	ú	/xFA
214	Ö	/xD6	251	û	/xFB
215	×	/xD7	252	ü	/xFC
216	Ø	/xD8	253	ý	/xFD
217	Ù	/xD9	254	þ	/xFE
218	Ú	/xDA	255	ÿ	/xFF

II

Hungarian Notation

Understanding complex code can be a difficult task, especially if it was written by someone else or even yourself some time ago. Any technique that can aid in simplifying code can be a great help, particularly when you're attempting to debug an application.

A programmer, Charles Simonyi, invented a technique known as Hungarian notation. Hungarian notation simply specifies that a prefix is added to variables and objects. This prefix denotes the type of variable or object being addressed. For example, the name property of a form may use the standard three-character prefix "frm" followed by the first letter of the object capitalized. Therefore, the central form may be named frmMain. In code, when the programmer encounters text such as frmMain.Show( ), there is no confusion about the type of object being addressed.

If applied consistently, Hungarian notation can greatly increase the readability of your code. It can also considerably simplify team development. The following is a list of the prefixes for the most common user interface items and variables/structures. The prefix, usually three letters, is followed by a generic object name as an example.

User Interface Items	Sample name	User Interface Items	Sample name
Animated Button	aniControl	Item	itmMyitem
Checkbox	chkControl	Label	lblControl
Class	clsClassname	Line	linControl
ComboBox	cboControl	Listbox	lstControl
CommandButton	cmdControl	Menu	mnuFile
DataControl	datControl	OLEControl	oleControl
DataGrid	grdMygrid	OptionButton	optControl
DirListBox	dlbControl	PictureBox	pbxControl
DriveListBox	drbControl	Remote Data Control	rdcControl
FileListBox	flbControl		
Form	frmForm	Shape	shpControl
Frame	fraControl	TextBox	txtControl
HScrollbar	hsbControl	Timer	tmrControl
Image	imgControl	VScrollbar	vsbControl

Variables and Structures	Sample name	Variables and Structures	Sample name
Byte	bNumber	Double	dNumber
Character string	strString	Flag Long	flFlag
		Flag Short	fsFlag
Constant	cName	Integer	iNumber
Currency	curCurrency	Return code	rcReturnvalue
Date/Time	dtDate	Single	sNumber

How To Code Examples

This How-To section provides some examples of problems commonly faced by programmers. By examining a simplified but complete example of a common function, you will be able to quickly construct the code that you need.

The following examples are as general as possible, so you can modify them to your particular circumstances. For brevity, most of the code does not provide lengthy comments or remarks. Examine the descriptions and Immediate window examples of individual commands in Part III for a complete explanation of the use of each particular command function used in the code.

- Reading a file into an array
- Adding data to an array from a database
- Filling a combo box from an array
- Drawing an analog clock
- Enabling user setting of the background color of the form
- Creating a browse file and checking if the file exists
- Using the Windows API to draw on a picture
- Using the Windows API to play a sound file
- Sending e-mail through Outlook
- Centering a form
- Accepting EXE-passed parameters
- Displaying a list of fonts in each style

Reading a File into an Array

Reading data files of various formats is a common need for Visual Basic programs. VB has the built-in capability of reading-in comma-delimited text files. Most spreadsheets can output a sheet in common text file format with comma delimiters (the CSV file extension).

1. Enter the following text and save it as a file named **vbr1.csv** in the root directory.

```
Joe,Girsh,10
John,Smith,11
Phil,Stewart,12
Dirk,Lumper,13
```

2. Create a new project in Visual Basic.

3. Add a command button and set the Name property of the button to **cmdReadFile.**

4. Enter the following code into the Click event of the button:

```
Private Sub cmdReadFile_Click()
    Dim a$(100), b$(100)
    Dim c(100) As Integer, i As Integer

    Open "c:\vbr1.csv" For Input As #1
    i = 0
    Do While Not EOF(1)
        Input #1, a$(i), b$(i), c(i)
        i = i + 1
    Loop
    MsgBox i & " entries loaded."
    Close #1
End Sub
```

5. Execute the application.

When executing, the code will load the information from the text file into the array. The example doesn't actually do anything with the data because this will vary from project to project. Note that the third variable, *c*, automatically loads the number for that column into a typed field (in this case an Integer). This same method may be used for other types, such as Date/Time.

Adding Data to an Array from a Database

Accessing the data within a database through the query interface can provide a powerful way of sorting or retrieving quantities of up-to-date information. Often, however, working with a small amount of data can be much more accessible if you read the data into a memory array. This example provides a self-expanding array that uses the ADO objects to load information from the Northwind database included with Visual Basic.

1. Create a new project in Visual Basic.

2. Under the References dialog box, select the Microsoft ActiveX Data Objects Library option for the ADO example, or Microsoft DAO Object Library for the DAO example.

3. Add a command button and set the Name property of the button to **cmdReadDB**.

4. Enter the following code into the Click event of the button.

ADO Example

```
Private Sub cmdReadDB_Click()
Dim myRS As New ADODB.Recordset
Dim myArray()

    ReDim myArray(0)
    ' Open Northwind sample
    Const ConnectStr = _
        "PROVIDER=Microsoft.Jet.OLEDB.3.51;" & _
        "Data Source=nwind.mdb;"

    Set myRS = New ADODB.Recordset

    myRS.ActiveConnection = ConnectStr
    myRS.Open "Select * from customers"

    If myRS.BOF And myRS.EOF Then
        MsgBox "Recordset is empty!", 16, _
        "Empty recordset"
    Else
        Do Until myRS.EOF
            myArray(i) = myRS!ContactName
            ReDim Preserve myArray(UBound(myArray) + 1)
```

```
      myRS.MoveNext
         i = i + 1
      Loop
      MsgBox "Found " & i & " records"
      myRS.Close
   End If
   Set myRS = Nothing
End Sub
```

DAO Example

```
Private Sub cmdReadDB_Click()
   Dim myDB As Database, myRS As Recordset
   Dim myArray()

   ReDim myArray(0)
   Set myDB = OpenDatabase("nwind.mdb")
   Set myRS = myDB.OpenRecordset( _
         "Select * from customers")

   If myRS.BOF And myRS.EOF Then
      MsgBox "Recordset is empty!", 16, _
         "Empty recordset"
   Else
      Do Until myRS.EOF
         myArray(I) = myRS!ContactName
         ReDim Preserve myArray(UBound(myArray) + 1)
         myRS.MoveNext
         I = I + 1
      Loop
      MsgBox "Found " & I & " records"
      myRS.Close
   End If
   Set myRS = Nothing

End Sub
```

5. Execute the application.

Filling a Combo Box from an Array

Arrays are often used to hold a variety of information, particularly a list of items. Unlike other development systems such as Visual FoxPro, there is no direct way of displaying the contents of an array in any type of user interface component for user selection. Therefore, the VB programmer often has to transport array data into controls like the ComboBox.

II

1. Create a new project in Visual Basic.

2. Add a ComboBox control to the form, and set the Name property to **cboMyCombo**.

3. Add a command button and set the Name property of the button to **cmdMakeCombo**.

4. Enter the following code into the Click event of the button.

```
Private Sub MakeCombo_Click()
    Dim myArray(10)
    For I = 0 To 9
        myArray(I) = Rnd * 100
    Next

    For I = 0 To UBound(myArray) - 1

        cboMyCombo.AddItem myArray(I)
    Next I
End Sub
```

5. Execute the application.

Drawing an Analog Clock

The PictureBox control contains a complete drawing environment that can be used for graphic display. This clock example demonstrates graphic commands, using the timer, using trigonometric functions, and converting the hours/minutes/seconds to graphic coordinates.

1. Create a new project in Visual Basic.

2. Add a Timer control to the form.

3. Add a PictureBox control to the form, and set the Name property to **pbxClock.**

4. Create a new procedure to the form called **DrawHand**, and add the following code:

```
Public Sub DrawHand(cx, cy, num, rad)
    Const pi = 3.14159

    x = rad * Sin((num * pi) / 30)
    y = rad * Cos((num * pi) / 30)

    pbxClock.Line (cx, cy)-(cx + x, cy - y)
End Sub
```

5. Set the ScaleMode property of the picture control to 3 – Pixel.

6. Enter the following code into the Timer event of the Timer control:

```
Private Sub Timer1_Timer()
    Dim cx As Integer, cy As Integer
    Dim rad As Integer

    ' Define center and radius
    cx = 100: cy = 100
    rad = 80

    pbxClock.FillStyle = 0
    pbxClock.FillColor = RGB(255, 255, 0)
    pbxClock.Circle (cx, cy), rad, RGB(0, 0, 0)
    ' Reset FillStyle
    pbxClock.FillStyle = 1
```

```
      pbxClock.DrawWidth = 3
      DrawHand cx, cy, Hour(Now), rad * 0.6
      DrawHand cx, cy, Minute(Now), rad * 0.9
      pbxClock.DrawWidth = 1
      DrawHand cx, cy, Second(Now), rad
   End Sub
```

7. Set the Interval property of the Timer control to **1000** (so it will activate every second).

8. Execute the application.

Enabling User Setting of the Background Color

The common dialog boxes included in Visual Basic provide a number of widely used capabilities for dialog boxes, including color selection, file opening and saving, printing, and font selection. The color dialog box provides a complete color selection interface to return a color in RGB selected format. This example enables the user to select a color for the background color of the form.

1. Create a new project in Visual Basic.

2. Add the Microsoft Common Dialog Control to the project using the Components dialog box.

3. Add a command button and set the Name property of the button to **cmdSelectColor.**

4. Enter the following code into the Click event of the button:

```
Private Sub cmdSelectColor_Click()
    CommonDialog1.CancelError = False
    CommonDialog1.Color = RGB(0, 0, 255)
    CommonDialog1.Flags = cdlCCRGBInit
    CommonDialog1.ShowColor
    Form1.BackColor = CommonDialog1.Color
End Sub
```

5. Execute the application.

The example sets the color to blue as the default before the window is displayed. Note that it also turns off the error generation routine that activates an error if the user selects the Cancel button within the window.

Creating a Browse File and Checking If the File Exists

The common dialog box has a dialog box to allow the selection of files to open or save. This example displays the Open dialog box and allows the user to select either from the files with the DAT extension or from all files in general. The nature of the Open file dialog box allows the user to enter a filename by hand as well.

Once the file is selected and the user clicks the OK button, the program code checks if the file actually does exist and displays a dialog box to notify the user.

1. Create a new project in Visual Basic.

2. Add the Microsoft Common Dialog Control in the Components window.

3. Add a TextBox control and set the Name property of the control to **txtFileName.**

4. Add a command button and set the Name property of the button to **cmdBrowse.**

5. Enter the following code into the Click event of the button:

```
Private Sub cmdBrowse_Click()
    CommonDialog1.CancelError = False
    CommonDialog1.Flags = cdlOFNHideReadOnly
    CommonDialog1.Filter = _
    "All Files (*.*)|*.*|Data Files" & _
    " (*.dat)|*.dat"
    CommonDialog1.FilterIndex = 2
    CommonDialog1.ShowOpen
    If CommonDialog1.filename <> "" Then
        ' Check if file exists
        If Dir(CommonDialog1.filename) <> "" Then
            MsgBox "File Exists: " & _
            CommonDialog1.filename, vbInformation
        txtFileName = CommonDialog1.filename
```

```
            Else
                MsgBox "File Not Found", vbCritical
            End If
        End If
    End Sub
```

6. Execute the application.

The common dialog boxes can be used to specify exactly the types of files to filter and allow for selection. There are also additional flags, such as the requirement to display the Read Only option. The available constant parameters are listed in the online documentation.

Using the Windows API to Draw on a Picture

The Windows API supports many advanced functions that are not supported by default in Visual Basic. Most of the complex drawing functions, including bitmap manipulation and complex polygon and printing functions, require the use of the API. This example provides a core example of using the API to draw onto a loaded bitmap and write it to a different file.

1. Create a new project in Visual Basic.

2. In the General Declarations area of the main form, enter the following code:

```
Const WHITE_PEN = 6
Const WHITENESS = &HFF0062
Const CCHDEVICENAME = 32
Const CCHFORMNAME = 32
Private Type DEVMODE
        dmDeviceName As String * CCHDEVICENAME
        dmSpecVersion As Integer
        dmDriverVersion As Integer
        dmSize As Integer
        dmDriverExtra As Integer
        dmFields As Long
        dmOrientation As Integer
        dmPaperSize As Integer
        dmPaperLength As Integer
        dmPaperWidth As Integer
        dmScale As Integer
        dmCopies As Integer
        dmDefaultSource As Integer
        dmPrintQuality As Integer
        dmColor As Integer
        dmDuplex As Integer
        dmYResolution As Integer
        dmTTOption As Integer
        dmCollate As Integer
        dmFormName As String * CCHFORMNAME
        dmUnusedPadding As Integer
        dmBitsPerPel As Integer
        dmPelsWidth As Long
        dmPelsHeight As Long
```

```
            dmDisplayFlags As Long
            dmDisplayFrequency As Long
End Type

Private Declare Function BitBlt Lib "gdi32" (ByVal
hDestDC As Long, ByVal x As Long, ByVal y As Long,
ByVal nWidth As Long, ByVal nHeight As Long, ByVal
hSrcDC As Long, ByVal xSrc As Long, ByVal ySrc As
Long, ByVal dwRop As Long) As Long
Private Declare Function CreateCompatibleDC Lib
"gdi32" (ByVal hdc As Long) As Long
Private Declare Function CreateDC Lib "gdi32"
Alias "CreateDCA" (ByVal lpDriverName As String,
ByVal lpDeviceName As String, ByVal lpOutput As
String, lpInitData As DEVMODE) As Long
Private Declare Function DeleteDC Lib "gdi32" (By-
Val hdc As Long) As Long
Private Declare Function DeleteObject Lib "gdi32"
(ByVal hObject As Long) As Long
Private Declare Function PatBlt Lib "gdi32" (ByVal
hdc As Long, ByVal x As Long, ByVal y As Long, By-
Val nWidth As Long, ByVal nHeight As Long, ByVal
dwRop As Long) As Long
Private Declare Function SelectObject Lib "gdi32"
(ByVal hdc As Long, ByVal hObject As Long) As Long
```

3. Add a command button and set the Name property of the button to **cmdSimpleBitmap**.

4. Enter the following code into the Click event of the button:

```
Private Sub cmdSimpleBitmap_Click()
    Dim hShadowDC, hShadowBMP, I
    Dim picMyMod As Object, result

    hShadowDC = CreateCompatibleDC(Form1.hdc)
    Set picMyMod = LoadPicture("c:\vb6\test.bmp")
    hShadowBMP = picMyMod
    hTempBitmap = SelectObject(hShadowDC, hShadowBMP)
    result = PatBlt(hShadowDC, 0, 0, 100, _
            100, WHITENESS)
```

```
    result = BitBlt(Form1.hdc, 0, 0, 320, 200, _
            hShadowDC, 10, 10, SRCCOPY)
    SavePicture picMyMod, "c:\mod.bmp"
    i = SelectObject(hShadowDC, hTempBitmap)
    i = DeleteObject(hShadowBMP)
    i = DeleteDC(hShadowDC)
End Sub
```

5. Execute the application.

This example expects a bitmap file named test.bmp in the VB6 folder. You can replace this reference with any qualified path to a bitmap, GIF, or JPEG file. The example writes the modified file to the root directory with a bitmap named mod.bmp.

Using the Windows API to Play a Sound File

Through the Multimedia control, many types of audio and visual files may be played. However, for user feedback or general background audio, playing a sound (WAV) file can be much more convenient. By use of the sndPlaySound API call, a WAV file is played through the default audio system.

1. Create a new project in Visual Basic.

2. In the General Declarations area of the main form, enter the following code:

```
Private Declare Function sndPlaySound Lib "WINMM.DLL"
Alias "sndPlaySoundA" _
        (ByVal lpszSoundName As String, ByVal uFlags
As Long) As Long

Const cSndSYNC = &H0, cSndASYNC = &H1
Const cSndNODEFAULT = &H2
Const cSndLOOP = &H8, cSndNOSTOP = &H10
```

3. Add a command button and set the Name property of the button to **cmdPlaySound.**

4. Enter the following code into the Click event of the button:

```
Private Sub cmdPlaySound_Click()
    SoundName$ = "c:\harpup.wav"
    result = sndPlaySound(SoundName$, _
        cSndASYNC Or cSndNODEFAULT)
End Sub
```

5. Execute the application.

Note that this code example expects a file named harpup.wav in the root directory. Change this path to point to a WAV file available on your system.

Sending E-mail Through Outlook

On many occasions, it is useful to be able to send e-mail from within Visual Basic. Through the Messaging API (MAPI), you can program the transmission of any type of message, but the programming is more complicated. Sending the e-mail through Outlook is simple, and it will be added to the Sent Items folder if you wish to track the mail sent.

1. Create a new project in Visual Basic.

2. Set the References dialog box to include Microsoft Outlook 98 Object Model.

3. Add a command button and set the Name property of the button to **cmdOutlookMail.**

4. Enter the following code into the Click event of the button:

```
Private Sub cmdOutlookMail_Click()
    Dim objOutlook As Object
    Dim objItem As MailItem

    Set objOutlook = _
            CreateObject("Outlook.Application")
    ' Create olMailItem
    Set objItem = objOutlook.CreateItem(olMailItem)
    With objItem
        .Subject = "VB Prog Ref"
        .To = danr@cvisual.com
        .CC = danr@coherentdata.com
        .Body = "I found this book useful"
        .Attachments.Add "c:\autoexec.bat"
        .Send
    End With
    Set objItem = Nothing
    Set objOutlook = Nothing
End Sub
```

5. Execute the application.

This example does not provide error detection, and it also assumes a file named autoexec.bat is located at the root directory on the C drive. The addresses in the example are in Internet address format, but you can use standard names such as "John Doe" from the address book just as you can when manually sending Outlook mail.

II

Centering a Form

One of the most common needs for central dialog windows or splash screens is to center the form within the current screen. This example retrieves the size of the screen from the Windows system through a Windows API call and then moves the current form to the appropriate location.

1. Create a new project in Visual Basic.

2. In the General Declarations area of the main form, enter the following code:

```
Private Type RECT
        Left As Long
        Top As Long
        Right As Long
        Bottom As Long
End Type

Const SPI_GETWORKAREA = 48

Private Declare Function SystemParametersInfo Lib
"user32" Alias _
  "SystemParametersInfoA" (ByVal uAction As Long, _
  ByVal uParam As Long, lpvParam As Any, _

  ByVal fuWinIni As Long) As Long
```

3. Add a command button and set the Name property of the button to **cmdCenterForm.**

4. Enter the following code into the Click event of the button:

```
Private Sub cmdCenterForm_Click()
    Dim screenRect As RECT
    Dim screenWidth As Integer
      Dim screenHeight As Integer

    result = SystemParametersInfo(SPI_GETWORKAREA, _
          0, screenRect, 0)
    If result Then
        With screenRect
            .Left = Screen.TwipsPerPixelX * .Left
            .Right = Screen.TwipsPerPixelX * .Right
```

```
            .Top = Screen.TwipsPerPixelY * .Top
            .Bottom = Screen.TwipsPerPixelY * .Bottom
            screenWidth = .Right - .Left
            screenHeight = .Bottom - .Top
            fx = .Left + _
                ((screenWidth - Me.Width) / 2)
            fy = .Top + _
                ((screenHeight - Me.Height) / 2)
            Me.Move fx, fy
        End With
    End If
End Sub
```

5. Execute the application.

The SystemParametersInfo function supplies a number of parameters, one of which is the rectangle of the current work area. The work area constitutes only the current window area and does not include the space taken by the taskbar.

For more of the values available from the SystemParametersInfo function, check the SPI constants available in the API Text Viewer included with Visual Basic.

Accepting EXE-Passed Parameters

When programs are launched from the Windows environment, they may include command-line parameters or the names of files that were dragged and dropped onto the EXE icon. Accessing the passed string enables you to allow input to the application before the complete environment execution has begun.

1. Create a new project in Visual Basic.

2. Enter the following code into the Load event of the main form:

```
Private Sub Form_Load()
    If Command$ <> "" Then
        MsgBox Command$
    End If
End Sub
```

3. Use the Make EXE option under the File menu to create an executable.

4. From the Windows system, drag and drop a file onto the EXE.

When execution occurs, the program checks to see if any parameters have been passed to the application. If parameters are present, they are displayed in a message box.

Displaying a List of Fonts in Each Style

Determining which fonts are on a display device is fairly simple if the Fonts property of the device is used. Either the Screen or the Printer objects can be queried to find out what fonts are available. In this example, the fonts for the screen device are detected as the name of each font is displayed in a picture box in its proper text face.

1. Create a new project in Visual Basic.

2. Draw a PictureBox control on the form.

3. Add a command button and set the Name property of the button to **cmdListFonts.**

4. Enter the following code into the Click event of the button:

```
Private Sub cmdListFonts_Click()
    Screen.MousePointer = 11
    For I = 0 To Screen.FontCount - 1

        Picture1.Font = Screen.Fonts(I)
        Picture1.Print Screen.Fonts(I)
    Next I
    Screen.MousePointer = 0
End Sub
```

5. Execute the application.

Because some of the fonts must be retrieved from the disk, you'll notice that the MousePointer is set to the hourglass until the display is finished. The PictureBox control is useful for displaying text as well as using geometric primitives (such as circles and lines) to draw onto a form.

Part III
Language Reference

!

III

Database field operator

Description

Using the exclamation command (!) allows access to a single
database field while bypassing a complete database field object
reference (using the Fields collection). The Immediate window
example requires a recordset created with the name "myRS" and
containing a field titled "LastName."

NOT AVAILABLE IN VB SCRIPT

Syntax
```
recordset!field
```

Parameters
recordset   Required. Recordset of dynaset, table, or snapshot type.

field   Required. Field contained in the recordset.

Returns
N/A

Immediate Window Sample
```
? myRS!LastName
```

> ## ➤ Programmer's Tip

The exclamation command can be used to quickly reference
fields in a database instead of using a complete
myRS.Fields("LastName") collection reference.

SEE ALSO   Fields, &

49

Double operator

Description
This operator will set the variable to be a Double type.

AVAILABLE IN VB SCRIPT

Syntax
a#

Parameters
a   Any permitted variable name

Returns
N/A

Immediate Window Sample
a# = 56

SEE ALSO   CDbl, DefDbl

Used to enclose a Date type

Description
Surrounding a Date or Time value with the # sign will generate the proper Date value.

AVAILABLE IN VB SCRIPT

Syntax
#date#

Parameters
date   Required. Any valid date or time.

Returns
Variant type

Immediate Window Sample
```
? #1/2/97#
```

SEE ALSO   CVDate

#Const

Conditional compile constant

Description
This operator creates a private constant in a module. The conditional compiler treats these constants as literals. Therefore, when the program is actually compiled, there is no speed difference from using the actual value.

NOT AVAILABLE IN VB SCRIPT

Syntax
```
#Const constname = expression
```

Parameters
constname   Any permitted variable name.

expression   Can include an operator (except Is) or a numeric value.

Returns
N/A

Immediate Window Sample
N/A

SEE ALSO   #if...#else...#endif, Const

#if...#else...#endif

Conditional compilation of a section of code

Description

Using the conditional compile adds the code encapsulated only if
the condition is True. This can be used to include or exclude demo
code or, in Visual Basic 4.0, to provide conditional code for a 16- or
32-bit compile. It also can check for execution on the Macintosh for
special Macintosh-related code. Compile time variables include
Mac and Win32 to determine the type of execution system.

NOT AVAILABLE IN VB SCRIPT

Syntax

```
#if condition-1 Then  [actions-1] : [#ElseIf
condition-2 Then] : [actions-2] : [#ElseIf
condition-n Then] : [actions-n] : [#Else] : [else-
actions] : #End If
```

Parameters

conditions   Required. Boolean expressions.

Returns

N/A

Immediate Window Sample

N/A

SEE ALSO   #Const

$

Sets the type of the variable to a string

Description

This string operator serves the same function as defining a variable
with the "Dim x As String" command. Once the operator is used in a
definition, the variable name without the operator can be used to

access the same variable (that is, myString$ and myString address the same variable).

AVAILABLE IN VB SCRIPT

Syntax
a$

Parameters
a Any permitted variable name

Returns
N/A

Immediate Window Sample
```
a$ = "Hello" & 2
? a$
? a
```

SEE ALSO CStr, Dim, DefStr

Sets the type of the variable to an integer

Description
This string operator serves the same function as defining a variable with the "Dim x As Integer" command. Once the operator is used in a definition, the variable name without the operator accesses the same variable.

AVAILABLE IN VB SCRIPT

Syntax
a%

Parameters
a Any permitted variable name

Returns
N/A

Immediate Window Sample
```
a% = 5.14
? a%
? a
```

SEE ALSO　CInt, DefInt

&

String combining or concatenation operator

Description
This operator is extremely powerful, because it automatically converts between types as it combines or concatenates into a resultant string. Therefore, it can be used to combine several different variable types into a string without any explicit conversion.

AVAILABLE IN VB SCRIPT

Syntax
```
a & b
```

Parameters
a, b　Any variant or data types

Returns
Variant

Immediate Window Sample
```
? "a" & 12 & 1.22 & #1/2/97#
```

> ### ➤ Programmer's Tip

The & operator can prevent database errors when you're dealing with Nulls. If you set a string to a field that contains a Null, as in myStr$ = myRS!myField, an error will occur. To prevent the error, use myStr$ = "" & myRS!myField.

SEE ALSO +, !, CStr

Remark command

Description

The apostrophe (') command can be used to mark code as a remark to be ignored by the compiler. In the Immediate window, Visual Basic will also ignore any command that follows it.

AVAILABLE IN VB SCRIPT

Syntax

```
' comment
```

Parameters

comment Any text

Returns

N/A

Immediate Window Sample

```
' ? "1"
```

> ## ➤ Programmer's Tip

During development, when a line of code isn't needed anymore, make the line a comment rather than deleting it. Then if conditions change before the project completes and the code is needed, you can remove the comment rather than rewrite the code.

SEE ALSO Rem

Multiplication operator

Description
This operator multiplies one number by another and provides the result.

AVAILABLE IN VB SCRIPT

Syntax
`a * b`

Parameters
a, **b**   Required. Any valid numeric expression.

Returns
Variant

Immediate Window Sample
`? 2.12 * 3.14`

SEE ALSO   ^, /, +, -, Mod, \

Addition operator

Description
This operator adds one number to another and provides the result.

AVAILABLE IN VB SCRIPT

Syntax
`a + b`

Parameters

a, **b**   Required. Any valid numeric expression.

Returns

Variant

Immediate Window Sample

```
? 2.12 + 3.14
```

SEE ALSO   ^, /, *, -, Mod, \

String addition operator

Description

The + operator can be used many times within a single line to
create a large combination of strings. Unlike using the & operator,
if you try to create a string using the + operator with multiple
variable types, a "Type Mismatch" error will occur. Use the &
operator to avoid the error.

AVAILABLE IN VB SCRIPT

Syntax

```
a + b
```

Parameters

a, **b**   Required. Any valid expression.

Returns

Variant

Immediate Window Sample

```
? "U.S. economy..." + "Status: " + "ok."
```

SEE ALSO   &, CStr

Subtraction or negation operator

Description
This operator subtracts one number from another and provides
the result.

AVAILABLE IN VB SCRIPT

Syntax
```
a - b
```

Parameters
a, b   Required. Any valid numeric expression.

Returns
Variant

Immediate Window Sample
```
? -1
? 5 - 3
? 3 - 5
```

SEE ALSO   ∧, /, *, +, Mod, \

Division operator

Description
This operator divides one number by another and provides the
result. The result of the division will be returned in the data type
appropriate to the result (that is, 10 / 3 will be returned as a Single).
Use the operator to force the return of an integer. Use the Mod
operator to return the remainder that results in an integer division.

AVAILABLE IN VB SCRIPT

Syntax
```
a / b
```

Parameters
a, **b**   Required. Any valid numeric expression.

Returns
Variant

Immediate Window Sample
```
? 9/3
? 9/2
```

SEE ALSO   ∧, +, *, -, Mod, \

Less-than operator

Description
Using the Less-than operator compares two numeric values and returns the Boolean True or False depending on the result. If you send this operator values such as strings, they will be evaluated by their alphabetical values, including case sensitivity. Some of the Immediate window operators demonstrate the nonintuitive results.

AVAILABLE IN VB SCRIPT

Syntax
```
a < b
```

Parameters
a, **b**   Required. Any valid numeric expression.

Returns
Variant

Immediate Window Sample
```
? 3 < 5
? 3 < 2
```

```
? "a" < "z"
? "z" < "a"
? "A" < "a"
? "21" < "200"
```

SEE ALSO   >, =, <>, >=, <=, Like, Not, And

Less-than or equal-to operator

Description
This operator compares two values for less-than or equivalent condition.

AVAILABLE IN VB SCRIPT

Syntax
a <= b

Parameters
a, b   Required. Any valid numeric expression.

Returns
Variant

Immediate Window Sample
```
? 1 <= 2
? 2 <= 1
```

SEE ALSO   =, <>, <, >, >=, Like, Not, And

Nonequality operator

Description
This operator compares two values for nonequivalent condition.

AVAILABLE IN VB SCRIPT

Syntax
```
a <> b
```

Parameters
a, b   Required. Any valid numeric expression.

Returns
Variant

Immediate Window Sample
```
? 1 <> 2
? 1 <> 1
```

SEE ALSO   =, >, <, >=, <=, Like, Not, And

=

Equality operator

Description
This operator compares two values for equivalent condition.

AVAILABLE IN VB SCRIPT

Syntax
```
a = b
```

Parameters
a, b   Required. Any valid numeric expression.

Returns
Variant

Immediate Window Sample
```
? 1 = 1
? 2 = 1
? True = False
```

SEE ALSO   <>, >, <, >=, <=, Like, Not, And

Greater-than operator

Description
This operator compares two values for the greater-than condition.

AVAILABLE IN VB SCRIPT

Syntax
`a > b`

Parameters
a, b   Required. Any valid numeric expression.

Returns
Variant

Immediate Window Sample
```
? 5 > 3
? 3 > 5
```

SEE ALSO   =, <>, <, >=, <=, Like, Not, And

Greater-than or equal-to operator

Description
This operator compares two values for greater-than or equivalent condition.

AVAILABLE IN VB SCRIPT

Syntax
```
a >= b
```

Parameters
a, b   Required. Any valid numeric expression.

Returns
Variant type

Immediate Window Sample
```
? 2 >= 1
? 2 >= 2
? 1 >= 2
```

SEE ALSO   =, <>, >, <, <=, Like, Not, And

?

Prints to the current or Immediate window

Description
For quick typing, the question mark can be used in place of the Print command.

AVAILABLE IN VB SCRIPT

Syntax
```
? a
```

Parameters
a   Any valid expression

Returns
N/A

Immediate Window Sample
```
? "Hello"
```

SEE ALSO   Print, Space, Space$, Tab

\

Integer division operator

Description

This performs like the traditional division (/) operator, except it returns the results as an integer. Before the division takes place, both numbers are converted to integers. The result is truncated rather than rounded to the nearest integer. Use the Mod operator to obtain the remainder of the division of two integers.

AVAILABLE IN VB SCRIPT

Syntax

a \ b

Parameters

a, b   Required. Any valid numeric expression.

Returns

Variant type

Immediate Window Sample

```
? 16 \ 8
? 16 \ 15
```

SEE ALSO   ^, +, *, -, Mod, /

^

Exponent or caret operator

Description

This returns the number raised to the power of the provided exponent.

AVAILABLE IN VB SCRIPT

Syntax
a ^ b

Parameters
a, b   Required. Any valid numeric expression.

Returns
Variant

Immediate Window Sample
```
? 2 ^ 1
? 2 ^ 2
? 2 ^ 8
? 2 ^ 0
```

SEE ALSO   +, *, -, Mod, \, /

Abs

Returns the absolute value of the parameter passed to it

Description
This function returns the absolute (positive) value of a number passed to it. The same type of number is returned that is passed to it (that is, pass a type Integer, and a type Integer is returned).

AVAILABLE IN VB SCRIPT

Syntax
Abs (num)

Parameters
num   Required. The value to convert to an absolute value.

Returns
Same as passed

Immediate Window Sample

```
? Abs(1)
? Abs(-1)
? Abs(-45.2334)
```

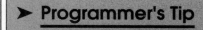

➤ Programmer's Tip

The Abs function can handle a Null value without causing an error. A Null is simply returned.

SEE ALSO   Imp, Int, Log, Mod, Fix

AddressOf

VB 6
Only

Returns the address of a procedure

Description

The AddressOf operator is used for Windows API calls when the API routine requires a call-back function to be passed to it. Most API functions execute and then return control to the Visual Basic application when execution is complete. When a call-back is required, this means that a function needs to be called while the API retains execution control. This operator is used like the ByRef or ByVal commands when passing a series of arguments to an API routine.

NOT AVAILABLE IN VB SCRIPT

Syntax

```
AddressOf procName
```

Parameters

procName   Required. The name of the procedure to be activated by the API function.

Returns

N/A

Immediate Window Sample
N/A

> ## ➤ Programmer's Tip
>
> This operator allows a call-back that before VB 6 was nearly
> impossible to do from Visual Basic. However, this function is
> very advanced and when used improperly could cause an
> execute fault. Be sure to study a Windows API manual before
> attempting to create a call-back function.

SEE ALSO   Call, Declare

And

Logical And

Description
This command can be used to compile two comparison expressions
or to logically combine two numbers. The And operator returns the
bitwise result of all bits that exist in both values.

AVAILABLE IN VB SCRIPT

Syntax
a And b

Parameters
a, b   Required. Any valid numeric expression.

Returns
Variant

Immediate Window Sample
```
? (2 > 1) And (2 > 0)
? (2 > 3) And (2 > 0)
? 15 And 8
```

```
? 16 And 8
? 256 And 8
```

SEE ALSO   Or, Imp, Eqv, Xor, True, False

AppActivate

Activates a specified application window

Description
This command shifts the focus to any application currently running under the Windows system. Either the title of the window or the application ID that is returned by the Shell command may be used. Note that activating the application does not change the collapsed or expanded state of the application.

NOT AVAILABLE IN VB SCRIPT

Syntax
```
AppActivate title[, wait]
```

Parameters
title   Required.

wait   Optional.

Returns
N/A

Immediate Window Sample
```
AppActivate "Microsoft Excel"
MyAppID = Shell("C:.EXE", 1)
AppActivate MyAppID
```

➤ Programmer's Tip

To avoid multiple instances of a single application executing, this command can be used. If an instance is already running, the new instance simply activates the existent application and shuts itself down.

SEE ALSO   Shell, Environ$

Array

Creates an array in memory containing the values passed in the
parameter list

III

Description
This extremely useful function can be used to automatically create
an array in memory and store a number of values into it. If no values
are specified, an empty array with zero elements is returned.

AVAILABLE IN VB SCRIPT

Syntax
```
Array(arglist)
```

Parameters
arglist   Required. The parameters to be contained as sequential
elements in the array.

Returns
Array passed in a variant

Immediate Window Sample
```
myArray = Array("McClane","Gennero","Gruber")

? myArray(1)
```

➤ Programmer's Tip

Use the Array command to test array code in the Immediate
window. Since the Immediate window does not accept
dimensioning commands, the Array command is the only way
to create an array on the fly.

SEE ALSO   Dim, ReDim

Asc

Returns the ASCII code of the first letter of the string

Description
This command is the exact opposite of the Chr( ) command that returns the character when given a numeric ASCII character value. When given a character, this command returns the numeric value.

AVAILABLE IN VB SCRIPT

Syntax
Asc(val)

Parameters
val   Required. String that contains the first letter that will be converted to a numeric.

Returns
Integer

Immediate Window Sample
```
? Asc("A")
? Asc("Abbey")
? Chr(Asc("A"))
```

➤ Programmer's Tip

If a string with multiple values is passed, any characters after the first are ignored. Use the Mid$( ) command to pull a specific character for conversion from a long string.

SEE ALSO   Chr, Mid$

Atn

VB 6
Only

Returns the arctangent of a given number in radians

Description

This function retrieves the arctangent value of a number of type Double. The Atn function is the inverse trigonometric function of the Tan function.

AVAILABLE IN VB SCRIPT

Syntax

Atn(val)

Parameters

val   Required. Ratio of two sides of a right triangle.

Returns

Double type

Immediate Window Sample

? Atn(1.2)

SEE ALSO   Tan, Cos, Sin, Sqr

Beep

Speaker beep

Description

The Beep command will simply beep the speaker. There is no other way to make sound with Visual Basic without using the Windows API routines or the Multimedia control. Use the Windows API (see

Declare statement) to play digitized sound (WAV files) or MIDI (MID files) sounds.

NOT AVAILABLE IN VB SCRIPT

Syntax
Beep

Parameters
N/A

Returns
N/A

Immediate Window Sample
Beep

➤ Programmer's Tip

The Beep command is excellent to place strategically in your code for debugging. By counting the number of beeps, you can determine what points of the program have executed before a problem occurred.

SEE ALSO   ?, Print, Declare

Call

Activates a procedure

Description
This executes a system or user-defined procedure. To call a subroutine, you can simply use the name of the procedure or precede the name with the Call statement to make the call more explicit in the code.

AVAILABLE IN VB SCRIPT

Syntax

```
Call name [argmentlist]
```

Parameters

name   Required. Current procedure name.

argmentlist   Optional. Any parameters required for the procedure.

Returns

N/A

Immediate Window Sample

```
Call Beep
Call MsgBox("Hello")
```

➤ Programmer's Tip

Although a procedure can be executed by simply typing its name, the Call command allows the use of parentheses around arguments (like a function) and makes calls to outside routines more apparent in your source code.

SEE ALSO   Function, Sub

CallByName

VB 6
Only

Enables run-time binding of a method or property

Description

This function enables a property or method to be accessed by passing a string. Use of a string allows the property or method to be chosen at run time for the string construction. This function can be used to get or set a property or to invoke a method.

NOT AVAILABLE IN VB SCRIPT

Syntax
```
CallByName(object,procName,callType,[arglist])
```

Parameters

object   Required. Object reference such as a control (that is, text box or check box) that will be used.

procName   Required. A string of the procedure or property that will be accessed.

callType   Required. Constant of the type of call being made including vbLet, vbGet, or vbMethod.

arglist   Optional. Arguments to pass to method if method is called.

Returns
Dependent on method/property

Immediate Window Sample
```
? CallByName(Screen, "MousePointer", vbGet)
```

➤ Programmer's Tip

Avoid using this command in speed-intensive routines. The selection of the method or property at run time is called *late binding* or *dynamic binding*. It slows execution.

SEE ALSO   Call

CByte

Converts to Byte data type

Description
A Byte data type takes up a single byte in the computer memory and has a value from 0 to 255. This data type is used mostly for file formats and data conversion. Converting a number greater than 255 or less than 0 results in an Overflow error.

AVAILABLE IN VB SCRIPT

Syntax
CByte(expression)

Parameters
expression   Required. Value to be converted.

Returns
Byte type

Immediate Window Sample
? CByte(3)
? CByte(3.2)

SEE ALSO   CDbl, CInt, CLng, CSng, CStr, CVar, DefByte

CCur

Converts the variable passed to the function to a Currency
type variable

Description
This conversion function can be used to ensure the type of a
particular variable. It is especially useful for converting variant
types to a specific variable type, which makes many routines up to
four times faster.

AVAILABLE IN VB SCRIPT

Syntax
CCur (expression)

Parameters
expression   Variant, Integer, Single, Double, String

Returns
Currency type

Immediate Window Sample

```
? CCur("10.5389")
```

SEE ALSO   CDbl, CInt, CLng, CSng, CStr, CVar, DefCur

CDbl

Converts to double floating-point number

Description

The Double type can hold from $-1.79769313486232E208$ to $-4.94065645841247E{-}324$ for negative numbers or from $4.94065645841247E{-}324$ to $1.79769313486232E208$ for positive numbers.

AVAILABLE IN VB SCRIPT

Syntax

```
CDbl(expression)
```

Parameters

expression   Required. Value to be converted.

Returns

Double type

Immediate Window Sample

```
myVar = 1
myDVar = CDbl(myVar)
myDVar = myDVar / 3
? myDVar
```

➤ Programmer's Tip

Double precision takes longer to calculate than the Single type. Therefore, use Single if you do not need the extra accuracy.

SEE ALSO   CCur, DInt, CLng, CSng, CStr, CVar, DefDbl

CDec

Converts to variable type Decimal

Description

The Decimal type contains numbers scaled to the power of ten. In the background, it optimizes for numbers that do or don't contain decimals. Without any decimals, the range is positive and negative 79,228,162,514,264,337,593,543,950,335. Numbers with decimal places have 28 decimal places between positive and negative 7.9228162514264337593543950335.

NOT AVAILABLE IN VB SCRIPT

Syntax

CDec(expression)

Parameters

expression   Required. Value to be converted.

Returns

Variant

Immediate Window Sample

```
? CDec(100)
? CDec(-5.231)
```

➤ Programmer's Tip

Currently you cannot specify a type with the As operator a Decimal. Use the CDec command to store a Decimal in a variant variable.

SEE ALSO   CDbl, CInt, CLng, CSng, CStr, CVar, DefDec

ChDir

Changes the default directory

Description

Use the change directory (ChDir) command to change the default directory location where Visual Basic searches for files without a fully qualified path. After you use this command, any open or file reference operations will access this specified folder first.

NOT AVAILABLE IN VB SCRIPT

Syntax

ChDir path$

Parameters

path$ Required. Any valid path.

Returns

N/A

Immediate Window Sample

ChDir("C:\")

SEE ALSO   ChDrive, CurDir, CurDir$, MkDir, RmDir, Open #, Dir$, Environ, Kill, MkDir, RmDir

ChDrive

Changes the currently default selected drive

Description

This command changes the current drive. This changes the default drive to the value passed in a string. If a multicharacter string is passed, only the first character is used.

NOT AVAILABLE IN VB SCRIPT

Syntax
```
ChDrive Drive$
```

Parameters
Drive$ Required. String that contains a valid drive.

Returns
N/A

Immediate Window Sample
```
ChDrive "c:"
ChDrive "alpha:"
```

SEE ALSO   ChDir, CurDir, CurDir$, MkDir, RmDir, Open #, Dir$, Environ, Kill

Choose

Returns a specified value for a list

Description
This function returns a value from a list of arguments based on an index number. Can be used to quickly return a selection without having to create an array.

NOT AVAILABLE IN VB SCRIPT

Syntax
```
Choose(index%,expression1[,expression2]...[expression13])
```

Parameters
index%   Required. Number of expression to be returned.

expression   Required. Any valid expression.

Returns
Variant

Immediate Window Sample
```
? Choose(3,"Draw","Paint","Write","Build")
```

SEE ALSO   IIf, Switch, Select...Case

Chr, Chr$

Returns the character string of the ASCII value passed to it

Description

This function can be used to return both normal and unprintable characters. Common characters such as a space (Chr(32)), a tab (Chr(9)), a carriage return (Chr(13)), or a linefeed (Chr(10)) can be added to a string.

AVAILABLE IN VB SCRIPT

Syntax

```
Chr$(AsciiCode%)
Chr(AsciiCode%)
```

Parameters

AsciiCode%   Required. An Integer or Long that defines the character.

Returns

String type

Immediate Window Sample

```
? Chr(86) + Chr(66) + Chr(65)
```

➤ Programmer's Tip

See the ASCII chart included in Part II of the book for a list of values.

SEE ALSO   Asc, ChrB, ChrW

ChrB

Converts to character string of type Byte

Description
This returns a single byte of a string. This byte conforms with the ASCII standard for files, as opposed to the newer Unicode standard, which uses two bytes per character to handle all of the international character sets.

AVAILABLE IN VB SCRIPT

Syntax
ChrB$(AsciiCode%)
ChrB(AsciiCode%)

Parameters
AsciiCode%   An Integer or Long that defines the character.

Returns
Byte type

Immediate Window Sample
? ChrB(65)

SEE ALSO   Chr, ChrW, Asc

ChrW

Converts to character type Unicode

Description
This returns a string of the character code. This string conforms with the Unicode standard, which uses two bytes per character to handle all of the international character sets.

AVAILABLE IN VB SCRIPT

Syntax

```
ChrW$(AsciiCode%)
ChrW(AsciiCode%)
```

Parameters

AsciiCode An Integer or Long that defines the character.

Returns

String type

Immediate Window Sample

```
? ChrW(65)
```

SEE ALSO Chr, ChrB, Asc

Converts the given expression to an integer

Description

This converts the expression to an Integer data type. A fractional part rounds to the nearest even number. The number 1.5 will round to 2, but 2.5 will round to 2 also. Integers can range from –32,768 to 32,767.

AVAILABLE IN VB SCRIPT

Syntax

```
CInt(expression)
```

Parameters

expression Required. Value to be converted.

Returns

Integer type

Immediate Window Sample

```
? CInt(1.25)
```

> ## ➤ Programmer's Tip

For your loops, make sure that you explicitly define the counter variables as Integer or Long numbers (that is, "Dim myVar as Integer"). This can make the loop up to four times faster than variables that are left as Variant variable types.

III

SEE ALSO   CCur, CDbl, CLng, CSng, CStr, CVar, Fix, Int, DefInt

CLng

Converts the given expression to a Long integer

Description

This converts the expression to a Long data type. A fractional part rounds to the nearest even number. The number 1.5 will round to 2, but 2.5 will round to 2 also.

AVAILABLE IN VB SCRIPT

Syntax
CLng(expression)

Parameters
expression   Required. Value to be converted.

Returns
Long type

Immediate Window Sample
? CLng(200000.5)

SEE ALSO   CCur, CDbl, CInt, CSng, CStr, CVar, Fix, Int, DefLng

Close

Closes all open files or the file specified by the file number

Description
If you omit the file number and issue the Close command, all open files will be closed.

NOT AVAILABLE IN VB SCRIPT

Syntax
```
Close [#][filenumber%][, [#]filenumber%]
```

Parameters
filenumber%   Required. Current file number to open.

Returns
N/A

Immediate Window Sample
```
Open "c:\vbtest.txt" for output as #1 :_
Print #1, "Hello World!" : Close #1
```

SEE ALSO   Open, Reset, Print #, Input, File System Objects (Part IV)

Command

Returns the commands passed to the Visual Basic program when it is executed

Description
This command is useful if you will have a file extension associated with your program. When the user double-clicks the document, your EXE is launched and the path and name of the document that was selected are passed in this string. If no commands were passed when the program was executed, this command will return an empty string.

NOT AVAILABLE IN VB SCRIPT

Syntax
Command$ Command

Parameters
N/A

Returns
String type

Immediate Window Sample
? Command

> ## ➤ Programmer's Tip
>
> Use this function to retrieve commands sent to the program at the DOS prompt, such as switches.

SEE ALSO   Environ, Environ$

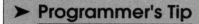

CommitTrans

Writes transactions to database

Description
This writes all currently queued transactions into the database since the BeginTrans command was activated. Committing the transactions will write them to the database, while the Rollback command will do the opposite by aborting all transactions.

NOT AVAILABLE IN VB SCRIPT

Syntax
CommitTrans

Parameters
N/A

Returns
N/A

Immediate Window Sample
N/A

SEE ALSO   BeginTrans, Rollback

Const

Declares a value as a Constant

Description
Like the Dim command, the Const command cannot be used in the
Immediate window. Defining a Const creates a read-only variable,
in contrast to the #Const command, which actually substitutes a
value at compile time. Note that the #Const command cannot be
used in VB Script.

AVAILABLE IN VB SCRIPT

Syntax
[Global] Const name = expression [,name = expression]

Parameters
name   Required. Any permitted variable name.

expression   Required. Any valid expression.

Returns
N/A

Immediate Window Sample
N/A

SEE ALSO   Enum, DefCur, DefDate, DefDbl, DefDec, DefInt,
DefLng, DefSng, DefStr, DefVar, Dim, Global, ReDim, Static, #Const

Cos

Returns the cosine of an angle specified in radians

Description
This command requires the angle to be passed in radians. The formula radians = (degrees * pi) / 180 can be used to determine the radians from a degree measure.

AVAILABLE IN VB SCRIPT

Syntax
Cos(angle)

Parameters
angle   Required. Any numeric expression holding a radian measure.

Returns
Double type

Immediate Window Sample
? Cos(3.14159)
? Cos((90*3.14159)/180)

SEE ALSO   Atn, Sin, Tan, Log, Exp, Sgn, Sqr

CreateObject

Creates an instance of an object

Description
Use this function to create a new instance of any OLE or ActiveX object. Either the qualified path name (that is, "excel.application") or the entire ClassID can be used to select the class library used to create the object.

AVAILABLE IN VB SCRIPT

Syntax
```
CreateObject(Class$)
```

Parameters
Class$　Required. Class name of the required object. Must be registered with the OLE Registry system.

Returns
Object reference

Immediate Window Sample
```
Set myObject = CreateObject("excel.application")
myObject.Visible = true
```

> ## ➤ Programmer's Tip
>
> Make sure that any objects you create are also eliminated by using the "Set myObject = Nothing" command. Garbage collection routines should eliminate instances when they go out of scope, but it is good programming practice to destroy the objects explicitly.

SEE ALSO　GetObject, Set, dot (.), Nothing

CreateObject

VB 6
Only

Creates an instance of an object on either the local or remote machine

Description
This version of the CreateObject call, new to Visual Basic 6, allows a machine to instantiate the object to be specified. Because the machine can be specified, DCOM can be used to reference remote objects.

NOT AVAILABLE IN VB SCRIPT

Syntax

```
CreateObject(Class$ [,serverName$])
```

Parameters

Class$ Required. Class name of the required object. Must be registered with the OLE Registry system.

serverName$ Optional. Name of the network server on which the object is located.

Returns

Object reference

Immediate Window Sample

```
Set myObject = CreateObject("Excel.Application")
myObject.Visible = true
```

➤ Programmer's Tip

Specifying the name of a remote server requires the use of a WINS name. Like referencing a shared directory, you use a reference such as "\\\\objectServer\\Public."

SEE ALSO   GetObject, Set, dot (.), Nothing

CSng

Converts the given expression to a Single precision floating-point number

Description

This converts to a Single data type that can hold negative numbers between −3.402823E38 and −1.401298E−45, or positive numbers between 1.401298E−45 and 3.402823E38.

AVAILABLE IN VB SCRIPT

Syntax
CSng(expression)

Parameters
expression   Required. Value to be converted.

Returns
Single type

Immediate Window Sample
? CSng(1.222)

SEE ALSO   CCur, CDbl, CInt, CLng, CStr, CVar, DefSng

CStr

Converts the given expression to a string

Description
This command can be used to convert any data type to a string. Most useful are the numeric- and date-to-string conversions.

AVAILABLE IN VB SCRIPT

Syntax
CStr(expression)

Parameters
expression   Required. Value to be converted.

Returns
String type

Immediate Window Sample
? CStr(12)
? CStr(1+2)

SEE ALSO   CCur, CDbl, CInt, CLng, CSng, CVar, Format, DefStr

CurDir, CurDir$

Returns the path for a specified drive

Description
This function, if passed no argument, returns the path of the selected drive. If passed a string with a drive letter, it returns the path of the requested drive.

NOT AVAILABLE IN VB SCRIPT

Syntax
CurDir$[(drive$)] CurDir[(drive$)]

Parameters
drive$ Optional. Single-letter string to indicate desired drive.

Returns
Variant type

Immediate Window Sample
? CurDir
? CurDir("C")

SEE ALSO   ChDir, ChDrive, MkDir, RmDir

CVar

Converts the given expression to a Variant

Description
This will convert a specific value to a Variant data type.

NOT AVAILABLE IN VB SCRIPT

Syntax
CVar(expression)

Parameters

expression   Required. Value to be converted.

Returns

Variant type

Immediate Window Sample

```
? CVar(1)
? CVar("Hello")
? CVar(Int(5/2))
```

SEE ALSO   CCur, CDbl, CInt, CLng, CSng, CStr, DefVar

CVDate

Converts the current expression into a Date type variable

Description

With this command, you can convert any number of data types and string formats into an actual date. A Date is a 64-bit (8-byte) value that may be between January 1, 1000, and December 31, 9999.

NOT AVAILABLE IN VB SCRIPT

Syntax

```
CVDate(expression)
```

Parameters

expression   Required. Value to be converted.

Returns

Date type

Immediate Window Sample

```
? CVDate("11/2/97")
? CVDate("November 2, 1997")
```

SEE ALSO   DateAdd, DateDiff, DatePart, DateSerial, DateValue, Date, Time, Format, Now, Day, IsDate, Month, Weekday

CVErr

VB 6
Only

Returns an error object of the type specified

Description

III

This command creates an error object based on the error type passed to the routines. It is used to create user-defined errors in user-created procedures. This will enable you to create routines that can return custom error types.

NOT AVAILABLE IN VB SCRIPT

Syntax
CVErr(errorNum)

Parameters
errorNum   Required. Error number specified by user.

Returns
Variant of type Error

Immediate Window Sample
N/A

SEE ALSO   Error

Date

Sets the current Date in the system

Description
This function sets the actual system date, so be careful with its use.

AVAILABLE IN VB SCRIPT

Syntax
Date = date

Parameters

date   Required. Date data type.

Returns

N/A

Immediate Window Sample

```
Date = #August 12, 1997#
```

SEE ALSO   CVDate, DateAdd, DateDiff, DatePart, DateSerial, DateValue, Time, Format, Now, Day, IsDate, Month, Weekday

Date, Date$

Returns the current date as a Date type or a String type

Description

This routine returns the current date of the system. The format of the date will be set to the format specified in the Windows Control Panel. Standard format will show the date in a format such as "6/28/98."

NOT AVAILABLE IN VB SCRIPT

Syntax

```
Date$
```

```
Date
```

Parameters

N/A

Returns

Variant or String type

Immediate Window Sample

```
? Date
```

SEE ALSO   CVDate, DateAdd, DateDiff, DatePart, DateSerial, DateValue, Date, Time, Format, Now, Day, IsDate, Month, Weekday

DateAdd

Adds a specified amount to the Date type variable passed to it

Description
The format returned by DateAdd is determined by the Windows
Control Panel settings. Intervals may be year (yyyy), quarter (q),
month (m), day of year (y), day (d), weekday (w), week (ww), hour
(h), minute (n), or second (s).

AVAILABLE IN VB SCRIPT

Syntax
```
DateAdd(interval$, number%, dateVar)
```

Parameters
interval$ Required. Interval to add to the specified datetime.

number%   Required. Multiplier of the interval.

dateVar   Required. The Date type to be used as the base of the
addition.

Returns
Date type

Immediate Window Sample
```
? DateAdd("m", 1, Now)
? DateAdd("ww", 2, Now)
? DateAdd("h", 5, Now)
```

SEE ALSO   CVDate, DateDiff, DatePart, DateSerial, DateValue,
Date, Time, Format, Now, Day, IsDate, Month, Weekday

DateDiff

Determines the difference between two dates in units of the
interval passed to it

Description

This function returns the number of intervals between the two periods. Intervals may be year (yyyy), quarter (q), month (m), day of year (y), day (d), weekday (w), week (ww), hour (h), minute (n), or second (s).

AVAILABLE IN VB SCRIPT

Syntax

```
DateDiff(interval$, date1, date2
[,firstdayofweek[,firstweekofyear]])
```

Parameters

interval$ Required. Interval to add to the specified datetime.

date1, **date2**   Required. The Date type.

firstdayofweek   Optional. Specifies first day of week (1 = Sunday (default), 2 = Monday, and so on).

firstweekofyear   Optional. Specifies the first week of the year (1 = Jan 1 (default)).

Returns

Variant type

Immediate Window Sample

```
? DateDiff("d",Now,#1/1/2000#)
```

SEE ALSO   CVDate, DateAdd, DatePart, DateSerial, DateValue, Date, Time, Format, Now, Day, IsDate, Month, Weekday

DatePart

Returns the part of the date specified by the interval string

Description

Intervals may be year (yyyy), quarter (q), month (m), day of year (y), day (d), weekday (w), week (ww), hour (h), minute (n), or second (s).

AVAILABLE IN VB SCRIPT

Syntax
```
DatePart(interval$, date)
```

Parameters
interval$ Required. Interval to derive from the specified datetime.

date   Required. The Date type to be used as the base of the conversion.

Returns
Variant

Immediate Window Sample
```
? DatePart("m",Now)
```

SEE ALSO   CVDate, DateAdd, DateDiff, DateSerial, DateValue, Date, Time, Format, Now, Day, IsDate, Month, Weekday

DateSerial

Returns a Date type for the specified values

Description
This routine allows the quick creation of a date from three integer values.

AVAILABLE IN VB SCRIPT

Syntax
```
DateSerial(year%, month%, day%)
```

Parameters
year%, **month%**, **day%**   Required. Integers.

Returns
Variant type

Immediate Window Sample
```
? DateSerial(1997,8,1)
```

SEE ALSO   DateAdd, DateDiff, DatePart, DateValue, Date, Time, Format, Now, Day, IsDate, Month, Weekday, CVDate

DateValue

Converts an expression to a Date type

Description
This function works very similarly to the CVDate function.

AVAILABLE IN VB SCRIPT

Syntax
```
DateValue(datestring$)
```

Parameters
datestring$ An expression representing a date

Returns
Variant type

Immediate Window Sample
```
? DateValue("August 15, 1997")
```

SEE ALSO   DateAdd, DateDiff, DatePart, DateSerial, Date, Time, Format, Now, Day, IsDate, Month, Weekday, CVDate, #

Day

Returns the day value from the passed date argument

Description
The returned day value will be an integer between 1 and 31 representing the day of the month.

AVAILABLE IN VB SCRIPT

Syntax
```
Day(dateVariant)
```

Parameters
dateVariant   Required. Date to be used to retrieve the requested day.

Returns
Integer type

Immediate Window Sample
```
? Day(Now)
```

SEE ALSO   DateAdd, DateDiff, DatePart, DateSerial, DateValue, Date, Time, Format, Now, IsDate, Month, Weekday, CVDate

DDB

Returns a depreciation value of an asset

Description
Depreciation is determined by use of a double-declining balance method, unless another factor is specified using the factor parameter. The double-declining balance uses the number 2 for the factor parameter.

NOT AVAILABLE IN VB SCRIPT

Syntax
```
DDB(cost@, salvage@, life%, period%[, factor])
```

Parameters
cost@   Required. Initial cost of asset as Double type.

salvage@   Required. Value at end of useful life as Double type.

life%   Required. Length of useful life as Double type.

period% Required. Period for which depreciation is calculated as Double type.

factor   Optional. Rate that balance declines (default = 2) as Variant type.

Returns
Double type

Immediate Window Sample
? DDB(10000,500,24,12)

SEE ALSO   FV, IPmt, IRR, MIRR, NPer, NPV, Pmt, PPmt, PV, Rate, SLN, SYD

Declare

Creates a reference to a procedure or function in an external DLL

Description
The Libname$ is the name of the DLL to be called. The DLL extension is optional and will be added automatically if omitted. The procedure name is case sensitive, so make sure the name you use in the declaration is exact. Visual Basic includes the API Text Viewer application that contains VB declarations for all Win32 API calls.

NOT AVAILABLE IN VB SCRIPT

Syntax
Declare Sub Procname Lib Libname$ [Alias aliasname$] [(argList)] Declare Function procname [Lib Libname$] [Alias aliasname$] [(arg-List)] [As type]

Parameters
Procname   Required. Case-sensitive name must match function name unless given in aliasname parameter.

Libname$ Name of library containing Sub or Function.

aliasname$ Name or ordinal number of the specified routine.

argList   Any parameters and their types that must be passed.

Returns
N/A

Immediate Window Sample
N/A

> ## ➤ Programmer's Tip
>
> The aliasname$ can also be an ordinal number to call the
> index of a DLL routine. For example, setting the aliasname$ to
> "#2" will call the second routine stored in the DLL.

SEE ALSO   Call

DefBool

Specifies default data types for arguments to Boolean for
specified settings

Description
This command can be used to automatically set the data type of a
variable based on the starting of the name. For example, "DefBool
B" would make any new untyped variables that begin with the
letter "B" Boolean type. The statement "BNum = 4" would be a
Boolean type. This is used at the module level.

NOT AVAILABLE IN VB SCRIPT

Syntax
```
DefBool letterRange[, letterRange]...
```

Parameters
letterRange   Range can be a single letter or from–to (such as A–Z)

Returns
N/A

Immediate Window Sample
N/A

SEE ALSO DefDate, DefDec, DefDbl, DefInt, DefLng, DefSng, DefStr, DefVar, CBool, CCur, CDbl, CInt, CLng, CSng, CStr, CVar

DefByte

Specifies default data types for arguments to Bytes for specified settings

Description
This command can be used to automatically set the data type of a variable based on the starting of the name. For example, "DefByte B" would make any new untyped variables that begin with the letter "B" Byte type. The statement "BNum = 4" would be a Byte type. This is used at the module level.

NOT AVAILABLE IN VB SCRIPT

Syntax
```
DefByte letterRange[, letterRange]...
```

Parameters
letterRange   Range can be a single letter or from–to (such as A–Z)

Returns
N/A

Immediate Window Sample
N/A

SEE ALSO DefCur, DefDate, DefDec, DefDbl, DefInt, DefLng, DefSng, DefStr, DefVar

DefCur

Specifies default data types for arguments to Currency for specified settings

Description

This command can be used to automatically set the data type of a variable based on the starting of the name. For example, "DefCur C" would make any new untyped variables that begin with the letter "C" Currency type. The statement "CNum = 4" would be a Currency type. This is used at the module level.

NOT AVAILABLE IN VB SCRIPT

Syntax
```
DefCur letterRange [, letterRange]...
```

Parameters
letterRange   Range can be a single letter or from–to (such as A–Z)

Returns
N/A

Immediate Window Sample
N/A

SEE ALSO   DefDate, DefDec, DefDbl, DefInt, DefLng, DefSng, DefStr, DefVar

DefDate

VB 6
Only

Specifies default data types for arguments to Date for specified settings

Description

This command can be used to automatically set the data type of a variable based on the starting of the name. For example, "DefDate D" would make any new untyped variables that begin with the letter "D" the Date type. The statement "DAzoria = #6/26/97#" would be a Date type. This is used at the module level.

NOT AVAILABLE IN VB SCRIPT

Syntax
```
DefDate letterRange [, letterRange]...
```

Parameters

letterRange   Range can be a single letter or from–to (such as A–Z)

Returns

N/A

Immediate Window Sample

N/A

SEE ALSO   DefCur, DefDec, DefDbl, DefInt, DefLng, DefSng, DefStr, DefVar

DefDbl

Specifies default data types for arguments to Double for specified settings

Description

This command can be used to automatically set the data type of a variable based on the starting of the name. For example, "DefDbl Z" would make any new untyped variables that begin with the letter "Z" the Double type. The statement "ZNum = 4" would be a Double type. This is used at the module level.

NOT AVAILABLE IN VB SCRIPT

Syntax

```
DefDbl letterRange[, letterRange]...
```

Parameters

letterRange   Range can be a single letter or from–to (such as A–Z)

Returns

N/A

Immediate Window Sample

N/A

SEE ALSO   DefBool, DefByte, DefCur, DefDate, DefDec, DefInt, DefLng, DefObj, DefSng, DefStr, DefVar

DefDec

VB 6
Only

Specifies default data types for arguments to Decimal for
specified settings

Description
This command can be used to automatically set the data type of a
variable based on the starting of the name. For example, "DefDec Z"
would make any new untyped variables that begin with the letter
"Z" the Decimal type. The statement "ZNum = 4" would be a Decimal
type. This is used at the module level.

NOT AVAILABLE IN VB SCRIPT

Syntax
DefDec letterRange[, letterRange]...

Parameters
letterRange   Range can be a single letter or from–to (such as A–Z)

Returns
N/A

Immediate Window Sample
N/A

SEE ALSO   DefCur, DefDate, DefDbl, DefInt, DefLng, DefSng,
DefStr, DefVar

DefInt

Specifies default data types for arguments to Integer for
specified settings

Description
This command can be used to automatically set the data type of a
variable based on the starting of the name. For example, "DefInt i"
would make any new untyped variables that begin with the letter

"i" Integer type. The statement "iNum = 4" would create an Int type. This is used at the module level.

NOT AVAILABLE IN VB SCRIPT

Syntax
DefInt letterRange[, letterRange]...

Parameters
letterRange Range can be a single letter or from–to (such as A–Z)

Returns
N/A

Immediate Window Sample
N/A

SEE ALSO DefBool, DefByte, DefCur, DefDbl, DefLng, DefObj, DefSng, DefStr, DefVar

DefLng

Specifies default data types for arguments to Long for specified settings

Description
This command can be used to automatically set the data type of a variable based on the starting of the name. For example, "DefLng L" would make any new untyped variables that begin with the letter "L" Long type. The statement "LNum = 4" would be a Long type. This is used at the module level.

NOT AVAILABLE IN VB SCRIPT

Syntax
DefLng letterRange[, letterRange]...

Parameters
letterRange Range can be a single letter or from–to (such as A–Z)

Returns
N/A

Immediate Window Sample
N/A

SEE ALSO   DefBool, DefByte, DefCur, DefDbl, DefInt, DefObj, DefSng, DefStr, DefVar

DefObj

Specifies default data types for arguments to Objects for specified settings

Description
This command can be used to automatically set the data type of a variable based on the starting of the name. For example, "DefObj O" would make any new untyped variables that begin with the letter "O" Object type. The statement "Dim OExcel" would be an Object type. This is used at the module level.

NOT AVAILABLE IN VB SCRIPT

Syntax
```
DefObj letterRange[, letterRange]...
```

Parameters
letterRange   Range can be a single letter or from–to (such as A–Z)

Returns
N/A

Immediate Window Sample
N/A

SEE ALSO   DefBool, DefByte, DefCur, DefDbl, DefInt, DefLng, DefSng, DefStr, DefVar

DefSng

Specifies default data types for arguments to Singles for specified settings

Description

This command can be used to automatically set the data type of a variable based on the starting of the name. For example, "DefSng G" would make any new untyped variables that begin with the letter "G" Single type. The statement "GNum = 4" would be a Single type. This is used at the module level.

NOT AVAILABLE IN VB SCRIPT

Syntax

DefSng letterRange[, letterRange]...

Parameters

letterRange   Range can be a single letter or from–to (such as A–Z)

Returns

N/A

Immediate Window Sample

N/A

SEE ALSO   DefCur, DefDbl, DefInt, DefLng, DefStr, DefVar

DefStr

Specifies default data types for arguments to Strings for specified settings

Description

This command can be used to automatically set the data type of a variable based on the starting of the name. For example, "DefStr S" would make any new untyped variables that begin with the letter "S" String type. The statement "SName = "Joe"" would be a String type. This is used at the module level.

NOT AVAILABLE IN VB SCRIPT

Syntax
```
DefStr letterRange[, letterRange]...
```

III

Parameters
letterRange   Range can be a single letter or from–to (such as A–Z)

Returns
N/A

Immediate Window Sample
N/A

SEE ALSO   DefCur, DefDbl, DefInt, DefLng, DefSng, DefVar

DefVar

Specifies default data types for arguments to Variants for specified settings

Description
This command can be used to automatically set the data type of a variable based on the starting of the name. For example, "DefVar U-W" would make any new untyped variables that begin with the letter "U" through "W" a Variant type. The statement "VNum = 4" would be a Variant type. This is used at the module level.

NOT AVAILABLE IN VB SCRIPT

Syntax
```
DefVar letterRange[, letterRange]...
```

Parameters
letterRange   Range can be a single letter or from–to (such as A–Z)

Returns
N/A

Immediate Window Sample
N/A

SEE ALSO   DefCur, DefDbl, DefInt, DefLng, DefSng, DefStr

DeleteSetting   VB 6 Only

Deletes a setting from the application's window registry entries

Description
Eliminates an individual key or all keys contained in a section of the Windows registry. An error will occur if you attempt to delete a key or section that doesn't exist.

NOT AVAILABLE IN VB SCRIPT

Syntax
DeleteSetting appName,section[,key]

Parameters
appName   Required. The name of the application in the registry where the key is stored.

section   Required. Name of the section within the application area that holds the key. If key is not passed, all keys within the section are deleted.

key   Optional. Name of the key to be deleted.

Returns
N/A

Immediate Window Sample
DeleteSetting "MyApp","Prefs"

> ## ➤ Programmer's Tip

Use the settings commands for newer applications. Microsoft is increasingly stressing the use of the registry instead of individual INI files. Therefore, use this and other settings commands to maintain persistent settings related to your application.

SEE ALSO   GetSetting, GetAllSettings, SaveSetting

Dim

Defines a variable

Description
This defines the variable and can set the type of the variable either with the As keyword or through the variable suffixes (such as $, %, and so on). This command cannot be used in the Immediate window.

AVAILABLE IN VB SCRIPT

Syntax
Dim [Shared] name [As [New] type] [, name [As [New] type]]

Parameters
name   Permitted names include alphanumerics and basic symbols (such as the underscore), but no spaces.

type   Required if As keyword is used. Can be type such as Double, Integer, Byte, String, Object, Single, Currency, or Long.

Returns
N/A

Immediate Window Sample
N/A

> ### ➤ Programmer's Tip
>
> Because Dim cannot be used in the Immediate window, define
> variables in the Immediate window implicitly (that is, "i = 5"),
> by use of the conversion functions (that is, "a = CStr(12)"), or
> by use of the array command (that is, "a = array(3,5,9)").

SEE ALSO   Global, Option Base, ReDim, Static, Type, Private,
Public, Const, VarType

Dir, Dir$

Returns the name of the file or path that matches the pattern
passed in the argument

Description
The first call to this function must contain the requested pattern. If
the next call omits the pattern argument, the next file or path that
matches the original pattern will be returned. An empty string will
be returned if none matching the pattern is found.

NOT AVAILABLE IN VB SCRIPT

Syntax
For the first call to Dir$ for a pattern:

```
Dir$(pattern$[,attributes])  Dir(pattern$)
```

For each successive call for the same pattern:

```
Dir$  Dir
```

Parameters
pattern$ Any path or filename. May include wildcards.

Returns
String type

Immediate Window Sample
```
? Dir("C:\WINDOWS\WIN.INI")
? Dir("C:\WINDOWS\*.INI")
? Dir()
```

III

➤ Programmer's Tip

This function may be used to effectively create a routine to determine if a file exists.

SEE ALSO   CurDir$, ChDir, ChDrive

Do...Loop

Cycles through a loop until the necessary condition is met

Description
The Do...Loop structure can continue cycling while a condition is True (While) or until it is True (Until). Favor the Do...Loop structure over the While...Wend statements.

AVAILABLE IN VB SCRIPT

Syntax
To test the condition at the top of a loop:

```
Do [While I Until condition] [statements] [Exit Do]
[statements] Loop
```

To test the condition at the bottom of the loop:

```
Do [statements] Loop [While I Until condition]
```

Parameters

condition   Required. Boolean condition that may be evaluated to either True or False.

Returns

N/A

Immediate Window Sample

```
i=0 : Do While i < 5 : ? i : i=i+1 : Loop
i=0 : Do Until i > 5 : ? i : i=i+1 : Loop
```

SEE ALSO   Exit, For...Next, While...Wend

DoEvents

Pauses to allow the system to process events

Description

A loop that is doing a great number of operations provides few processing resources for the rest of the system for tasks such as screen updates. This command pauses for the system to process other tasks.

NOT AVAILABLE IN VB SCRIPT

Syntax

```
DoEvents() 'function
DoEvents 'statement
```

Parameters

N/A

Returns

N/A

Immediate Window Sample

```
DoEvents
```

> ### ➤ Programmer's Tip

When creating program status indicators, you will often need to use the DoEvents command to pause for the system to redraw text boxes, progress bars, and so on. This will slow execution, but will allow users to see what progress has taken place.

SEE ALSO   Stop, End

End

Stops execution or ends a definition of a Function, If structure, Select statement, Subroutine, or Type definition

Description

The End command is used to terminate either execution or a definition. Only the End If statement will automatically insert the necessary space when it is typed (automatically converting "endif" to "End If").

NOT AVAILABLE IN VB SCRIPT

Syntax

```
End [Function | If | Select | Sub | Type]
```

Parameters

N/A

Returns

N/A

Immediate Window Sample

```
End
```

> ## ➤ Programmer's Tip
>
> Use the End command by itself to completely stop execution
> of a program, such as when the user selects the Exit option on
> the File menu.

SEE ALSO   Function, If...Then...Else, Select Case, Stop, Sub, Type

Enum

VB 6
Only

Used to create an enumeration set of constants

Description

Like the Type...End Type commands, enumeration enables you to
create a set of variables that are referenced together. Variables and
parameters can be declared with the Enum type, although
assigned values cannot be modified at run time.

NOT AVAILABLE IN VB SCRIPT

Syntax

```
Enum setName
    constName1 = val1
    constName2 = val2
End Enum
```

Parameters

setName   Required.

constName1 , **constName2**   Optional. Any number of constant
names.

val1, val2   Optional. Values to assign to the enumerated constants.

Returns

N/A

Immediate Window Sample

N/A

> ➤ **Programmer's Tip**

Using enumeration is a great way to organize the constants used by your projects. Since Public enumerations become part of the type library, they are convenient for the use of class libraries.

SEE ALSO   Const

Environ, Environ$

Returns information on the current environment

Description

The operating system stores a great deal of information available through this function. These variables include such information as the Path statement, the Prompt information, the Temp directory, and so on. Each returned string begins with the environmental variable, followed by an = sign, followed by the current setting.

NOT AVAILABLE IN VB SCRIPT

Syntax

```
Environ$(entry-name$ | entry-position%)
Environ(entry-name$ | entry-position%)
```

Parameters

entry-name$ The name of the environmental variable to retrieve.

entry-position%   The index of the environmental variable.

Returns

String type

Immediate Window Sample

```
? Environ("path")
? Environ(1)
? Environ(2)
? Environ(3)
```

SEE ALSO Command, Command$

EOF

Returns the End-of-File condition

Description

This function may be used effectively with a Do...Loop to process a file. The Immediate window example requires a file Test.txt located at the root of C: to function properly. Change the file and path names to use a different file.

NOT AVAILABLE IN VB SCRIPT

Syntax

```
EOF(file-number)
```

Parameters

file-number The current file number assigned when the file was opened.

Returns

Integer type

Immediate Window Sample

```
Open "C:\test.txt" for Input as #1 : ? EOF(1) :_
Close #1
```

➤ Programmer's Tip

You may check this function when a file is initially opened with a True condition indicating that the file is empty.

SEE ALSO Close, Get, Input #, Line Input #, Loc, LOF, Open

Eqv

Logical equivalence operator

Description
This operator essentially performs a bitwise And on two numeric expressions.

AVAILABLE IN VB SCRIPT

Syntax
a Eqv b

Parameters
a, b   Required. Numeric expressions.

Returns
Boolean type

Immediate Window Sample
? 8 Eqv 8
? True Eqv False

SEE ALSO   And, Or, Imp, Xor, True, False

Erase

Clears the current contents of the array

Description
This clears the values of fixed-size arrays and releases the memory of a dynamic array.

AVAILABLE IN VB SCRIPT

Syntax
```
Erase arrayname [, arrayname]
```

Parameters
arrayname   Required. The name of the array to be cleared.

Returns
N/A

Immediate Window Sample
```
myArray = array(1,5,7,9)
? myArray(2)
Erase myArray
? myArray(2)
```

➤ Programmer's Tip

In Visual Basic, arrays start at a lower bound of 0. Any arrays defined automatically have an index member of 0. VBA, however, starts at zero (0) in newer versions, but older versions use 1 as the lower bound. Check the VBA documentation for information on the version you use.

SEE ALSO   Dim, ReDim, Array

Err Object

Contains complete information about an error that has occurred

Description
The Clear method will clear the current error, while the Description and Number properties describe the error itself. The Err object is mostly used in conjunction with an On Error routine within a procedure or function.

NOT AVAILABLE IN VB SCRIPT

Syntax
`Err.Raise errornum`

Parameters
errornum   Required. Integer with error code to be generated.

Returns
N/A

Immediate Window Sample
`Err.Clear Err.Raise 6`

SEE ALSO   Error, Error$, On Error GoTo, Resume

Error

Generates an error of the specified type in the system

Description
This statement causes the Visual Basic system to receive an error of the type specified.

NOT AVAILABLE IN VB SCRIPT

Syntax
`Error errorcode%`

Parameters
errorcode%   Required. Integer error code number.

Returns
N/A

Immediate Window Sample
`Error 6`

➤ **Programmer's Tip**

You can use these errors yourself when debugging by
generating exactly the type error you need to document
problems the user is having.

SEE ALSO   Err, Error$, On Error GoTo, Resume

Error, Error$

Returns the error message that corresponds to the passed
argument

Description
This function returns the technical English explanation of the error
type passed in the errorcode argument.

NOT AVAILABLE IN VB SCRIPT

Syntax
```
Error$[(errorcode%)]  Error[(errorcode%)]
```

Parameters
errorcode%   Required. Integer representing an error code number.

Returns
String type

Immediate Window Sample
```
? Error$(6)
```

SEE ALSO   Err, Error, On Error GoTo, Resume

Event

Creates a user-defined event

Description

Once you define an event, the RaiseEvent command may generate that event to activate the routine. This command is not available in VBA or VB Script, only in the complete Visual Basic development environment.

NOT AVAILABLE IN VB SCRIPT

Syntax

```
[Public] Event procedurename [arglist]
```

Parameters

procedurename   Required. Any permitted name for the event.

arglist   Optional. Any arguments that are to be passed to the event.

Returns

N/A

Immediate Window Sample

N/A

SEE ALSO   Sub, Function, Property Let, Property Get, Property Set

Exit

Terminates the current operation before the conditions are complete

Description

You can use the Exit Do to exit a Do...Loop before the final conditions have been met. The same is possible with For...Next loops, subroutines, and functions.

AVAILABLE IN VB SCRIPT

Syntax

```
Exit Do
Exit For
Exit Sub
Exit Function
```

Parameters
N/A

Returns
N/A

Immediate Window Sample
N/A

SEE ALSO   Do...Loop, For...Next, Function, Sub

Exp

Raises the base of natural logarithms (e) to a specified power

Description
The function (known as an antilogarithm) returns a Double type based on the results of the passed exponent. The constant e is approximately 2.718282.

AVAILABLE IN VB SCRIPT

Syntax
Exp(power)

Parameters
power   Required. Double type to be used as the exponent.

Returns
Double type

Immediate Window Sample
? Exp(1)
? Exp(20)

SEE ALSO   Log

False

Logical False

Description

This constant can be used in most expressions, bitwise operations, and comparisons.

AVAILABLE IN VB SCRIPT

Syntax
```
False
```

Parameters
N/A

Returns
N/A

Immediate Window Sample
```
? (2=2) = False
? (2=2) = True
```

SEE ALSO   And, Or, Imp, Eqv, Xor, True

FileAttr

Returns the mode (input, output, and so on) of the specified file

Description

This function can be used to determine the current attributes of an open file. The mode can be input (1), output (2), random (4), append (8), or binary (32).

NOT AVAILABLE IN VB SCRIPT

Syntax

```
FileAttr(filenumber%[, infotype%])
```

Parameters

filenumber%   Required. Any valid file number ID.

infotype%   Optional. On 32-bit systems, must be equal to 1. On 16-bit systems, a type 2 will return a system file handle.

Returns

Long type

Immediate Window Sample

```
Open "C:\test.txt" for Input as #1 : ? FileAttr(1) _
: Close #1
```

SEE ALSO   Open, Input #, Print #, Close

FileCopy

Copies a file from the source to the destination

Description

This routine acts as the traditional file-copy operating system call and makes a duplicate of the file (with path) described in the source$ to the file (with path) denoted in the second string.

NOT AVAILABLE IN VB SCRIPT

Syntax

```
FileCopy source$, dest$
```

Parameters

source$, dest$ Required. Strings containing paths and filenames.

Returns

N/A

Immediate Window Sample
```
FileCopy "C:\test.txt" "C:\testdup.txt"
```

➤ Programmer's Tip

Use of the FileCopy command is an effective way to create database templates. Because it is difficult to dynamically construct a database, you can keep a blank structured database in the program folder. When you need a copy, use FileCopy to create it.

SEE ALSO   ChDir, ChDrive, CurDir, Open, Close, MkDir, RmDir, Kill

FileDateTime

Returns the date and time when a specified file was last modified

Description
Simply passing a valid filename and path will return the last modified date of any accessible file.

NOT AVAILABLE IN VB SCRIPT

Syntax
```
FileDateTime(filename$)
```

Parameters
filename$ Required. Any valid path and filename.

Returns
Variant (Date) type

Immediate Window Sample
```
? FileDateTime("C:\test.txt")
```

SEE ALSO   GetAttr, FileLen, ChDir, ChDrive, CurDir, Open, Close, MkDir, RmDir, Kill

FileLen

Returns the length in bytes of a particular file

Description

This routine can determine the length of any file available to the system. The file does not need to be opened with any of the disk access commands to get its length.

NOT AVAILABLE IN VB SCRIPT

Syntax

```
FileLen(filename$)
```

Parameters

filename$ Required. Any valid path and filename.

Returns

Long type

Immediate Window Sample

```
? FileLen("C:\test.txt")
```

SEE ALSO   FileDateTime, GetAttr, ChDir, ChDrive, CurDir, Open, Close, MkDir, RmDir, Kill

Filter

VB 6
Only

Filters a current array and returns a new array that qualifies for the filter criteria

Description

This function uses criteria passed to it to filter an array. A new array is created and returned that only contains the data that qualifies under the filter specifications.

AVAILABLE IN VB SCRIPT

Syntax
```
Filter(strArray,pattern [,include[,compare]]
```

Parameters
strArray   Required. Array of source strings.

pattern   Required. String used as search string.

include   Optional. Boolean to indicate whether to return strings that contain the string. A False value (default) requires the string to match the pattern.

compare   Optional. Type of comparison to perform, such as vbUseCompareOption (–1), vbBinaryCompare (0), vbTextCompare (1), or vbDatabaseCompare (2).

Returns
Array type

Immediate Window Sample
```
a = Array("Cussler", "Hill", "Burgess", "Wordsworth")
b = Filter(a,"Hill")
? b(0)
```

➤ Programmer's Tip

Use of this routine provides a quick and effective alternative to placing a short list of values in a database for searching.

SEE ALSO   Array, Join, Split

Fix

Returns an integer of the passed value

Description
This function works almost exactly like the Int( ) function, except when concerning negative numbers. Fix returns the first negative

number greater than or equal to the passed value. Int( ) returns the
first negative number that is less than or equal to the value.
Fix(−1.4) would return the value −1, while Int(−1.4) would return
the value −2.

AVAILABLE IN VB SCRIPT

Syntax
```
Fix(numericExpression)
```

Parameters
numericExpression   Required. Any valid numeric expression.

Returns
Integer type

Immediate Window Sample
```
? Fix(1.4)
? Fix(-1.4)
```

➤ Programmer's Tip

While both the Fix and Int commands are available to VBA
and VB Script environments, if you are using VB 6, you might
consider using the new Round command, as it provides a
great deal of flexibility for rounding.

SEE ALSO   CInt, Int, Round

For Each...Next

Cycles through an entire collection of objects or items in an array

Description
The For Each...Next structure will cycle through all the elements,
even if they are not in numeric order. In an object collection, the
element variable is set to reference the current object.

AVAILABLE IN VB SCRIPT

Syntax

```
For Each element In group [statements] Next [element]
```

Parameters

element   Required. A variable that will hold the current reference to the selected object or array item.

group   An array or collection reference.

Returns

N/A

Immediate Window Sample

```
myArray = array(5,8,10,98)
For Each myItem in myArray : ? myItem : Next
```

➤ Programmer's Tip

Use this command for accessing the objects in a collection, because it can process nonsequential objects lists much more effectively than using an index with a traditional For...Next loop.

SEE ALSO   Do...Loop, Exit, While...Wend, For...Next, CreateObject, GetObject

---

For...Next

Loops until necessary value is reached

Description

The For...Next structure will cycle through the statements in the loop until the endvalue parameter is reached.

AVAILABLE IN VB SCRIPT

Syntax

```
For counter = startvalue To endvalue [Step increment]
    [statements]
    [Exit For]
    [statements]
Next [counter] [, counter] ...
```

Parameters

counter   Required. Variable that keeps the current increment.

startvalue   Required. Begin value of loop.

endvalue   Required. End value of loop.

Step   Optional. Amount that counter is increased every time through the loop.

Returns

N/A

Immediate Window Sample

```
For i = 1 to 10 : ? i : Next i
For i=10 to 1 step -1 : ? i : Next
```

SEE ALSO   Do...Loop, Exit, While...Wend, For Each...Next

Format, Format$

Returns a string formatted in a number of ways, including string, date, time, currency, and other formats

Description

The Format command is one of the most powerful commands for easily and quickly generating output in a desired format. Use the # within the editPattern to indicate a placeholder.

AVAILABLE IN VB SCRIPT

Syntax

```
Format$(numericExpression, editPattern$)
```

Parameters

numericExpression   Required. Valid expression including dates.

editPattern$ Required. Pattern required for output.

Returns

Variant or String type

Immediate Window Sample

```
? Format(Now, "hh:mm:ss AMPM")
? Format(Now, "h:m:s")
? Format(Now, "mmm d yyyy")
? Format(2534.64,"##,##0")
? Format(2534.64,"##,##0.00")
? Format(2534.64,"##,###.##")
? Format(-2534.64,"$##,##0.00;($##,##0.00)")
```

SEE ALSO   DateSerial, Now, Str, Str$, TimeSerial, CVDate, Val, CStr, &, DateValue, FormatCurrency, FormatDateTime, FormatNumber, FormatPercent

FormatCurrency

VB 6
Only

Returns a string formatted in a specified currency format

Description

This command is a new specialized formatting command for easily and quickly generating output in a currency format. The character conventions of the standard Format command also apply to this command. The currency symbol that is specified in the control panel is used for formatting.

AVAILABLE IN VB SCRIPT

Syntax

```
FormatCurrency(numericExpression [,numDecimalPlaces
[,includeLeadDigit [,useParensforNegs [,groupDigits]]]])
```

Parameters

numericExpression   Required. Value to be formatted.

NumDecimalPlaces   Optional. Number of decimal places to appear to the right of the decimal. If left blank, −1 will be used to indicate that the default number will be used.

includeLeadDigit   Optional. Tristate value to specify whether leading zero will be displayed for fractional values.

useParensforNegs   Optional. Tristate value to specify whether to show parentheses for negative numbers.

groupDigits   Optional. Tristate value to specify whether to group digits using the group delimiter specified in the computer's regional settings.

Returns
Variant or String type

Immediate Window Sample
? FormatCurrency(123.1232)

➤ Programmer's Tip

This command uses the Tristate setting for some of the typically Boolean expressions. The Tristate value is an integer where −1 = True, 0 = False, and −2 = Use computer's default regional setting.

SEE ALSO   Format, FormatDateTime, FormatNumber, FormatPercent

---

FormatDateTime
VB 6
Only

Returns a string formatted in a specified date and time format

Description
This command is a new specialized formatting command for easily and quickly generating output in a date and time format. The character conventions of the standard Format command also apply to this command.

AVAILABLE IN VB SCRIPT

Syntax
```
FormatDateTime(date [,namedFormat])
```

Parameters
date   Required.

namedFormat   Optional. This specifies the format type based on one of five constants: vbGeneralDate (0), vbLongDate (1), vbShortDate (2), vbLongTime (3), or vbShortTime (4).

Returns
String type

Immediate Window Sample
```
? FormatDateTime(Now, 0)
? FormatDateTime(Now, vbLongDate)
```

> ## ➤ Programmer's Tip
>
> Use this command if you want quick date and time formatting. However, if your code will need to be translated to VBA, use the Format function to specify a custom date and time format.

SEE ALSO   Format, FormatCurrency, FormatNumber, FormatPercent

FormatNumber
VB 6
Only

Returns a string formatted in a specified numeric format

Description
This command is a new specialized formatting command for easily and quickly generating output in a numeric format. The character conventions of the standard Format command also apply to this command.

AVAILABLE IN VB SCRIPT

Syntax

```
FormatNumber(numericExpression [,numDecimalPlaces
[,includeLeadDigit [,useParensforNegs [,groupDig-
its]]]])
```

Parameters

numericExpression   Required. Value to be formatted.

numDecimalPlaces   Optional. Number of decimal places to appear to the right of the decimal. If left blank, −1 will be used to indicate that the default number will be used.

includeLeadDigit   Optional. Tristate value to specify whether leading zero will be displayed for fractional values.

useParensforNegs   Optional. Tristate value to specify whether to show parentheses for negative numbers.

groupDigits   Optional. Tristate value to specify whether to group digits using the group delimiter specified in the computer's regional settings.

Returns

Numeric type

Immediate Window Sample

```
? FormatNumber(129.222,1)
```

> ## ➤ Programmer's Tip

This command uses the Tristate setting for some of the typically Boolean expressions. The Tristate value is an integer where −1 = True, 0 = False, and −2 = Use default setting.

SEE ALSO   Format, FormatCurrency, FormatDateTime, FormatPercent

FormatPercent

Returns a string formatted in a specified percentage format

Description

This command is a new specialized formatting command for easily and quickly generating output in a percentage format. The character conventions of the standard Format command also apply to this command. The formatted percentage is returned as the value passed multiplied by 100 (that is, .987 = 98.7%).

AVAILABLE IN VB SCRIPT

Syntax

```
FormatPercent(numericExpression [,numDecimalPlaces
[,includeLeadDigit [,useParensforNegs [,groupDigits]]]])
```

Parameters

numericExpression   Required. Value to be formatted.

numDecimalPlaces   Optional. Number of decimal places to appear to the right of the decimal. If left blank, −1 will be used to indicate that the default number will be used.

includeLeadDigit   Optional. Tristate value to specify whether leading zero will be displayed for fractional values.

useParensforNegs   Optional. Tristate value to specify whether to show parentheses for negative numbers.

groupDigits   Optional. Tristate value to specify whether to group digits using the group delimiter specified in the computer's regional settings.

Returns

Variant or String type

Immediate Window Sample

```
? FormatPercent(123.456,2)
```

> ➤ **Programmer's Tip**

This command uses the Tristate setting for some of the typically Boolean expressions. The Tristate value is an integer where −1 = True, 0 = False, and −2 = Use default setting.

SEE ALSO Format, FormatCurrency, FormatDateTime, FormatNumber

FreeFile

Returns the next valid free file number

Description

This function returns the next available number for use as a file. Use this command if a program needs to manually specify the index number of a file to be opened. If you've been letting the system supply the file number, checking this value will reveal how many files have been opened this session.

NOT AVAILABLE IN VB SCRIPT

Syntax

```
FreeFile
```

Parameters

N/A

Returns

Integer type

Immediate Window Sample

```
? FreeFile
```

SEE ALSO Open, Close, Print #, Input #, ChDir, ChDrive, CurDir, Get, Put, GetAttr, MkDir, RmDir

FreeLocks

Allows background processing to occur to keep open dynasets current

Description

If processing is too intense, calling this function will activate any processing required on dynasets to keep them current. This routine is obsolete and included in Visual Basic only for backward compatibility.

NOT AVAILABLE IN VB SCRIPT

Syntax

```
FreeLocks
```

Parameters

N/A

Returns

N/A

Immediate Window Sample

N/A

SEE ALSO   DoEvents

Friend

Like the Public keyword, but limits accessibility to within project

Description

Using the Public keyword makes a procedure accessible throughout the project and exposes it outside the project. The Friend keyword allows the procedure to be called within the project, but hides it from the outside. For example, you may need a function in a form module or class to be available within the project, but hide it from final compilation as an ActiveX control.

NOT AVAILABLE IN VB SCRIPT

Syntax
```
Friend procedureName
```

Parameters
procedureName   Required. Name of procedure to make public within a project.

Returns
N/A

Immediate Window Sample
N/A

➤ Programmer's Tip

This keyword is perfect if you want to hide methods much as internal properties may be hidden. Use the Friend keyword in a way similar to the use of the Property Let, Get, and Set commands to restrict direct access to methods within the control.

SEE ALSO   Private, Public

Function...End Function

Creates a function in a module or form

Description
This command enables definition of a function that may include the types of arguments that will be received by the function as well as the arguments that will be returned.

AVAILABLE IN VB SCRIPT

Syntax

```
[Static] [Private] Function function-name [(arguments)]
[As type] [Static var[,var]...] [Dim var[,var]...]
    [statements]
    [function-name = expression]
    [Exit Function]
    [statements]
    [function-name = expression]
End Function
```

Parameters

arguments   Required. Any arguments to be received by the function.

Returns

Any defined type

Immediate Window Sample

N/A

➤ Programmer's Tip

A single value may be returned by a function. Setting the name of the function to a value, within the function, sets the return value. To return the value 5 from the function myFunction, the code "myFunction = 5" would appear within the body of the function.

SEE ALSO   End, Exit, Sub

FV

Returns the future value of an annuity

Description

The value that is returned is calculated from the period, the fixed payments, and the fixed interest rate.

NOT AVAILABLE IN VB SCRIPT

Syntax

```
FV(rate!, numPeriods%, payment@, presentValue@, whenDue%)
```

Parameters

rate!   Required. Double type of interest rate per period.

numPeriods%   Required. Integer of total number of payments.

payment@   Required. Double type of the amount of each payment.

presentValue@   Optional. Variant of the present value.

whenDue%   Optional. 0 = Payments due at end of period, 1 = Beginning of the period.

Returns

Double type

Immediate Window Sample

```
? FV(.0081,48,-1500.75)
```

SEE ALSO   DDB, IPmt, IRR, MIRR, NPer, NPV, Pmt, PPmt, PV, Rate, SLN, SYD

Get

Retrieves information from an open file and places it in a variable

Description

The Get command reads the data usually written into the file by a Put statement. All data types are supported. The Immediate window example assumes a file named Test.txt at the C: root directory contains at least eight characters of data to read.

NOT AVAILABLE IN VB SCRIPT

Syntax
```
Get [#]filenumber%,[position&], recordbuffer
```

Parameters
filenumber%   Required. Any valid open file number.

position&   Optional. Specifies record number in a Random file or a byte number in a Binary file where writing should occur.

recordbuffer   Required. A valid variable that will have its contents read from the file.

Returns
N/A

Immediate Window Sample
```
b$ = String(8," ")
Open "C:\test.txt" for Binary as #1: Get #1,,b$ : Close #1
? b$
Close #1
```

➤ Programmer's Tip

If you have a sequence of variables in a particular order that need to be input, you can define a structure using the Type...End Type commands. When a variable is defined with the structure that you've created, all of the variables in that structure can be loaded with a single Get.

SEE ALSO   LOF, Open, Put, Type, FileLen, Input #, Line Input #

GetAllSettings
VB 6
Only

Retrieves all of the settings from a section of the Windows registry

Description
This command will return a list of key settings within a section of the application's registry area. The settings are returned in a

two-dimensional array where the first column contains the key name and the second contains the value of the related key.

NOT AVAILABLE IN VB SCRIPT

Syntax
```
GetAllSettings(appName,section)
```

Parameters
appName   Required. Application area within the Windows registry to access.

section   Required. Section of the registry to be retrieved.

Returns
Array type

Immediate Window Sample
```
SaveSetting "myApp", "Prefs", "Velo", 500
a = GetAllSettings("myapp","Prefs")
```

➤ Programmer's Tip

Use the settings commands for newer applications. Microsoft is increasingly stressing the use of the registry instead of individual INI files. Therefore, use this and other settings commands to maintain persistent settings related to your application.

SEE ALSO   DeleteSetting, GetSetting, SaveSetting

GetAttr

Returns the attributes of a given file

Description
As opposed to FileAttr, which returns information about open files, GetAttr returns such information as Normal (0), ReadOnly (1),

Hidden (2), System (4), Directory (16), or Archive (32) designations about a file on the disk.

NOT AVAILABLE IN VB SCRIPT

Syntax
GetAttr(fileName$)

Parameters
fileName$ Required. A valid path and filename.

Returns
Integer type

Immediate Window Sample
? GetAttr("c:\test.txt")

SEE ALSO   FileDateTime, FileLen, FileAttr, Open, Close, EOF, LOF, Loc

GetAutoServerSettings

VB 6
Only

Retrieves the OLE registry condition of an ActiveX component

Description
This command can be used to establish whether an ActiveX control has been registered on the current system or will execute from a remote machine. It returns one of four values: 1 = component is registered remotely, 2 = remote machine name, 3 = RPC network protocol name, and 4 = RPC authentication level.

NOT AVAILABLE IN VB SCRIPT

Syntax
object.GetAutoServerSettings([progID],[classID])

Parameters
progID   Optional. Specifies the ProgID for the component.

classID   Optional. Specifies the unique identifier class ID (CLSID) of the component.

Returns

Integer type

Immediate Window Sample

```
set myObject = CreateObject("excel.application")
? myObject.GetAutoServerSettings()
```

➤ Programmer's Tip

For intensive processing, it may be a good idea to query objects to determine if they are remotely used. If so, make sure you place backup error checking for object re-creation if a remote fault would lose the object connection, making the object disappear.

SEE ALSO CreateObject, GetObject

GetObject

Returns a reference to a current object or creates the object if unavailable

Description

This function checks whether an instance of the object exists and uses the current one. If no object is available in memory, it attempts to instantiate it. GetObject can also be used to open a file that has an ActiveX/OLE Automation server.

In the Immediate window example, the GetObject statement expects the Excel application to already be launched and open. A reference is then created to the Application object.

AVAILABLE IN VB SCRIPT

Syntax

```
GetObject([pathName] [,className])
```

Parameters

pathName   Optional. Path to the file that will be opened with the GetObject.

className   Optional. Class of OLE Automation Server to be used.

Returns
N/A

Immediate Window Sample

```
Set myObject = GetObject(,"Excel.Application")
Set myObject = GetObject("test.xls","Excel.Application")
```

➤ Programmer's Tip

To avoid multiple instances of a single application executing, this command can be used. If an instance is already running, the new instance simply activates the existent object and uses it.

SEE ALSO   CreateObject, Set, dot (.), Nothing

GetSetting

Reads a key setting from the application's area of the Windows registry

Description

This function will return the key value given the application, section, and key name from the Windows registry. If no value is included as the default and the key is not found, a zero-length string ("") is returned.

NOT AVAILABLE IN VB SCRIPT

Syntax

```
GetSetting(appName,section,key [,default])
```

Parameters

appName   Required. Name of the application for the proper area of the Windows registry.

section   Required. Name of the section where the key will be retrieved.

key   Required. Name of the key.

default   Optional. Value to return if no key is found.

Returns

Variant

Immediate Window Sample

N/A

➤ Programmer's Tip

Use the settings commands for newer applications. Microsoft is increasingly stressing the use of the registry instead of individual INI files. Therefore, use this and other settings commands to maintain persistent settings related to your application.

SEE ALSO   GetAllSettings, SaveSetting, DeleteSettings

Global

Declares a variable globally available to all forms and modules in a project

Description

The Global command can only be used in a module. To make a method or property of a form available to the project, use the Public keyword.

NOT AVAILABLE IN VB SCRIPT

Syntax

For declaring the data type of a simple variable:

```
Global name [As [New] type] [, name [As [New] type]]
```

For declaring an array:

```
Global name[(subscript-range)] [As [New] type]
[, name[(subscript-range)] [As [New] type]
```

Parameters

name   Permitted names including alphanumerics and basic symbols (such as the underscore), but no spaces.

type   Required. Can be type such as Double, Integer, Byte, String, Object, Single, Currency, or Long.

Returns

N/A

Immediate Window Sample

N/A

➤ Programmer's Tip

Although Global variables are extremely useful in particular situations, try to avoid their use as much as possible. By making a variable Public and attaching it to a particular object, you will be able to more successfully manage your project. Object-oriented programming seeks to encapsulate variables within their related structures. This is a good methodology to adopt.

SEE ALSO   Const, Dim, Option Base, Static, Public, Private

GoSub...Return

This command can be used to jump within a subroutine or function to a piece of code

Description

Use of the GoSub breaks the flow of the program by allowing
in-subroutine jumps. The LineLabel or Linenumber parameter sets
the anchors for the top of the sub-subroutines.

NOT AVAILABLE IN VB SCRIPT

Syntax

```
GoSub LineLabel | Linenumber
LineLabel: | Linenumber : [statement-block] : Return
```

Parameters

LineLabel | Linenumber   Required. Numeric or alphanumeric
anchor that a GoSub command can jump to.

Returns

N/A

Immediate Window Sample

N/A

➤ Programmer's Tip

Try to avoid the use of GoSub and GoTo commands—they
remain in Visual Basic mostly for compatibility with older
versions. They make code difficult to read and expensive
to maintain.

SEE ALSO   On...GoSub, Sub

GoTo

This command will jump execution within a procedure or function

Description

Use the GoTo command to jump to an out-of-sequence set of code.

NOT AVAILABLE IN VB SCRIPT

Syntax

```
GoTo [linenumber | linelabel]
```

Parameters

linelabel | linenumber   Required. Numeric or alphanumeric
anchor that a GoTo command can jump to.

Returns

N/A

Immediate Window Sample

N/A

> ➤ **Programmer's Tip**
>
> Try to avoid the use of GoSub and GoTo commands, as they
> remain in Visual Basic mostly for compatibility with older
> versions. They make code difficult to read and expensive
> to maintain.

SEE ALSO   GoSub

Hex, Hex$

Converts a number to its hexadecimal equivalent

Description

This function will create a string containing the hexadecimal (base
16 number) from the passed value. Each value may contain the
numbers 0–9 and the letters A–F.

AVAILABLE IN VB SCRIPT

Syntax

```
Hex$(numericExpression) Hex(numericExpression)
```

Parameters
numericExpression   Required. Any numeric expression.

Returns
String type

Immediate Window Sample
```
? Hex(9)
? Hex(10)
? Hex(255)
? Hex(256)
```

➤ Programmer's Tip

When using a hexadecimal number, you can easily define a constant using the &H command. For example, the code "Const myHex = &HFF" will set the constant "myHex" to the decimal value "255."

SEE ALSO   Oct, Oct$

Hour

Returns the hour portion of a date and time value

Description
The returned hour value will be an integer between 0 and 23 representing the hour of the day.

AVAILABLE IN VB SCRIPT

Syntax
```
Hour(dateVariant)
```

Parameters
dateVariant   The date that the hour is to be extracted from.

Returns

Integer type

Immediate Window Sample

? Hour(Now)

SEE ALSO Now, TimeSerial, TimeValue, Time, Minute, Second

III

If...Then...ElseIf...End If

Conditional execution of statements

Description

The If...Then structure enables evaluation of conditions for a
change in the program flow. If the statements to be executed are
placed on a single line (without using the : command to simulate
multiple lines), the End If statements must be eliminated.
However, for code clarity, it is often a good idea to include them.

AVAILABLE IN VB SCRIPT

Syntax

```
If condition-1 Then
    [actions-1]
[ElseIf condition-2 Then]
    [actions-2]
[ElseIf condition-n Then]
    [actions-n]
[Else]
    [else-actions]
End If
```

Parameters

conditions Required. Boolean expressions.

Returns

N/A

Immediate Window Sample

```
a = 1
If a = 1 Then ? "Equal" else ? "Not equal"
a = 2
If a = 1 Then ? "Equal" else ? "Not equal"
```

➤ Programmer's Tip

If the valuation or multiple valuation is simple, consider using the Choose, IIf, or Switch commands instead. These usually will make the code much simpler in certain situations.

SEE ALSO   If...Then...Else, Select Case, IIf, Choose, Switch

---

IIf

Returns one of two values depending on the evaluation of an expression

Description

This function, like Switch, compactly and quickly returns a value based on the evaluation of an expression. The IIf works very well to substitute Null values.

NOT AVAILABLE IN VB SCRIPT

Syntax

```
IIf(expression, valueIfTrue, valueIfFalse)
```

Parameters

expression   Required. Any expression that can be resolved to a Boolean condition.

valueIfTrue, valueIfFalse   Required. Values to be returned from the function depending on the expression.

Returns

Variant

Immediate Window Sample

```
a=1
? IIf(a=1,"It's true","It's not true")
a=2
? IIf(a=1,"It's true","It's not true")
a=Null
? IIf(IsNull(a),0,a)
```

III

➤ Programmer's Tip

The IIF function requires the Financial DLL. The command is not included with the Visual Basic run time and must be installed separately if you're shipping a Visual Basic solution to customers.

SEE ALSO   If...Then...Else, Select Case, Choose, Switch

IMEStatus

For East Asian versions of VB, retrieves the Input Method Editor

Description

This command retrieves an integer detailing the Input Method Editor (IME) for either the Japanese or Chinese versions. See the Visual Basic 6 manual for all of the possible settings.

NOT AVAILABLE IN VB SCRIPT

Syntax

IMEStatus

Parameters

N/A

Returns
Integer type

Immediate Window Sample
```
? IMEStatus
```

SEE ALSO   Environ$

Returns logical implication from two values

Description
Order is important when using the Imp operator, as the bitwise comparison between the two values sets the corresponding bit in the result.

AVAILABLE IN VB SCRIPT

Syntax
```
a Imp b
```

Parameters
a, b   Required. Valid numeric expressions.

Returns
Variant

Immediate Window Sample
```
? 1 Imp 0
? 1 Imp 1
? 0 Imp 1
? 0 Imp 0
```

SEE ALSO   And, Or, Eqv, Xor, True, False

Implements

Activates a specified interface or class implemented within a
class module

Description

In Visual Basic, an interface is automatically created for all Public
procedures. The Implements command causes the class to accept
COM QueryInterface calls for an interface ID.

NOT AVAILABLE IN VB SCRIPT

Syntax

```
Implements name
```

Parameters

name   Required. Either the name of the interface or the class to be
exposed.

Returns

N/A

Immediate Window Sample

N/A

➤ Programmer's Tip

Don't use this command unless you need an advanced C++
level call interface. Otherwise, interaction with the VB COM
object is much more effective through the OLE Automation
interface.

SEE ALSO   Shell, Environ$

Input

Returns a string from the open stream of an Input or Binary file

Description
By use of the Open command, once a file's open, the input stream can be read. The Input command can read directly into the specified variable.

NOT AVAILABLE IN VB SCRIPT

Syntax
```
Input #filenumber, var1[, var2]
```

Parameters
filenumber   Required. File to read input stream.

var1   Required. Variable name to read input.

Returns
N/A

Immediate Window Sample
```
Open "c:.txt" for Input as #1 : Input #1, a$_
: Close #1

? a$
```

➤ Programmer's Tip

Since Input # can read a line at a time, it provides the easiest way to load text-based formats such as SYLK or DIF files.

SEE ALSO   Input, Input$, Write #

Input, Input$

Reads a specified number of bytes from an Input or Binary file

Description

In contrast to the Input # statement made for text files, the Input function can read a specific number of bytes into memory, which is ideal for Binary files.

NOT AVAILABLE IN VB SCRIPT

Syntax

```
Input$(inputlength%,[#]filenumber%)
```

Parameters

inputlength%   Required. Number of bytes to read.

filenumber%   Required. Current file number to read from.

Returns

String type

Immediate Window Sample

```
Open "c:\test.txt" for Input as #1 : _
a$ = Input(50,#1) : Close #1

? n$
```

➤ Programmer's Tip

Use the LOF and the EOF functions to determine the current place in the file relative to the end.

SEE ALSO   InputB #, Write #, Open, Close, InputB

InputB, InputB$

Reads a specified number of bytes from an Input or Binary file

Description
In contrast to the Input # statement made for text files, the InputB function can read a specific number of bytes into memory, which is ideal for Binary files.

NOT AVAILABLE IN VB SCRIPT

Syntax
```
InputB(inputlength%,[#]filenumber%)
InputB$(inputlength%,[#]filenumber%)
```

Parameters
inputlength%   Required. Number of bytes to read.

filenumber%   Required. Current file number to read from.

Returns
String type

Immediate Window Sample
```
Open "c:\test.txt" for InputB as #1 : _
a$ = InputB(50,#1) : Close #1
```

➤ Programmer's Tip

Use the LOF and the EOF functions to determine the current place in the file relative to the end.

SEE ALSO   Input, Input #, Write #

InputBox, InputBox$

Presents an input dialog box that allows the user to enter text information

Description
InputBox functions in much the same way as MsgBox( ). If the user clicks the Cancel button, the returned string will be empty.

AVAILABLE IN VB SCRIPT

Syntax
```
InputBox$(msg$[, [title$][, [default$][,xpos%, ypos%]]])
InputBox(msg$[, [title$][, [default$][, xpos%, ypos%]]])
```

Parameters
msg$ Required. String that contains the message to display in the input box.

title$ Optional. Title of the dialog box that will be shown.

default$ Optional. Default string to place in the input box.

xpos%, ypos%   Optional. The x and y position where the input box should be displayed.

Returns
String type

Immediate Window Sample
```
a = InputBox("Please enter your name:","Name Entry")
? a
```

SEE ALSO   MsgBox, MsgBox$

InStr

Returns the first place within a string that another string occurs

Description

This function can be used to search for the occurrence of a string and its location within a larger string. The startpos parameter begins the search at a particular position with the string.

AVAILABLE IN VB SCRIPT

Syntax

```
InStr([startpos&], string1$, pattern$)
```

Parameters

startpos&   Optional. The position within the string to begin search.

string1$ Required. String that is to be searched.

pattern$ Required. The pattern string that the function attempts to locate.

Returns

Long type

Immediate Window Sample

```
? InStr("Hello World from Dan","Dan")
? InStr(3,"Hello World from Dan","World")
```

SEE ALSO   InStrB, InStrRev, Left$, Right$, Option Compare, Upper, Lower

InStrRev

Returns the first place within a string that another string occurs from the end of the string

Description

This function can be used to search for the occurrence of a string and its location within a larger string. The reverse InStr works almost like the InStr function, but starts at the end of the string.

AVAILABLE IN VB SCRIPT

Syntax

```
InStrRev(string1$, pattern$ [,startpos&] [,compare])
```

Parameters

string1$ Required. String that is to be searched.

pattern$ Required. The pattern string that the function will attempt to locate.

startpos&   Optional. The position within the string to begin search.

compare   Optional. Type of comparison to perform, such as vbUseCompareOption (–1), vbBinaryCompare (0), vbTextCompare (1), or vbDatabaseCompare (2).

Returns

Long type

Immediate Window Sample

```
? InStrRev("Hello World from Dan","Dan")
? InStrRev("Hello World from Dan","World",6)
```

SEE ALSO   InStr, Left$, Right$, Option Compare, Upper, Lower

Int

Converts a number to an Integer data type

Description

This function works almost exactly like the Fix( ) function, except when concerning negative numbers. Int returns the first negative number less than or equal to the passed value. Int( ) returns the first negative number less than or equal to the value. Fix(−1.4) would return the value −1, while Int(−1.4) would return the value −2.

AVAILABLE IN VB SCRIPT

Syntax
```
Int(numericExpression)
```

Parameters
numericExpression   Required. Any valid numeric expression.

Returns
Integer type

Immediate Window Sample
```
? Int(1.4)
? Int(-1.4)
```

SEE ALSO   CInt, CStr, CDbl, CVar, CStr, Fix, Round

IPmt

Returns the interest rate per period calculated from an annuity

Description
The payment is calculated from the values of periodic fixed payments and fixed interest rate. The rate returns the interest rate per period given the other factors.

NOT AVAILABLE IN VB SCRIPT

Syntax
```
IPmt(rate!, currentPeriod%, totalPeriods%,
presentValue@, [FutureValue@, whenDue%])
```

Parameters
rate!   Required. Interest rate for the calculations.

currentPeriod%   Required. Must be greater than 1 and less than totalPeriods%.

totalPeriods%   Required.

presentValue@   Required. Current value of payments.

futureValue@   Optional. Final cash value desired.

whenDue%   Optional. End (0) or beginning (1) of payment period.

Returns
Double type

Immediate Window Sample
```
? IPmt(.0081,2,48,20000)
```

SEE ALSO   FV, DDB, IRR, MIRR, NPer, NPV, Pmt, PPmt, PV, Rate, SLN, SYD

IRR

Returns the Return Rate of a series of payments or receipts

Description
This financial function will use an array that must contain at least one negative (payment) and one positive (receipt) value to estimate the Return Rate value. You may include a guess as to the final value which, if omitted, is set to 0.1 (10 percent).

NOT AVAILABLE IN VB SCRIPT

Syntax
```
IRR(valuesArray(),guess!)
```

Parameters
valuesArray   Required. An Array containing positive (receipt) and negative (payment) information.

guess!   Optional. Your estimate of the Return Rate final value.

Returns
Double type

Immediate Window Sample

```
myArray = array(-50000#,12000#,15000#,10000#)
? IRR(myArray)
```

SEE ALSO FV, IPmt, DDB, MIRR, NPer, NPV, Pmt, PPmt, PV, Rate, SLN, SYD

Is

Compares two objects

Description

This determines whether both object references point to the same object.

AVAILABLE IN VB SCRIPT

Syntax

```
a Is b
```

Parameters

a, b Required. Any valid object references.

Returns

Boolean

Immediate Window Sample

```
Set A = CreateObject("Excel.Application")

? A Is B
Set A = B
? A Is B
```

SEE ALSO GetObject, Set, CreateObject

IsArray

VB 6
Only

Determines whether variable holds a reference to an array

Description

This command indicates if an array is stored within the given variable.

AVAILABLE IN VB SCRIPT

Syntax

```
IsArray(varName)
```

Parameters

varName   Required. Name of the variable to be evaluated.

Returns

Boolean type

Immediate Window Sample

```
? IsArray(a)
a = Array("Philips","Velo")
? IsArray(a)
```

➤ Programmer's Tip

This command tells you if there is an array at all, but not if the array is empty. Use the ALen command to determine the length of the array. If zero, the array is empty.

SEE ALSO   ALen, Array, Dim

IsDate

Returns whether the value contains a valid date

Description

This function checks the value passed to it (string, variant, and so on) and determines whether there is either a valid date or time contained in it.

AVAILABLE IN VB SCRIPT

Syntax
```
IsDate(variant)
```

Parameters
variant   Required. Variant or variable data type.

Returns
Boolean type

Immediate Window Sample
```
? IsDate(#1/2/97#)
? IsDate("1/2/97")
? IsDate("")
```

SEE ALSO   IsEmpty, IsNull, IsNumeric, DateAdd, DateDiff, DatePart, DateSerial, DateValue, Date, Time, Format, Now, Month, Weekday, CVDate

IsEmpty

Determines if variable is empty

Description
The IsEmpty function is most often used for data field entry confirmation.

AVAILABLE IN VB SCRIPT

Syntax
```
IsEmpty(variant)
```

Parameters
variant   Required. Variant or variable data type.

Returns
Boolean type

Immediate Window Sample
```
? IsEmpty("a")
? IsEmpty("")
```

SEE ALSO   IsDate, IsNull, IsNumeric, VarType

IsError

VB 6
Only

Determines whether the passed variable is a valid error

Description
This command will check the passed number against all valid error codes and determine if it is a valid error.

NOT AVAILABLE IN VB SCRIPT

Syntax
IsError(val)

Parameters
val   Required. Value of error to be evaluated.

Returns
Boolean type

Immediate Window Sample
? IsError(13)

SEE ALSO   Error, CVErr

IsMissing

VB 6
Only

Determines whether optional passed argument is available

Description
For procedures that allow optional arguments, this function determines if a value for the argument was passed.

NOT AVAILABLE IN VB SCRIPT

Syntax
IsMissing(argName)

Parameters
argName   Required. Name of optional argument.

Returns
Boolean

Immediate Window Sample
N/A

SEE ALSO   Environ$, Private, Public

IsNull

Determines if variable contains a Null

Description
This is usually used for database fields, which often contain Nulls. Nulls cannot be detected with traditional comparison operators such as "If a = Null then beep."

AVAILABLE IN VB SCRIPT

Syntax
```
IsNull(variant)
```

Parameters
variant   Required. Variant or variable data type.

Returns
Boolean type

Immediate Window Sample
```
? IsNull("")
? IsNull(Null)
```

> ## ➤ Programmer's Tip

You can also use the & command to circumvent database errors. By use of the command, such as a = "" & myRS!LastName, even if the field contains a Null value, no error is generated.

SEE ALSO   IsDate, IsEmpty, IsNumeric, VarType, Null, IIf

IsNumeric

Determines if variable contains a numeric value

Description
The IsNumeric function is most often used for user field entry confirmation.

AVAILABLE IN VB SCRIPT

Syntax
```
IsNumeric(variant)
```

Parameters
variant   Required. Variant or variable data type.

Returns
Boolean type

Immediate Window Sample
```
? IsNumeric("123")
? IsNumeric("abc")
```

SEE ALSO   IsDate, IsEmpty, IsNull

IsObject

VB 6
Only

Determines whether variable is valid object variable

Description
This command determines whether the variable holds a variant data type of Object, but does not determine whether the object itself is valid.

AVAILABLE IN VB SCRIPT

Syntax
IsObject(varName)

Parameters
varName Required. Name of variable to be evaluated.

Returns
N/A

Immediate Window Sample
? IsObject(myObject)

Set myObject = GetObject(,"excel.application")
? IsObject(myObject)

SEE ALSO CreateObject, GetObject

Join

Concatenates strings contained in an array into a single string

Description
This command is the opposite of the Split command in that it reforms all the individual strings from an array into a single string.

AVAILABLE IN VB SCRIPT

Syntax

```
Join(array [,delimiter])
```

Parameters

array   Required. One-dimensional array containing strings.

delimiter   Optional. The string to be placed between each entry. If not specified, a single space is used.

Returns

String type

Immediate Window Sample

```
a = Array("Osborne","books","are","great!")

? Join(a)
```

SEE ALSO   Array, Split

Kill

Deletes the file specified

Description

The Kill command supports the wildcard characters * (multiple character) and ? (single character) to delete one or more filenames. If an attempt to delete an open file occurs, an error will be generated.

NOT AVAILABLE IN VB SCRIPT

Syntax

```
Kill filename$
```

Parameters

filename$ Required. Any valid path and filename may be used.

Returns

N/A

Immediate Window Sample
```
Kill "c:\test.txt"
```

SEE ALSO   Name, Open, RmDir, MkDir, ChDir, ChDrive, FileLen, EOF

LBound

Returns the lowest subscript available in the array

Description
This function can be used to determine the lower bound of an array. If the array is multidimensional, use the dimension argument to specify the lower bounds to be returned.

AVAILABLE IN VB SCRIPT

Syntax
```
LBound(arrayname[, dimension%])
```

Parameters
arrayname   Required. The name of the array required to determine the limit.

dimension%   Optional. The subscript dimension of a multidimensional array.

Returns
Long type

Immediate Window Sample
```
myArray = array(6,4,2,5,2,4,6)
? LBound(myArray)
```

SEE ALSO   UBound, Array, Dim, Option Base

LCase, LCase$

Returns an all-lowercase string

Description

This function converts all of the characters in the passed string to lowercase. This function is effective when you're comparing two strings to make sure the case matches.

AVAILABLE IN VB SCRIPT

Syntax

```
LCase$(expression$) LCase(expression$)
```

Parameters

expression$ Required. Any valid string.

Returns

String type

Immediate Window Sample

```
? LCase("hElLo")
```

SEE ALSO   UCase, UCase$

Left, Left$

Returns a string containing the amount of the left portion of the passed string

Description

This function can be used to take any specified substring from the left to the right and to return it as a separate string.

AVAILABLE IN VB SCRIPT

Syntax
```
Left$(expression$, Length&)
```

Parameters
expression$ Any string expression

Length& Number of characters to return in the substring

Returns
String

Immediate Window Sample
```
? Left("Hello World",4)
```

SEE ALSO Mid, Mid$, Right, Right$, InStr$, Format$, LTrim, RTrim, Str, Len, LenB

Len

Returns the length of a specified string

Description
This function is used to determine the length in characters of a string. Either a string itself or a variable containing the string may be passed to this routine.

AVAILABLE IN VB SCRIPT

Syntax
```
Len(variable-name)
```

Parameters
variable-name Required. Any valid string.

Returns
Long type

Immediate Window Sample

```
a$ = "Hello World"
? Len(a)
```

SEE ALSOH   LenB, Left, Mid, Mid$, Right, Right$, InStr$, Format$, LTrim, RTrim, Str

LenB

III

Length of string or variable in bytes

Description

This function is used to determine the length in bytes of a string. Either a string itself or a variable containing the string may be passed to this routine. In contrast to the Len function (which supports Unicode, where each character uses two bytes), the LenB function will return the actual bytes used.

AVAILABLE IN VB SCRIPT

Syntax

```
LenB(variable-name)
```

Parameters

variable-name   Required. Any valid string.

Returns

Long type

Immediate Window Sample

```
a$ = "Hello World"
? LenB(a)
```

SEE ALSO   Left, Right, Mid, ChrB

Let

Sets a variable to a particular value

Description

The Let command is most often implicit when defining variables. It can be used sometimes for code clarification.

NOT AVAILABLE IN VB SCRIPT

Syntax

```
[Let] variablename = expression
```

Parameters

variablename   Required. A variable name that follows standard naming practices.

expression   Required. The expression that will be evaluated to set the variable.

Returns

N/A

Immediate Window Sample

```
Let i = 1
```

SEE ALSO   LSet, RSet, Set

Like

Compares a string with a pattern

Description

The Like command supports a number of wildcard characters to create the pattern string to search the primary string. These characters include ? = Single character, * = Zero or more characters, # = Any single digit, [charlist] = Any char in charlist, [!charlist] = Any single character not in charlist.

NOT AVAILABLE IN VB SCRIPT

Syntax

```
a Like b
```

Parameters

a Required. String to search.

b Required. Pattern to search for.

Returns

String type

Immediate Window Sample

```
? "c:\myFile.txt" Like "*.txt"
```

SEE ALSO   Option Compare Text, Option Compare Binary, =, Is, <>, <, >=, <=, Not, And, InStr$

Line Input

Reads a single line from a Sequential file

Description

This command will read directly into a variable a single line delimited by a Chr(13) carriage return or Chr(13) + Chr(10) linefeed and carriage return. The carriage return + linefeed combination is not included with the returned string.

NOT AVAILABLE IN VB SCRIPT

Syntax

```
Line Input #filenumber%, variable
```

Parameters

filenumber%   Required. Any valid open file number.

variable   Required. The String variable that will receive the new information.

Returns

N/A

Immediate Window Sample

```
Open "c:\test.txt" for Input as #1 : _
     Line Input #1, d$ : Close #1
? d$
```

SEE ALSO Input #, Print #

Load

Loads a form or control object, but doesn't show it

Description

Use the Load command to read a control or form. The Show method of the object can then be used to make it visible.

NOT AVAILABLE IN VB SCRIPT

Syntax

For a form:

```
Load form-name
```

For a control:

```
Load control-name(index)
```

Parameters

form-name, **control-name**   Required. Name to reference desired object.

Returns

N/A

Immediate Window Sample

N/A

> ## ➤ Programmer's Tip

If you set the form property Visible to False, the Load command can be used to make an application more responsive. While your application is originally loading and the splash screen is displayed, you can use the Load command to bring all the commonly used forms into memory. When the user selects the form, it can simply be made visible without requiring any disk access.

SEE ALSO   Unload

LoadPicture

Loads a picture from the specified file for manipulation or placement in a Picture or Image control

Description

The LoadPicture command can be used to load WMF, BMP, or ICO format pictures. This command is not included in VBA.

NOT AVAILABLE IN VB SCRIPT

Syntax

To load a picture into a form or picture box:

```
LoadPicture(picturefile$)
```

To clear a picture from a form or picture box:

```
LoadPicture
```

Parameters

picturefile$ Required. Valid path to a current picture file.

Returns
Variant

Immediate Window Sample
```
a = LoadPicture("c:\windows\rivets.bmp")
```

➤ Programmer's Tip

When used in conjuction with the SavePicture command, this command can be used as a simple conversion routine. Pictures of almost any format (BMP, GIF, JPEG, and so on) can be loaded into a Picture control, and the SavePicture command can then be used to write these pictures back to the disk in BMP format.

SEE ALSO   SavePicture

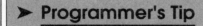

LoadResData
VB 6
Only

Loads data from a resource file (RES)

Description
The LoadResData command will load a specified resource and return a byte array of the information. The data loaded from a resource with this command may not exceed 64K.

NOT AVAILABLE IN VB SCRIPT

Syntax
```
LoadResData(index,format)
```

Parameters
index   Required. Integer specifying the ID of the resource to be loaded within the resource file.

format   Required. Type of resource to be loaded specified with a numeric identifier: 1 = cursor, 2 = bitmap, 3 = icon, 4 = menu, 5 = dialog box, 6 = string, 7 = font directory, 8 = font, 9 =

accelerator table, 10 = user-defined, 12 = group cursor, and
14 = group icon.

Returns
Array type

Immediate Window Sample
N/A

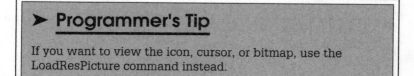

> ➤ **Programmer's Tip**
>
> If you want to view the icon, cursor, or bitmap, use the
> LoadResPicture command instead.

SEE ALSO   LoadResPicture, LoadResString

LoadResPicture
VB 6
Only

Loads a picture from a resource file (RES)

Description
Loads a bitmap, icon, or cursor from a resource file. This command
can be used in place of the LoadPicture command for retrieving
images from the disk.

NOT AVAILABLE IN VB SCRIPT

Syntax
```
LoadResPicture(index,format)
```

Parameters
index   Required. Integer specifying the ID of the resource to be
loaded within the resource file.

format   Required. Type of resource to be loaded specified with a
numeric identifier: 0 = bitmap, 1 = icon, and 2 = cursor.

Returns
N/A

Immediate Window Sample
N/A

> ➤ **Programmer's Tip**
>
> The resource file is an excellent way to store information external to the executable. This makes a resource file ideal for internationalization if menus, text, and other items are stored within the file. A single executable can then be created, and only the resource file need be changed for other language versions.

SEE ALSO   LoadResData, LoadResString

LoadResString

| VB 6 |
| Only |

Loads a string from a resource file (RES)

Description
This command can be used to load a string and can be used to provide a string without using a string literal.

NOT AVAILABLE IN VB SCRIPT

Syntax
```
LoadResString(index)
```

Parameters
index   Required. Integer ID of resource to be loaded.

Returns
String

Immediate Window Sample
N/A

➤ Programmer's Tip

The resource file is an excellent way to store information
external to the executable. This makes a resource file ideal
for internationalization if menus, text, and other items are
stored within the file. A single executable can then be
created, and only the resource file need be change for other
language versions.

SEE ALSO   LoadResData, LoadResPicture

Loc

Sets the current read or write position with the open file

Description
This function positions the current read or write access to an exact
record (Random), current byte position divided by 128 (Sequential),
or exact byte location (Binary).

NOT AVAILABLE IN VB SCRIPT

Syntax
Loc(filenumber%)

Parameters
filenumber%   Any valid open file number.

Returns
Long type

Immediate Window Sample
? Loc(1)

> ➤ **Programmer's Tip**
>
> Since the Loc will change with every read or write to the file, this command can also be used to track the expanding file size as a file is being stored to disk. Especially when variables are being written to a sequential file, the number of bytes can be easily determined by use of this method.

SEE ALSO   EOF, LOF, Open, FileLen, Read, Write, Get, Print #

Lock...Unlock

Locks or unlocks access to parts of the current file for other processes

Description

These commands may be used to control access to a single file to ensure no data is corrupted or destroyed by concurrent reads or writes.

NOT AVAILABLE IN VB SCRIPT

Syntax

```
Lock [#]filenumber%[,startpos&][ To endpos&] :
[statements] : Unlock [#]filenumber%[,startpos&]
[ to endpos&]
```

Parameters

filenumber%   Required. Any valid open file number.

startpos&   Number of first byte or record.

endpos&   Number of last byte or record.

Returns

N/A

Immediate Window Sample
N/A

SEE ALSO   Get, Put, Open, Close, Loc

Returns the length of a currently open file

Description
This function, when passed a file number, returns the size, in bytes, of the open file.

NOT AVAILABLE IN VB SCRIPT

Syntax
LOF([#]filenumber%)

Parameters
filenumber%   Required. Any valid file number.

Returns
Long type

Immediate Window Sample
? LOF(1)

SEE ALSO   EOF, Loc

Returns the logarithmic expression for the given expression

Description
This function returns the natural log of the passed expression.

AVAILABLE IN VB SCRIPT

Syntax
Log(numericExpression)

Parameters
numericExpression   Required. Any valid numeric expression.

Returns
Double type

Immediate Window Sample
? Log(1.3)

SEE ALSO   Exp

LSet

Left-justifies string within the destination and fills the remainder with spaces

Description
This command essentially copies the sourcevariable into the resultvariable padded with spaces if the resultvariable is longer. For example, if the length of resultvariable is ten characters, a five-character sourcevariable would be copied to it and padded with five space characters. See this example in the Immediate window. This command can also be used to copy from one user-defined variable to another of the same length.

NOT AVAILABLE IN VB SCRIPT

Syntax
LSet resultvariable = sourcevariable

Parameters
resultvariable   Required. Destination for the new string.

sourcevariable   Left-justified string to copy.

Returns
N/A

Immediate Window Sample
```
a$ = "1234567890"
LSet a$ = "Hello"
? a$ + " <--end"
```

> ### ➤ Programmer's Tip
>
> You can use LSet for advanced number operations such as a
> binary file import. LSet will let you copy the actual bytes from
> one data type to another without conversion. However, using
> this technique may sacrifice cross-platform portability.

SEE ALSO   Let, RSet, LTrim, LTrim$, Input, Input #

LTrim, LTrim$

Returns a substring with the leading spaces from left to right
removed from the passed string

Description
The LTrim function is the complement of the RTrim function, but
returns a string taken from left to right. Any spaces on the left side
of the string are removed.

AVAILABLE IN VB SCRIPT

Syntax
```
LTrim$(stringExpression$) LTrim(stringExpression$)
```

Parameters
stringExpression$ Required. Any valid string.

Returns
String type

Immediate Window Sample
```
? LTrim(" Hello")
```

SEE ALSO   RTrim, RTrim$, Trim, Trim$, Left, Left$, Right, Right$, Mid$

Me Property

This command returns to the currently active form

Description
Use the Me command to write code that will work independently of the form on which it is executed. The Immediate window example needs to be executed when a form is shown on the screen and the execution is paused.

NOT AVAILABLE IN VB SCRIPT

Syntax
```
Me
```

Parameters
N/A

Returns
N/A

Immediate Window Sample
```
Me.Hide
```

SEE ALSO   Load, Show, Hide

Mid, Mid$

Returns a substring of the passed string of specified length and start position

Description

This function allows *access* to an exact substring within a string. The start argument determines where the desired string should begin. The lowest character position is 1. The length, if omitted, will be automatically set to the remaining length of the string.

The Mid, Mid$ functions can also have a different usage; see the next function definition.

AVAILABLE IN VB SCRIPT

Syntax

```
Mid$(stringExpression$, start&[, Length&])
Mid(stringExpression$, start&[, Length&])
```

Parameters

stringExpression$ Required. Any valid string.

start&   Required. Start position within stringExpression$. Must be equal to 1.

Length&   Optional. Length of substring to return.

Returns

String type

Immediate Window Sample

```
? Mid$("Hello",2)
? Mid$("Hello",2,3)
```

SEE ALSO   Left, Left$, Right, Right$, Len

Mid, Mid$

Replaces a substring of the passed string of specified length and start position

Description

This function allows *replacement* of a substring within a string. The start argument determines where the desired string should begin. The lowest character position is 1. The length, if omitted, will be automatically set to the remaining length of the string.

The Mid, Mid$ functions can also have a different usage; see the previous function definition.

AVAILABLE IN VB SCRIPT

Syntax

```
stringExpression$ Mid(result-string$, start&[, Length&])
= stringExpression$
```

Parameters

result-string$ Required. Any valid string.

start&   Required. Start position within stringExpression$. Must be equal to 1.

Length&   Optional. Length of substring to return.

stringExpression$ Required. Any valid string.

Returns

N/A

Immediate Window Sample

```
a$ = "My new world"
Mid$(a$,4,3) = "big"
? a$
```

SEE ALSO   Left, Left$, Right, Right$, Mid (previous definition), Mid$ (previous definition)

Minute

Returns the minute portion of the date and time passed to it

Description

The Minute function will return the minute portion of a Date type. An integer between 0 and 59 is returned.

AVAILABLE IN VB SCRIPT

Syntax
```
Minute(dateVariant)
```

Parameters
dateVariant   Required. The date from which the minute value will be extracted.

Returns
Integer type

Immediate Window Sample
```
? Minute(Now)
```

SEE ALSO   Now, TimeSerial, TimeValue, Hour, Second

MIRR

Returns the modified internal rate of return

Description
This function works similarly to the IRR( ) function. The finance and reinvestment rate is supplied to complete the calculations.

NOT AVAILABLE IN VB SCRIPT

Syntax
```
MIRR(valuesArray(), financeInterestRate!,
reinvestmentInternalRate!)
```

Parameters
valuesArray   Required. An Array containing at least one positive (receipt) and one negative (payment) item.

financeInterestRate!   Required. The cost of accounting interest rate.

reinvestmentInternalRate!   Required. The capital gains interest received from cash reinvestment.

Returns
Double type

Immediate Window Sample
```
myArray = array(-50000#,12000#,15000#,10000#)
? MIRR(myArray)
```

SEE ALSO   FV, IPmt, IRR, DDB, NPer, NPV, Pmt, PPmt, PV, Rate,
SLN, SYD

MkDir

Creates a new directory at specified path

Description
This command will create a single directory. The command
requires all directories leading up to where the new one is going to
be created to already exist. If current path information is omitted,
the directory will be created in the default path.

NOT AVAILABLE IN VB SCRIPT

Syntax
```
MkDir dirname$
```

Parameters
dirname$ Any valid path string

Returns
N/A

Immediate Window Sample
```
MkDir "C:\vbtemp"
```

SEE ALSO   ChDrive, ChDir, RmDir, FileCopy, Open, Kill,
Environ, CurDir

Mod

Modulo arithmetic operator

Description
The Mod operator allows you to obtain the remainder if the divisor doesn't divide evenly.

AVAILABLE IN VB SCRIPT

Syntax
B Mod C

Parameters
B, **C**   Any numeric expressions

Returns
Integer type

Immediate Window Sample
? 9 Mod 5
? 9 Mod 2
? 9 Mod 3

➤ Programmer's Tip

This operator is perfect for finding a row number within a greater set. If a record in a sheet is seven rows long, use of the Mod operator can instantly tell the row within the sheet as follows: "? ActiveCell.Row Mod 7".

SEE ALSO   Int, CInt, \, /

Month

Returns the Month portion of the passed Date type

Description
This function will return an integer value between 1 and 12 that represents the month of the date passed to it.

AVAILABLE IN VB SCRIPT

Syntax
```
Month(dateVariant)
```

Parameters
dateVariant   A valid date from which the Month will be extracted

Returns
Integer type

Immediate Window Sample
```
? Month(Now)
```

SEE ALSO   DateSerial, DateValue, Now, Day, IsDate, WeekDay, DateAdd, DateDiff, CVDate, Year

MonthName

Provides a string of the specified month

Description
This command will return the name of the month specified by its numeric equivalent (1 = January, 2 = February, and so on). It can provide either the full month name or the abbreviation.

AVAILABLE IN VB SCRIPT

Syntax
```
MonthName(num[, abbreviate])
```

Parameters

num   Required. Number of the month.

abbreviate   Optional. Boolean to determine if returned string is month abbreviation. Default is False.

Returns

String type

III

Immediate Window Sample

```
? MonthName(3)
? MonthName(12,True)
```

SEE ALSO   Date, Format

MsgBox

Displays a dialog box presenting information and possibly retrieving a user selection

Description

The message box is one of the most useful functions in the Visual Basic language because it can quickly present information to the user or retrieve simple information without requiring the construction of a complete form. Since the MsgBox command can be used as either a function or a statement, the Immediate window example shows many of the ways it can be called.

Box types are numbers that represent the types of buttons shown, the icons displayed, and the modal setting. The buttons can include the OK button (0); the OK and Cancel buttons (1); the Abort, Retry, and Ignore buttons (2); the YesNoCancel buttons (3); the Yes and No buttons (4); or the Retry and Cancel buttons (5).

Icons include the Critical (16), the Question (32), the Exclamation (48), and the Information (64) icons. Including a SystemModel setting (4096) suspends all applications until the user dismisses the message box. Returned values include OK (1), Cancel (2), Abort (3), Retry (4), Ignore (5), Yes (6), and No (7).

AVAILABLE IN VB SCRIPT

Syntax

```
MsgBox(message$[, boxtype%][, windowtitle$])
```

Parameters

message$ Required. A String containing the message to be displayed.

boxtype%   Optional. The compilation of all the box type numbers to display the desired buttons, icons, and dialog type.

windowtitle$ Optional. Title of the message box.

Returns

Integer type

Immediate Window Sample

```
MsgBox "Hello World"
Call MsgBox("Hello World")
a = MsgBox("Hello World")
a = MsgBox("What should I do?",2+16+4096,"Proceed?")
```

SEE ALSO   InputBox, InputBox$

Name

Renames a file, directory, or folder

Description

The new path name and old path name must match except for the final change value. You cannot change the name of an open file.

NOT AVAILABLE IN VB SCRIPT

Syntax

```
Name oldname As newname
```

Parameters

oldname, newname   Required. Oldname must be a valid path or file.

Returns

N/A

Immediate Window Sample
```
Name "test.txt" as "test2.txt"
```

SEE ALSO   Kill, ChDir, Environ, Open, CurDir, ChDir, ChDrive

Not

Logical negation

Description
Using the Not operator on a number will actually create its bitwise negative, but this is not the same as a true negative. Try using the Not in the Immediate window to demonstrate this yourself.

AVAILABLE IN VB SCRIPT

Syntax
```
Not expression
```

Parameters
expression   A valid mathematical expression.

Returns
Variant

Immediate Window Sample
```
? Not True
? Not 2=2
? Not 10
```

SEE ALSO   And, Or, Xor, Exp

Now

Returns the current system date and time

Description
This function will return a Date type value containing the current date and time of the system.

AVAILABLE IN VB SCRIPT

Syntax
Now

Parameters
N/A

Returns
Variant type

Immediate Window Sample
? Now

SEE ALSO Day, Hour, Minute, Month, Second, WeekDay, Year, IsDate, Time, Timer, TimeValue, TimeSerial, DateSerial, DateAdd, DateDiff, DateValue, Date, Time

NPer

Returns the number of periods in an annuity

Description
The returned value is based on periodic fixed payments and a fixed interest rate. The interestRate must specify the rate per period, such as 0.0821 per month. The periodicPayment specifies the size of payment made each period. The presentValue determines the value of a series of future receipts and payments.

The futureValue is the desired cash value you wish to have once all of the payments are complete. The whenDue parameter instructs the function to calculate whether the payments are due at the end of the period (0), the default, or at the beginning of the period (1).

NOT AVAILABLE IN VB SCRIPT

Syntax
```
NPer(interestRate!, periodicPayment@, presentValue@
[, futureValue@, whenDue%])
```

Parameters

interestRate!   Required. Interest rate for the calculations.

periodicPayment@   Required. Size of each payment.

presentValue@   Required. Current value of payments.

futureValue@   Optional. Final cash value desired.

whenDue%   Optional. End (0) or beginning (1) of payment period.

Returns

Double type

Immediate Window Sample

```
? NPer(.0821,400,2000)
```

SEE ALSO   FV, IPmt, IRR, MIRR, DDB, NPV, Pmt, PPmt, PV, Rate, SLN, SYD

```
NPV
```

Returns the net present value based on payments, receipts, and discount rate

Description

This function determines the current value of the future series of investments. These include the cash flow values of payments (negatives) and receipts (positives). The discountRate is stated as a percentage over the life of the investment.

NOT AVAILABLE IN VB SCRIPT

Syntax

```
NPV(discountRate, valuesArray())
```

Parameters

discountRate   The rate of interest expressed as a decimal (that is, 5 percent = .05).

valuesArray   Required. Array that must contain at least one payment and one receipt.

Returns
Double type

Immediate Window Sample
```
myArray = array(-50000#,12000#,15000#,10000#)
? NPV(.05, myArray)
```

SEE ALSO   FV, IPmt, IRR, MIRR, NPer, DDB, Pmt, PPmt, PV, Rate, SLN, SYD

Oct, Oct$

Converts a number to its octal equivalent

Description
This function will create a string containing the hexadecimal (base 16 number) from the passed value. Each value may contain the numbers 0–9 and the letters A–F.

AVAILABLE IN VB SCRIPT

Syntax
```
Oct$(numericExpression) Oct(numericExpression)
```

Parameters
numericExpression   Required. Any numeric expression.

Returns
String type

Immediate Window Sample
```
? Oct(7)
? Oct(8)
? Oct(63)
? Oct(64)
```

SEE ALSO   Hex, Hex$, Val

On Error...

Creates error-trapping routine and jumps to prespecified areas of code when an error occurs

Description

The On Error routine will seize control when an error occurs. If the On Error routine instructs, the GoTo command will jump to a specified error-handler or line number. The On Error Resume Next command will simply ignore the error and execute the instruction that follows it. The On Error GoTo 0 command will disable the current error handler in the procedure or function.

Note that only the On Error Resume Next command of the On Error commands is available in VB Script.

NOT AVAILABLE IN VB SCRIPT

Syntax

```
On Error GoTo error-handler
error-handler:
    [statements]
Resume [[0] | Next | line-number | line-label ]
```

To cause the Err flag to be set:

```
On Error Resume Next
```

or

```
On Error GoTo 0
```

Parameters

error-handler   Label to indicate location of the error handler.

Returns

N/A

Immediate Window Sample

N/A

SEE ALSO   Err, Error, Error$, Resume

On...GoSub

Jumps to a subroutine of code within a procedure or function based on the value of a numeric index

Description

Using a numeric index, the On...GoSub will jump to the routine in the GoSub list in the index slot specified. A GoSub allows execution to return to the originator, where the On...GoTo routine changes the execution path.

NOT AVAILABLE IN VB SCRIPT

Syntax

```
On numericExpression GoSub Line1[, Line 3][, line255]
```

Parameters

numericExpression   Required. Specifies the number in the list that follows to branch to.

Returns

N/A

Immediate Window Sample

N/A

SEE ALSO   On...GoTo, SelectCase

On...GoTo

Changes execution to a subroutine of code within a procedure or function based on the value of a numeric index

Description

By use of a numeric index, the On...GoTo will jump to the routine in the GoTo list in the index slot specified.

NOT AVAILABLE IN VB SCRIPT

Syntax

```
On NumericExpression GoTo Line1[, Line 2][, line 3]
[, Line255]
```

Parameters

numericExpression   Required. Specifies the number in the list that follows to branch to.

Returns

N/A

Immediate Window Sample

N/A

SEE ALSO   On...GoSub, SelectCase

Open

Opens a file for reading or writing

Description

This command is used to open a file with particular access options. Files of types Sequential, Binary, and Random may be opened.

NOT AVAILABLE IN VB SCRIPT

Syntax

```
Open filename$ [for mode] [Access access] [locktype]
As [#]filenumber [Len=recordLength]
```

Parameters

filename$ Required. Any valid path and filename.

mode   May include Input, Output, Binary, Append, and Random.

access   May include Read, Write, or Read Write.

locktype   May include Shared, Lock Read, Lock Write, and Lock Read Write.

filenumber Required. Any valid file number between 1 and 511 as long as it isn't already in use.

recordLength Number of characters buffered (Sequential) or record length (Random).

Returns
N/A

Immediate Window Sample
```
Open "C:\test.txt" for Output as #1 : _
Print #1,"Hello";Spc(20);"Hello2" : Close #1
```

> ## ➤ Programmer's Tip
>
> Keep in mind that when you open a file in Binary mode, if the file doesn't exist, it will be created as a blank file. To avoid an error when reading from a file that was just created, use the EOF command to determine if the end has already been reached.

SEE ALSO Close, FreeFile, Get, Input, Input$, Line Input #, Put, Write, File System Objects (Part IV)

Option Base

Sets the default lower bounds for arrays

Description
Using this command allows you to define, at a module level, the lower bounds for an array. The default is typically 0, and the Dim command can be used to set the lower bounds on individual arrays.

NOT AVAILABLE IN VB SCRIPT

Syntax
```
Option Base 0 | 1
```

Parameters
0 | 1   A lower bound of 0 or 1.

Returns
N/A

Immediate Window Sample
N/A

SEE ALSO   Dim, Global, ReDim

Option Compare

Sets the default comparison method for strings

Description
When strings are being compared, they can be compared by use of the Binary method, which differentiates between case, foreign alphabets, and so on, and the Text method, which does not. The default is set to Binary mode.

NOT AVAILABLE IN VB SCRIPT

Syntax
```
Option Compare (Binary | Text)
```

Parameters
Binary | Text   Required. Specifies the comparison method.

Returns
N/A

Immediate Window Sample
N/A

SEE ALSO   StrComp, Option Explicit

Option Explicit

Requires that all variables be explicitly defined

Description

The Option Explicit command makes any execution generate an error if a variable is not explicitly defined with a Dim command.

AVAILABLE IN VB SCRIPT

Syntax

```
Option Explicit
```

Parameters

N/A

Returns

N/A

Immediate Window Sample

N/A

➤ Programmer's Tip

Although frequently annoying because of the strict definition requirements, this command can save you hours of debugging time. Variables are always defined, so misspellings or misreferences become much less frequent.

SEE ALSO   Dim

Option Private

Prevents the method of a module being referenced from outside it

Description

Using the Option Private command is primarily useful for VBA projects where multiple projects may be loaded at one time. Excel, for example, can contain a project with each spreadsheet, so this option will protect modules from interproject access. This statement must appear at the top of the General Declarations section before any variable definitions.

NOT AVAILABLE IN VB SCRIPT

Syntax

```
Option Private Module
```

Parameters

N/A

Returns

N/A

Immediate Window Sample

N/A

SEE ALSO Option Base, Option Compare, Option Explicit

Or

Logical Or

Description

The Or operator will perform a logical Or on two numbers, or will do a logical truth on two Boolean values.

AVAILABLE IN VB SCRIPT

Syntax

```
a Or b
```

Parameters

a, b Required. Any valid numeric expressions.

Returns
Variant

Immediate Window Sample
```
? True Or False
? True Or True
? False Or False
? 1=2 Or 1=1
```

SEE ALSO　　And, Imp, Eqv, Xor, True, False, Not

Partition

Returns a string denoting where the passed number occurs within the ranges

Description
This function calculates ranges and the particular range in which the specified number falls. The returned string describes the range in the format *start:end*.

NOT AVAILABLE IN VB SCRIPT

Syntax
```
Partition(number&, startRange&, endRange&, interval&)
```

Parameters
number&　　Required. Number that will be evaluated against the ranges.

startRange&　　Required. Number. The number 0 is used as the beginning of the overall range.

endRange&　　Required. Number. The endRange is used as the end of the overall range.

interval&　　Required. Number. The number 1 is used as the interval spanned by each range.

Returns
String type

Immediate Window Sample
? Partition(20,0,400,30)

SEE ALSO   InStr$

Pmt

Returns a payment value for an annuity

Description
The payment is calculated from the values of periodic fixed
payments and fixed interest rate. The interestRate is specified in a
decimal percentage for each period.

NOT AVAILABLE IN VB SCRIPT

Syntax
Pmt(interestRate!, numberOfPayments%, presentValue@
[, futureValue@, whenDue%])

Parameters
interestRate!   Required. Interest rate for the calculations.

numberOfPayments%   Required. Total number of payments.

presentValue@   Required. Current value of payments.

futureValue@   Optional. Final cash value desired.

whenDue%   Optional. End (0) or beginning (1) of payment period.

Returns
Double type

Immediate Window Sample
? Pmt(.0081,48,10000)

SEE ALSO   FV, IPmt, IRR, MIRR, NPer, NPV, DDB, PPmt, PV, Rate,
SLN, SYD

PPmt

Returns the principal payment value for an annuity

Description
This function calculates the principal payment based on periodic payments and a fixed interest rate.

NOT AVAILABLE IN VB SCRIPT

Syntax
```
PPmt(interestRate!, whichPeriod%, totalPeriods%,
presentValue@[, futureValue@, whenDue%])
```

Parameters
interestRate!   Required. Interest rate for the calculations.

whichPeriod%   Required. Total number of payments.

totalPeriods%   Required.

presentValue@   Required. Current value of payments.

futureValue@   Optional. Final cash value desired.

whenDue%   Optional. End (0) or beginning (1) of payment period.

Returns
Double type

Immediate Window Sample
```
? PPmt(.0081,12,48,10000)
```

SEE ALSO   FV, IPmt, IRR, MIRR, NPer, NPV, Pmt, DDB, PV, Rate, SLN, SYD

Print

Writes data to a specified Sequential file

Description

The Print # statement outputs variables or formatted text to the file denoted by the file number.

NOT AVAILABLE IN VB SCRIPT

Syntax

```
Print #filenumber, [[Spc(n)|Tab(m)]expres-
sion[;|,]...]
```

Parameters

filenumber   Required. Any valid open file number.

outputlist   Required. Any number of items may be included in the output list, such as strings, spaces, tabs, or expressions.

Returns

N/A

Immediate Window Sample

```
Open "C:\test.txt" for Output as #1 : _
Print #1,"Hello";Spc(20);"Hello2" : Close #1
```

SEE ALSO   Input, Input #, Write #

Private

Makes the variable scope private to a particular form, module, or routine

Description

Use of the Private statement will limit the scope of the form, module, procedure, or function.

NOT AVAILABLE IN VB SCRIPT

Syntax

```
Private [Function|Sub|variablename]
```

Parameters

N/A

Returns

N/A

Immediate Window Sample

N/A

SEE ALSO   Public, Dim, Sub, Function, Property Get, Property Let, Property Set, Friend

Property Get

Declares a property retrieval routine

Description

Use of the Property Get/Set/Let statements allows the program to minimize the direct access to internally used properties. In object-oriented programming, using these statements is known as "information hiding." By creation of an indirect method to access properties, internal changes do not affect programs that access properties. Also, bounds checking can be performed before changes are made to the properties.

NOT AVAILABLE IN VB SCRIPT

Syntax

```
[Public|Private] [Static] Property Get name
[(arglist)] [As type] [statements] [Exit Property]
End Property
```

Parameters

name   Required. Any valid name expression. Can be the same as Property Let and Property Set names.

arglist   Required. List of variables to be passed to the Get statement when it is called.

Returns

N/A

Immediate Window Sample
N/A

> ➤ **Programmer's Tip**
>
> If you are beginning to use object-oriented methods such as
> information hiding, make sure you use this structure to
> optimize your solution.

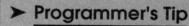

SEE ALSO   Sub, Function, Property Let, Property Set

Property Let

Declares a property definition routine

Description
Use of the Property Get/Set/Let statements allows the program to
minimize the direct access to internally used properties. In
object-oriented programming, using these statements is known as
"information hiding." By creation of an indirect method to access
properties, internal changes do not affect programs that access
properties. Also, bounds checking can be performed before
changes are made to the properties.

NOT AVAILABLE IN VB SCRIPT

Syntax
```
[Public|Private] [Static] Property Let name
[(arglist)] [As type] [statements] [Exit Property]
End Property
```

Parameters
name   Required. Any valid name expression. Can be the same as
Property Get and Property Set names.

arglist   Required. List of variables to be passed to the Let
statement when it is called.

Returns
N/A

Immediate Window Sample
N/A

➤ Programmer's Tip

If you are beginning to use object-oriented methods such as information hiding, make sure you use this structure to optimize your solution.

SEE ALSO   Sub, Function, Property Get, Property Set

Property Set

Declares a property reference routine

Description
Use of the Property Get/Set/Let statements allows the program to minimize the direct access to internally used properties. In object-oriented programming, using these statements is known as "information hiding." By creation of an indirect method to access properties, internal changes do not affect programs that access properties. Also, bounds checking can be performed before changes are made to the properties.

NOT AVAILABLE IN VB SCRIPT

Syntax
```
[Public|Private] [Static] Property Set name
[(arglist,) reference] [statements] [Exit Property]
End Property
```

Parameters
name   Required. Any valid name expression. Can be the same as Property Let and Property Get names.

arglist   Required. List of variables to be passed to the Set statement when it is called.

Returns
N/A

Immediate Window Sample
N/A

III

➤ Programmer's Tip

If you are beginning to use object-oriented methods such as information hiding, make sure you use this structure to optimize your solution.

SEE ALSO   Sub, Function, Property Let, Property Get

Public

Makes the variable scope Public for access outside a form or module

Description
Using the Public statement will increase the scope of the form, module, procedure, or function so that it may be accessed from another object. References to a Public member from an external object require the hosting object name to be referenced (that is, "myPublicForm.myPublicSub").

NOT AVAILABLE IN VB SCRIPT

Syntax
`Public [Function|Sub|variablename]`

Parameters
N/A

Returns
N/A

Immediate Window Sample
N/A

SEE ALSO   Dim, Sub, Function, Property Get, Property Let, Property Set, Private, Friend

Put

Writes a variable to a current file

Description
The Put command works very much like the Print # command, except it outputs the contents of a single variable and provides no automatic formatting to the output.

NOT AVAILABLE IN VB SCRIPT

Syntax
```
Put [#]filenumber%, [position&],variablename
```

Parameters
filenumber%   Required. Any valid open file number.

position&   Optional. Specifies record number in a Random file or byte number in a Binary file where writing should occur.

variablename   Required. A valid variable that will have its contents written to the file.

Returns
N/A

Immediate Window Sample
```
a$ = "Hello World"
Open "C:.txt" for Binary as #1 : _
Put #1,,a$ : Close #1
```

SEE ALSO   Get, LOF, Open, Type

PV

Returns the present value of an annuity

Description
This function calculates the present value based on periodic payments and a fixed interest rate.

NOT AVAILABLE IN VB SCRIPT

Syntax
```
PV(interestRate!, totalPeriods%, payment@
[,futureValue@,whenDue%])
```

Parameters
interestRate!   Required. Interest rate for the calculations.

totalPeriods%   Required.

payment@   The amount of payment to be made each period.

futureValue@   Optional. Final cash value desired.

whenDue%   Optional. End (0) or beginning (1) of payment period.

Returns
Double type

Immediate Window Sample
```
? PV(.0081,48,2000)
```

SEE ALSO   FV, IPmt, IRR, MIRR, NPer, NPV, Pmt, PPmt, DDB, Rate, SLN, SYD

QBColor

Returns a standard Long color value from a QuickBasic color

Description

This command provides quick access to simple colors that are supported in the QuickBasic system included with most versions of Windows 3.1. QuickBasic color values include black (0), blue (1), green (2), cyan (3), red (4), magenta (5), yellow (6), white (7), gray (8), light blue (9), light green (10), light cyan (11), light red (12), light magenta (13), light yellow (14), and bright white (15).

NOT AVAILABLE IN VB SCRIPT

Syntax

QBColor(color-number%)

Parameters

color-number% Required. A number between 0 and 15.

Returns

Long value

Immediate Window Sample

? QBColor(7)

> ## ➤ Programmer's Tip
>
> QBColor is excellent for quick color setting when you don't know the exact RGB values of a particular shade. By simply using a single constant, you can use this function to retrieve the RGB Long value.

SEE ALSO RGB, Line

RaiseEvent

Simulates an event occurrence for user-created events

Description
This command will create an event for a form, class, or document. The event must be a user-defined event that is explicitly declared within the module.

NOT AVAILABLE IN VB SCRIPT

Syntax
```
RaiseEvent eventName [(argList)]
```

Parameters
eventName   Required. Name of the event to be activated.

argList   Optional. List of any arguments to be passed to the event.

Returns
N/A

Immediate Window Sample
N/A

➤ Programmer's Tip

Although the RaiseEvent function does not allow normal events (such as a Click event) to be activated with it, you can execute these events like any other function. For example, to activate the Click event on a command button named Button1, you can simply call the routine using a statement such as "Call Button1_Click( )."

SEE ALSO   Call

Randomize

Initializes the seed of the random generator

Description

This statement sets the random seed to a new number. Call this function before the first call to the Rnd( ) function to have a fairly random outcome.

AVAILABLE IN VB SCRIPT

Syntax

```
Randomize [seed]
```

Parameters

seed   Optional. Any valid numeric expression. If seed is omitted, the system timer is used for the seed.

Returns

N/A

Immediate Window Sample

```
Randomize
? Rnd
```

➤ Programmer's Tip

To create an identical random sequences, call the Rnd( ) function with a negative value and then call the Randomize function with the same numeric argument. Calling Randomize with the same number as previously used does not create the same sequence.

Many programmers mistakenly think the Rnd( ) function is a number rounding function. For rounding, see the Int, Fix, Format, and CInt functions.

SEE ALSO   Rnd, Timer

Rate

Returns the interest rate per period calculated from an annuity

Description
The payment is calculated from the values of periodic fixed payments and a fixed interest rate. The Rate function returns the interest rate per period given the other factors.

NOT AVAILABLE IN VB SCRIPT

Syntax
```
Rate(totalPeriods%,payment@,presentValue@
[,futureValue@, whenDue%, guess!])
```

Parameters
totalPeriods%   Required.

payment@   The amount of payment to be made each period.

presentValue@   Required. Current value of payments.

futureValue@   Optional. Final cash value desired.

whenDue%   Optional. End (0) or beginning (1) of payment period.

guess!   Optional. Your estimate of the rate. If omitted, guess is set to 0.1 (10 percent).

Returns
Double type

Immediate Window Sample
```
? Rate(24,-2000,12000)
```

SEE ALSO   FV, IPmt, IRR, MIRR, NPer, NPV, Pmt, PPmt, PV, DDB, SLN, SYD

ReDim

Redimensions an array size that can leave the data within the array intact

Description

This command can be used to resize an array. If the array is made bigger, the new array items are left blank. If smaller, the array is truncated and values outside the new array size are lost.

AVAILABLE IN VB SCRIPT

Syntax

```
ReDim [Preserve] name[subscript-range][As type]
[, namesubscript-range)As type]]...
```

Parameters

Preserve   Optional. Preserve the data that exists with the array.

Returns

N/A

Immediate Window Sample

N/A

SEE ALSO   Dim, Erase, Global, Option Base

Rem

Makes any text following it on the current line invisible to the compiler

Description

The remark command can be used anywhere on a code line. Any text that follows it until the end of the line will be ignored.

AVAILABLE IN VB SCRIPT

Syntax

```
Rem comment
' comment
```

Parameters

comment   Optional. Any text.

Returns

N/A

Immediate Window Sample

N/A

> ## ➤ Programmer's Tip
>
> The remark command is very useful when you're testing code.
> Rather than delete the code, which you may need later, simply
> make it a comment.

SEE ALSO   ' (apostrophe)

Replace

Returns a string with the replacement

Description

This command will shift the focus to any application currently
running under the Windows system. Either the title of the window
or the application ID that is returned by the Shell command may be
used. Note that activating the application does not change the
collapsed or expanded state of the application.

AVAILABLE IN VB SCRIPT

Syntax

```
Replace(str, find, replaceWith [,start [,count
[,compare]]])
```

Parameters

str   Required. Initial string to search for replacements.

find   Required. The string to search for within the string.

replaceWith   Required. The string to replace the found strings.

start   Optional. Character position where the searching is to begin.

count   Required. Number of substitutions to perform. If omitted, all found replacements are made.

compare   Required. Type of comparison used for replacement. Use one of the constants: vbUseCompareOption (–1), vbBinaryCompare (0), vbTextCompare (1), or vbDatabaseCompare (2).

Returns

String

Immediate Window Sample

```
Replace "Hello ab this ab is ab a ab test ab.", "ab", "**"
```

SEE ALSO   InStr

Reset

Closes all open files

Description

Any files that were opened using the Open command will be closed, and their file buffers will be written to disk. This works in the same manner as the Close command when Close is not passed any parameters.

NOT AVAILABLE IN VB SCRIPT

Syntax

```
Reset
```

Parameters

N/A

Returns
N/A

Immediate Window Sample
N/A

SEE ALSO   Open, Close, End, FreeFile, ChDir, ChDrive

Resume

Resumes execution after an error-handling routine has completed processing

Description
The Resume command can resume to the beginning of the procedure (Resume 0), with the next available statement (Resume Next), or with a particular anchor line or label.

NOT AVAILABLE IN VB SCRIPT

Syntax
```
Resume [[0] | Next | line-number | line-label ]
```

Parameters
line-number | line-label   An anchor where execution is to resume.

Returns
N/A

Immediate Window Sample
N/A

SEE ALSO   On Error...

Return

Returns for a GoSub call within a subroutine

Description

The Return command moves execution back to the original call of the subroutine by its line or label.

NOT AVAILABLE IN VB SCRIPT

Syntax

```
Return
```

Parameters

N/A

Returns

N/A

Immediate Window Sample

N/A

SEE ALSO   GoSub, On...GoSub

RGB

Returns a Long value representing the three RGB values passed to it

Description

This function converts a Red value, a Green value, and a Blue value into the Long format typically used by the Windows system for everything from drawing to window background colors.

AVAILABLE IN VB SCRIPT

Syntax

```
RGB(red%, green%, blue%)
```

Parameters

red%   Integer value between 0 and 255.

green%   Integer value between 0 and 255.

blue%   Integer value between 0 and 255.

Returns
Long type

Immediate Window Sample
```
? RGB(0,255,0)
```

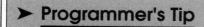

➤ Programmer's Tip

Use the QBColor command to quickly generate an RGB color of Long type for a standard setting.

SEE ALSO QBColor, Line

Right, Right$

Returns a string containing the amount of the right portion of the passed string

Description
This function can be used to take any specified substring from the right to the left and to return it as a separate string.

AVAILABLE IN VB SCRIPT

Syntax
```
Right$(expression$, Length&)
```

Parameters
expression$ Any string expression.

Length& Number of characters to return in the substring.

Returns
String type

Immediate Window Sample
```
? Right("Hello World",4)
```

> ## ➤ Programmer's Tip

The Right$ function can be used to easily check a filename that the user entered to determine if he or she added the correct extension. For example, for a text file, the last four characters should equal ".TXT".

SEE ALSO   Left, Left$, Mid, Mid$

RmDir

Removes the specified empty directory

Description
The directory to be removed must not contain any files. You can use the Kill command to delete the files before removing the directory.

NOT AVAILABLE IN VB SCRIPT

Syntax
RmDir dirname$

Parameters
dirname$ String must be in the format of
[drive:][dir[subdir][subdir]...

Returns
N/A

Immediate Window Sample
RmDir "c:\tempdir"

SEE ALSO   CurDir, CurDir$, MkDir, Kill

Rnd

Returns a random number

Description

This function returns a Single number between 0 and 1 that contains a seeded random number. You may include a specific seed for the random number. For random numbers within a range, use Int((ub − lb + 1) * Rnd + lb), where lb = lower bound and ub = upper bound.

AVAILABLE IN VB SCRIPT

Syntax

```
Rnd[(numericExpression#)]
```

Parameters

numericExpression#   Any valid numeric expression.

Returns

Single type

Immediate Window Sample

```
? Rnd
? Int((25-5+1)*Rnd+5)
```

➤ Programmer's Tip

Many programmers mistakenly think the Rnd( ) function is a number rounding function. For rounding, see the Int, Fix, Format, Round, and CInt functions.

SEE ALSO   Randomize

Rollback

Aborts operations currently in the transaction cycle

Description
When a transaction has begun with BeginTrans, Rollback will reverse all current operations within the transaction and abort it.

NOT AVAILABLE IN VB SCRIPT

Syntax
```
Rollback
```

Parameters
N/A

Returns
N/A

Immediate Window Sample
N/A

SEE ALSO   BeginTrans, CommitTrans

Round   VB 6
                                                       Only

Rounds the passed number to the specified decimal places

Description
This function will round a numeric expression (including Int, Double, Single, and Variant types) to a specified number of decimal places. If the number of decimal places is not specified, a rounded integer will be returned.

NOT AVAILABLE IN VB SCRIPT

Syntax
```
Round(num [,numDecimalPlaces]
```

Parameters

num   Required. Number to round.

numDecimalPlaces   Optional. Number of places to the right of the decimal to include in the answer.

Returns

Number

Immediate Window Sample

```
? Round(1.2268)
? Round(1.2268,2)
```

> ➤ **Programmer's Tip**
>
> For basic integer rounding, you can also use the Fix and Int commands. For string formatting of decimal places, you can use the Format command.

SEE ALSO   Format, Fix, Int

RSet

Right-justifies string within the destination and fills the remainder with spaces

Description

This command essentially copies the sourcevariable into the resultvariable padded with spaces if the resultvariable is longer. For example, if the length of resultvariable is ten characters, a five-character sourcevariable would be copied to it and padded with five space characters. See this example in the Immediate window. This command can also be used to copy from one user-defined variable to another of the same length.

NOT AVAILABLE IN VB SCRIPT

Syntax

```
RSet resultvariable = sourcevariable
```

Parameters

resultvariable   Required. Destination for the new string.

sourcevariable   Right-justified string to copy.

Returns

N/A

Immediate Window Sample

```
a$ = "1234567890"
RSet a$ = "Hello"
? a$ + "<--end"
```

SEE ALSO   Let, LSet

RTrim, RTrim$

Returns a substring with the trailing spaces from the right removed from the passed string

Description

The RTrim function is the complement of the LTrim function, but returns a string taken from right to left. Any spaces on the right side of the string are removed.

AVAILABLE IN VB SCRIPT

Syntax

```
RTrim$(stringExpression$)

RTrim(stringExpression$)
```

Parameters

stringExpression$ Required. Any valid string.

Returns

String type

Immediate Window Sample

```
? Rtrim("Hello ") + "<-end"
```

SavePicture

Saves the graphic stored in a Picture or Image control

Description

NOT AVAILABLE IN VBA. The SavePicture statement accepts the object reference to the picture, as well as a destination path and filename to store the file. SavePicture cannot save JPEG or GIF formats, so pictures in these formats are saved as bitmaps. Note that the Immediate window example requires that a form is executing but paused, and contains a Picture control named Picture1.

NOT AVAILABLE IN VB SCRIPT

Syntax

```
SavePicture objectReference, picturefile$
```

Parameters

objectReference   Required. The object reference stored in the Picture property of a control.

picturefile$ Required. A valid filename and path to store the picture.

Returns

N/A

Immediate Window Sample

```
SavePicture Picture1.Picture, "c:\myPict.bmp"
```

SEE ALSO   LoadPicture

SaveSetting

VB 6 Only

Writes an entry into the Windows registry

Description
This writes an entry into the Windows registry in the specified application section.

NOT AVAILABLE IN VB SCRIPT

Syntax
```
SaveSetting appName, section, key, setting
```

Parameters
appName   Required. Name of the application section in the registry.

section   Required. Section in which the setting is to be stored.

key   Required. Name of the key to be saved.

setting   Required. The value to be stored in the key.

Returns
N/A

Immediate Window Sample
```
SaveSetting "myApp", "Prefs", "Velo", 500
```

SEE ALSO   DeleteSetting, GetAllSettings, GetSetting

Second

Returns the seconds portion of the date and time passed to it

Description
The Second function will return the seconds portion of a Date type. An integer between 0 and 59 is returned.

AVAILABLE IN VB SCRIPT

Syntax
`Second(dateVariant)`

Parameters
dateVariant   Required. The date from which the second value will be extracted.

Returns
Integer type

Immediate Window Sample
`? Second(Now)`

SEE ALSO   Now, TimeSerial, TimeValue, Hour, Minute, Time

Seek

Returns the current read/write position of an open file

Description
When passed a file number, this will return a Long value that varies depending on the type of file accessed. If the file is a Random file, the number of the next record is returned. If a Binary, Output, Append, or Input file is used, the byte position (beginning at byte 1) will be returned.

NOT AVAILABLE IN VB SCRIPT

Syntax
As a function:

`Seek(filenumber%)`

As a statement:

`Seek [#]filenumber%, position&`

Parameters
filenumber%   Required. Number of a currently open file.

position&   Required. Position to move the read/write pointer as a record number (Random files) or byte offset number.

Returns
Long

Immediate Window Sample
```
? Seek(1)
```

SEE ALSO   Get, Open, Put, FileLen, Loc

Select Case

Executes a group of statements when an expression equals the testexpression

Description
The Select Case statement is an advanced form of an If...Then...Else structure, where one expression is entered and compared against multiple values. The Case Else statement allows statements to be executed if none of the values matches.

AVAILABLE IN VB SCRIPT

Syntax
```
Select Case testexpression
   Case expression1
       [statements]
   [Case expression2]
       [statements]
   [Case Else]
       [statements]
End Select
```

Parameters
testexpression   Main value used for all comparisons.

expression   Value to be compared with testexpression.

Returns
N/A

Immediate Window Sample

```
a = 3
Select Case a : Case 1 : ? "1" : Case 2 : _
? "2" : Case Else : ? "Other" : End Select
```

> ➤ **Programmer's Tip**

For simpler selection of multiple values, consider using the Switch command instead. Using Switch can often lead to more elegant code.

SEE ALSO   If...Else, If...Else...End If, IIf, Choose, Switch

---

SendKeys

Sends keystrokes to the active window

Description

This can be used to simulate keyboard entry and to access system functions, such as Cut, Copy, and Paste, not normally available to a Visual Basic program.

NOT AVAILABLE IN VB SCRIPT

Syntax

```
SendKeys keystrokes$ [, wait%]
```

Parameters

keystrokes$ Required. String containing the keystrokes to be sent to the window.

wait%   Optional. If True, control is not returned to the program until keys have been processed. For immediate control to be returned, False (the default) may be used.

Returns

N/A

Immediate Window Sample

```
SendKeys "ENTER"
SendKeys "F1"
SendKeys "PrtSc"
```

SEE ALSO DoEvents

Set

Creates a reference to an object

Description

The Set command does not create the object instance, but merely points the variable at the object. More than one reference to a particular object may exist. Use the New command to create a new instance of the object.

AVAILABLE IN VB SCRIPT

Syntax

```
Set objectVariableName = [New] objectExpression
Set objectVariableName = Nothing
```

Parameters

objectVariableName Required. Name of the variable that will receive the object reference.

objectExpression Required. Expression to create a new object or to reference an existing one.

Returns

N/A

Immediate Window Sample

```
Set a = GetObject("Excel.Application")
a.Visible = True
```

SEE ALSO Let, GetObject, CreateObject, With...End With

SetAttr

Sets the attributes of a file given a proper filename and path

Description
SetAttr designates the information of files as Normal (0), ReadOnly (1), Hidden (2), System (4), Directory (16), or Archive (32). These attributes can be set for any file on the disk. The Immediate window sample hides the Test.txt file.

NOT AVAILABLE IN VB SCRIPT

Syntax
```
SetAttr fileName$, attributeBits%
```

Parameters
fileName$ Required. A valid path and filename.

attributeBits%   Required. New attribute settings.

Returns
N/A

Immediate Window Sample
```
SetAttr "c:\test.txt", vbReadOnly
```

SEE ALSO   GetAttr

SetDataAccess

Sets the location of the current workgroup setting for a database

Description
This is used to set the location of the data access options. It is obsolete and only available for backward compatibility.

NOT AVAILABLE IN VB SCRIPT

Syntax
```
SetDataAccess option%, value
```

Parameters
option%   Numeric option of data access type (1 = Set the name and path of the application INI file).

value   Parameter for the specified option.

Returns
N/A

Immediate Window Sample
N/A

SEE ALSO   SetDefaultWorkspace

SetDefaultWorkspace

Sets the default user name and password for accessing secure databases

Description
This command will set a default user name and password that will be automatically passed to the database when a secure database is opened. It is obsolete and only available for backward compatibility.

NOT AVAILABLE IN VB SCRIPT

Syntax
```
SetDefaultWorkspace userName$, password$
```

Parameters
userName$ Valid user name.

password$ Valid password.

Returns
N/A

Immediate Window Sample
N/A

SEE ALSO   SetDataAccess

Sgn

Returns the sign (+/-) of the number passed to it

Description
The Sgn function can be used to determine the sign of a number. A positive number returns a 1, a negative number returns a −1. If the passed value is 0, a 0 is returned.

AVAILABLE IN VB SCRIPT

Syntax
Sgn(numericExpression)

Parameters
numericExpression   Required. Any valid numeric expression.

Returns
Integer type

Immediate Window Sample
```
? Sgn(5)
? Sgn(-5)
? Sgn(0)
```

SEE ALSO   Abs, Tan, Atn, Sin, Cos, Log, Exp

Shell

Executes a command at the command prompt

Description

Use of the Shell command gives complete access to all command-prompt (MS-DOS) functions. This command is most often used to launch another program. Using traditional command-line parameters, you can use this command to pass information including toggle commands or parameters to the launching application.

A taskID is returned if the command is successful. The mode enables you to control the execution window so it's hidden (0), normal with focus (1), minimized with focus (2), maximized with focus (3), normal without focus (4), or minimized without focus (6).

NOT AVAILABLE IN VB SCRIPT

Syntax

```
Shell(programname$[, mode%])
```

Parameters

programname$ Required. Fully qualified path and filename.

mode%   Optional. Specifies in what mode to execute the command.

Returns

Double type

Immediate Window Sample

```
Shell "c:\windows\calc.exe"
```

SEE ALSO   AppActivate

Show Method

Makes the current window visible

Description

This method can be used on a nonload form to load and display it. If the Form window was previously hidden or opened with the Load command, the Show method will make it visible.

AVAILABLE IN VB SCRIPT

Syntax

```
window.Show
```

Parameters

window   Required. The Name property of a window within the project.

Returns

N/A

Immediate Window Sample

N/A

SEE ALSO   Load, Unload

Sin

Returns the sine of an angle specified in radians

Description

This command requires the angle to be passed in radians. The formula radians = (degrees * pi) / 180 can be used to determine the radians from a degree measure.

AVAILABLE IN VB SCRIPT

Syntax

```
Sin(angle)
```

Parameters

angle   Required. Any numeric expression holding a radian measure.

Returns

Double type

Immediate Window Sample

```
? Sin(3.14159)
? Sin((90*3.14159)/180)
```

SEE ALSO Abs, Tan, Atn, Sgn, Cos, Log, Exp, Sqr

SLN

Returns the value for a single period of straight line depreciation

Description

Depreciation is determined by use of a double-declining balance method unless specified by use of the factor parameter.

NOT AVAILABLE IN VB SCRIPT

Syntax

```
SLN(initialCost@, salvageValue@, lifeSpan%)
```

Parameters

initialCost@   Required. Initial cost of asset as Double type.

salvageValue@   Required. Value at end of useful life as Double type.

lifeSpan%   Required. Length of useful life as Double type.

Returns

Double

Immediate Window Sample

```
? SLN(10000,500,24)
```

SEE ALSO FV, IPmt, IRR, MIRR, NPer, NPV, Pmt, PPmt, PV, Rate, DDB, SYD

Space, Space$

Returns a string containing the number of spaces specified

Description

This function can be used for formatting to pad any number of spaces required.

Syntax

```
Space$(number-of-spaces&)
Space(number-of-spaces&)
```

Parameters

number-of-spaces&   Required. Numeric expression containing the number of spaces to create.

Returns

String type

Immediate Window Sample

```
? Space(10);"Hello"
```

SEE ALSO   Spc, String, String$, Print, ?

Spc

Adds spaces for formatting specifically for Print and Print # commands

Description

The Spc function adds spaces to the current print position. If the number of spaces exceeds the line width, the spaces will be placed on the next line in the next print position.

NOT AVAILABLE IN VB SCRIPT

Syntax

```
Spc(number-of-spaces%)
```

Parameters

number-of-spaces%   Required. Numeric expression containing the number of spaces to create.

Returns

N/A

Immediate Window Sample

```
Open "C:\test.txt" for Output as #1 : _
Print #1,"Hello";Spc(20);"Hello2" : Close #1
```

SEE ALSO   Space, Space$, Tab

Split

Splits a string into a number of smaller strings between delimiter

Description

This function will take a string and break it into an array of
substrings. If the delimiter is set to an empty string (""), the entire
string will be returned in the first index position of the array.

AVAILABLE IN VB SCRIPT

Syntax

```
Split(str [,delimit [,count [,compare]]])
```

Parameters

str   Required. String to be processed.

delimit   Optional. Delimiting string that if not specified, a space is
being used.

count   Optional. Number of strings to be returned.

compare   Optional. Type of comparison specified by a constant:
vbUseCompareOption (–1), vbBinaryCompare (0), vbTextCompare
(1), or vbDatabaseCompare (2).

Returns

Array

Immediate Window Sample

```
a = Split("This is a test")
? a(0)
? a(1)
```

> ## ➤ Programmer's Tip

This function is excellent for file processing. By use of tabs or commas as the delimiting string, individual lines can easily be processed.

III

SEE ALSO　Array, Dim, Input #, Join

Sqr

Returns the square root of a given number

Description

The square root function will return the square root of any number greater than or equal to zero.

AVAILABLE IN VB SCRIPT

Syntax
Sqr(numericExpression)

Parameters
numericExpression　Required. Any valid numeric expression.

Returns
Double type

Immediate Window Sample
```
? Sqr(9)
? Sqr(2)
```

SEE ALSO　Sin, Abs, Tan, Atn, Sgn, Cos, Log, Exp

Static

Makes a variable persistent even after the procedure has completed executing

Description

The Static command will make a variable that is local to a particular routine keep its value. The next execution of the routine can access the remaining value.

NOT AVAILABLE IN VB SCRIPT

Syntax

For declaring the data type of a simple variable:

```
Static name [As type] [, name [As type]]...
```

For declaring an array:
```
Static name[(subscript-range)][As type]
[, name [(subscript-range)][As type] syntax as type]...
```

Parameters

Standard variable definitions.

Returns

N/A

Immediate Window Sample

N/A

SEE ALSO Dim, Global, Option Base, ReDim, Type

Stop

Halts execution of the program

Description

Placing a Stop command in your program essentially places a semipermanent breakpoint so the debugger will be activated when the Stop is executed. Since breakpoints don't save with a file, the Stop command allows the creation of a breakpoint that will be stored in the program.

NOT AVAILABLE IN VB SCRIPT

Syntax

Stop

Parameters

N/A

Returns

N/A

Immediate Window Sample

N/A

SEE ALSO   End

Str, Str$

Converts an expression to a string

Description

The Str function will return a string representation and only recognizes the period (.) as a decimal separator.

AVAILABLE IN VB SCRIPT

Syntax

Str$(numericExpression)

Parameters

numericExpression   Required. Any valid numeric expression.

Returns
String type

Immediate Window Sample
```
? Str$(5)
? Str$(5+10)
```

SEE ALSO   Val, InStr$, CStr, Format

StrComp

Compares two strings

Description
This function will compare two strings using a specified method and return a result of the comparison. The compareType can be a binary comparison (0, default), a textual comparison (1), or, for Microsoft Access, a comparison based on information in a database. The results returned by the comparison can indicate that string1 < string2 (–1), string1 = string2 (0), string1 > string2 (1), or string1 or string2 = Null (Null).

AVAILABLE IN VB SCRIPT

Syntax
```
StrComp(string1$, string2$ [, compareType%])
```

Parameters
string1$, string2$ Required. Any valid strings.

compareType%   Optional. Specifies comparison method.

Returns
Integer

Immediate Window Sample
```
? StrComp("Hello","hello")
? StrComp("Hello","hello",1)
? StrComp("Hello","jello",1)
```

SEE ALSO   InStr$, Option Compare, =

StrConv

VB 6
Only

Converts the passed string in a number of ways, such as
uppercase, lowercase, international, and so on.

III

Description

This command is powerful in its ability to make conversions of the
entire string for common needs. Passing a conversion type constant
determines how the string will be converted: vbUppercase (1);
vbLowercase (2); vbPropercase (3)—first letter of every word is
capitalized; vbWide (4)—changes byte character string to two-byte
character string; vbNarrow (8)—converts two-byte character string
to byte character string; vbKatakana (16)—converts Hirigana to
Katakana; vbHirigana (32)—converts Katakana to Hirigana;
vbUnicode (64); or vbFromUnicode (128).

NOT AVAILABLE IN VB SCRIPT

Syntax
StrConv(str, convertType[, LCID])

Parameters

str   Required. String to be converted.

convertType   Required. Value indicating the type of conversion.

LCID   Optional. Locale ID if different conversion is desired from
the one set in the System Locale ID.

Returns
String

Immediate Window Sample
? StrConv("Demon Baby",1)
? StrConv("Demon Baby",vbLowercase)

> **➤ Programmer's Tip**
>
> If a Byte array contains characters in ASCII standard format,
> you can use the StrConv function to convert it to a string.

SEE ALSO   LenB, LenW

StrReverse

Reverses the string that is passed to it

Description
Reverses the string character by character and returns the reversed
string. If the string passed to this function is a Null, an error will
occur.

AVAILABLE IN VB SCRIPT

Syntax
```
StrReverse(str)
```

Parameters
str   Required.

Returns
String

Immediate Window Sample
```
? StrReverse("Reef Brazil")
```

> **➤ Programmer's Tip**
>
> Use the ampersand (&) with an empty string ("") before
> passing your string to avoid generating an error if the passed
> string might contain a Null value.

String, String$

Creates a repeating string of the specified character

Description
The function can be passed a length, and a string or ASCII code that will be duplicated until the string length is reached.

AVAILABLE IN VB SCRIPT

Syntax
```
String$(number-of-characters&, ascii-code%)
String$(number-of-characters&, character$)
String(number-of-characters&, ascii-code%)
String(number-of-characters&, character$)
```

Parameters
number-of-characters&   Required. Length the returned string will be.

ascii-code%   The ASCII value of a character to be repeated to fill the string.

character$ A single-character string to be repeated.

Returns
String type

Immediate Window Sample
```
? String$(20,65)
? String$(25,"B")
```

SEE ALSO   Space, Space$, Asc, Chr

Sub...End Sub

Creates a subroutine in a module or form

Description

This command allows definition of a subroutine that may include the types of arguments that will be received when the routine is called.

AVAILABLE IN VB SCRIPT

Syntax

```
[Static] [Private] Sub sub-name[(arguments)]
[Static var[,var]...]  [Dim var[,var]...]
[ReDim var[,var]...] [statements] [Exit Static]
    [statements]
End Sub
```

Parameters

arguments   Required. Any arguments to be received by the function.

Returns

N/A

Immediate Window Sample

N/A

SEE ALSO   Call, End, Exit, Function

Switch

Evaluates the passed expressions and returns the expression for the first True expression

Description

The Switch function can be used to perform a quick series of related comparisons. The Immediate window example demonstrates converting from an abbreviation to a complete string.

AVAILABLE IN VB SCRIPT

Syntax

```
Switch(expression1, value [, expression2, value2
[,. . . expression7, value7])
```

Parameters

expression   Boolean. Can be an evaluative expression.

value   Any valid Variant type variable.

Returns

Variant type

III

Immediate Window Sample

```
a$ = "CA"
? Switch(a$="WI","Wisconsin",a$="OR","Oregon", _
a$="CA","California")
```

➤ Programmer's Tip

If the value to be selected is a numeric index, consider using the Choose command instead of Switch. Evaluation of numeric constants will execute faster using the Choose command.

SEE ALSO   Choose, IIf, Select Case

SYD

Returns the sum depreciation of the years digits of an asset

Description

Depreciation is determined by use of a double-declining balance method unless specified by use of the factor parameter.

NOT AVAILABLE IN VB SCRIPT

Syntax

```
SYD(initialCost@, salvageValue@, Lifespan%, period%)
```

Parameters

initialCost@   Required. Initial cost of asset as Double type.

salvageValue@   Required. Value at end of useful life as Double type.

Lifespan%   Required. Length of useful life as Double type.

period%   Required. Period for which depreciation is calculated as Double type.

Returns
Double type

Immediate Window Sample
```
? SYD(10000,500,24,12)
```

SEE ALSO   DDB, FV, IPmt, IRR, MIRR, NPer, NPV, Pmt, PPmt, PV, Rate, SLN

Tab

Adds a tab to the formatting for a Print or Print # statement

Description
Tab can be used to properly format columns for output to files. If the position specified in the column has already passed, the characters will automatically be aligned with the next column position.

NOT AVAILABLE IN VB SCRIPT

Syntax
```
Tab([column%])
```

Parameters
column%   Optional. Integer that specifies the column to tab into.

Returns
N/A

Immediate Window Sample
```
? Tab + "Hello"
? Tab(5) + "Hello"
```

SEE ALSO   Print #, Spc, Print, ?

Tan

Returns the tangent of an angle specified in radians

Description

This command requires the angle to be passed in radians. The formula radians = (degrees * pi) / 180 can be used to determine the radians from a degree measure.

AVAILABLE IN VB SCRIPT

Syntax

```
Tan(angle)
```

Parameters

angle   Required. Any numeric expression holding a radian measure.

Returns

Double type

Immediate Window Sample

```
? Tan(3.14159)
? Tan((90*3.14159)/180)
```

SEE ALSO   Atn, Cos, Sin, Sqr

Time

Sets the current system time

Description

This function sets the actual system time, so be careful with its use.

AVAILABLE IN VB SCRIPT

Syntax
```
Time = time-string$
```

Parameters
time-string$ Required. String containing a valid time setting.

Returns
N/A

Immediate Window Sample
```
Time = "2:40"
? Time
```

SEE ALSO   Time$, Date$, Date, Now

Time$

Retrieves the time from the current system

Description
This returns a string that contains the current system time.

AVAILABLE IN VB SCRIPT

Syntax
```
Time$
```

Parameters
N/A

Returns
String type

Immediate Window Sample
```
? Time$
```

SEE ALSO   Date, Date$, Now, TimeValue

Timer

Returns the number of seconds that have elapsed since midnight

Description
This function, available in both VBA and VB Script, where there are no Timer controls available, can be used to track time values.

AVAILABLE IN VB SCRIPT

Syntax
Timer

Parameters
N/A

Returns
Single type

Immediate Window Sample
```
? Timer
a = Timer
? Timer - a
```

➤ Programmer's Tip

To time the speed of programs, the Timer function can be very useful. Simply set a variable equal to the current timer (that is, a = Timer), execute the routine, and then figure the time elapsed (that is, myTime = Timer – a).

SEE ALSO   Randomize

TimeSerial

Returns a time based on serial parameters passed to it

Description
This routine allows the quick creation of a datetime value from three integer values.

AVAILABLE IN VB SCRIPT

Syntax
```
TimeSerial(hour%, minute%, second%)
```

Parameters
hour%. minute%, second%   Required. Integers.

Returns
Variant (Date) type

Immediate Window Sample
```
? TimeSerial(14,34,15)
```

SEE ALSO   DateSerial, TimeValue, DateValue, Day, Month, Now, Year, Date, Time, Format, CVDate

TimeValue

Creates a Date type value holding the specified time

Description
This function can be used to create a date and time value from a string containing a time string.

AVAILABLE IN VB SCRIPT

Syntax
```
TimeValue(time-string$)
```

Parameters
time-string$ Required. Any valid string holding a time value.

Returns
Variant (Date) type

Immediate Window Sample
```
? TimeValue("2:15:23 PM")
```

SEE ALSO   Now, TimeSerial

Trim, Trim$

Returns a string with both leading and trailing spaces removed

Description
Just as the LTrim command removes leading space and the RTrim removes trailing spaces, Trim removes both.

AVAILABLE IN VB SCRIPT

Syntax
```
Trim$(stringExpression$) Trim(stringExpression)
```

Parameters
stringExpression$ Required. Any valid string.

Returns
String type

Immediate Window Sample
```
? Trim(" Hello ")
```

SEE ALSO   LTrim, LTrim$, RTrim, RTrim$

True

Logical True

Description

This constant can be used in most expressions, bitwise operations, and comparisons.

AVAILABLE IN VB SCRIPT

Syntax

True

Parameters

N/A

Returns

N/A

Immediate Window Sample

```
? (2=2) = False
? (2=2) = True
```

SEE ALSO   And, Or, Imp, Eqv, Xor, False

Type...End Type

Creates a user-defined variable type

Description

User-defined types are ideal when you need to format a set of information into a single structure such as rectangle data, data records, and so on.

NOT AVAILABLE IN VB SCRIPT

Syntax

```
Type type-name element As type [element As type] : : End Type
```

Parameters

type-name   Required. Any valid name.

element   Required. The name of the structure member.

type   Required. Any valid data type.

Returns
N/A

Immediate Window Sample
N/A

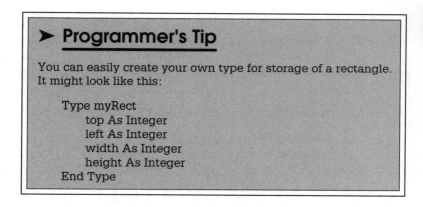

> ## ➤ Programmer's Tip
>
> You can easily create your own type for storage of a rectangle.
> It might look like this:
>
>   Type myRect
>   top As Integer
>   left As Integer
>   width As Integer
>   height As Integer
>   End Type

SEE ALSO   Dim, Global, ReDim, Static

TypeName
VB 6
Only

Returns a string of the variable type passed to the function

Description
This function receives a variable name and returns the data type
specified by the variable name. Data types such as Double, Date,
Null, and others are returned as a string.

NOT AVAILABLE IN VB SCRIPT

Syntax
TypeName(varName)

Parameters
varName   Required. The variable to be typed.

Returns
String

Immediate Window Sample
```
a = CStr("Hello") : b = CInt(53)
? TypeName(a)
? TypeName(b)
```

SEE ALSO   #, %, Dim

UBound

Returns the highest subscript available in the array

Description
This function can be used to determine the upper bound of an array. If the array is multidimensional, use the dimension argument to specify the upper bound to be returned.

AVAILABLE IN VB SCRIPT

Syntax
```
UBound(arrayname[, dimension%])
```

Parameters
arrayname   Required. The name of the array required to determine the limit.

dimension%   Optional. The subscript dimension of a multidimensional array.

Returns
Long type

Immediate Window Sample
```
myArray = array(6,4,2,5,2,4,6)
? UBound(myArray)
```

SEE ALSO   LBound, Array, Dim

UCase, UCase$

Returns a completely uppercase string

Description

III

This function converts all the characters in the passed string to uppercase.

AVAILABLE IN VB SCRIPT

Syntax
UCase$(expression$)
UCase(expression$)

Parameters
expression$ Required. Any valid string.

Returns
String type

Immediate Window Sample
? UCase("hElLo")

SEE ALSO   LCase, LCase$

Unload

Unloads a form or control object from memory

Description
Use the Unload command to release a control or form. Memory used by the form or control will be flushed, and any property setting will be lost.

NOT AVAILABLE IN VB SCRIPT

Syntax

```
UnLoad form-name
UnLoad control-name (index)
```

Parameters

form-name, control-name   Required. Name to reference desired object.

Returns

N/A

Immediate Window Sample

N/A

➤ Programmer's Tip

Some programmers use the Unload command on the central form of an application to stop execution. It is recommended that you use the End command instead. If there is one form invisible, but still loaded, unloading the central form will not end the application. By use of End, all forms that are visible or invisible are closed and the application exits.

SEE ALSO   Load, Show

Val

Returns the value contained in a string

Description

This function will convert the value contained within a string to a numeric value. If there is no numeric value contained in the string, a zero will be returned.

NOT AVAILABLE IN VB SCRIPT

Syntax
```
Val(stringExpression$)
```

Parameters
stringExpression$ Required. Any string containing a numeric value.

Returns
Variant

Immediate Window Sample
```
? Val("100")
? Val("54.55")
```

SEE ALSO   Str, Str$, Format, &

Value Property

Holds the value for a specific control property

Description
The Value property is the most common property available for objects. It typically holds the central data for the control. For example, in a scroll bar control, the Value property holds the current thumb position.

AVAILABLE IN VB SCRIPT

Syntax
```
object.Value [= value]
```

Parameters
value   Dependent on the object type.

Returns
N/A

Immediate Window Sample
```
? myScroll1.Value
```

SEE ALSO   . (dot)

VarType

Returns the type of variable stored in the passed reference

Description

Since Visual Basic variables may be defined implicitly, this function can be used to determine the type of variable being used. The returned type number may indicate Empty (0), Null (1), Integer (2), Long (3), Single (4), Double (5), Currency (6), Date (7), String (8), Object (9), Error (10), Boolean (11), Variant (12), Data Object (13), Decimal (14), Byte (17), or Array (8192).

AVAILABLE IN VB SCRIPT

Syntax

```
VarType(variant)
```

Parameters

variant   Required. A value to be evaluated.

Returns

Integer type

Immediate Window Sample

```
a$ = "Hello"
? VarType(a)
b% = 15
? VarType(b)
```

SEE ALSO   Dim, CInt, CStr, CDbl, CByte

WeekDay

Returns the weekday portion of the passed Date type

Description
This function will return an Integer value between 1 (Sunday) and 7 (Saturday) that represents the weekday of the date passed to it.

AVAILABLE IN VB SCRIPT

Syntax
WeekDay(dateVariant)

Parameters
dateVariant A valid date from which the weekday will be extracted.

Returns
Integer type

Immediate Window Sample
? WeekDay(Now)

SEE ALSO   DateSerial, DateValue, Day, Month, Year, Now, Format

WeekdayName

VB 6
Only

Returns a string with the name of the weekday

Description
This command will return a string with the specified day of the week in the format specified. The weekDay and firstDayoftheWeek parameters are specified using one of the following constants: vbUseSystem (0), vbSunday (1), vbMonday (2), vbTuesday (3), vbWednesday (4), vbThursday (5), vbFriday (6), or vbSaturday (7).

AVAILABLE IN VB SCRIPT

Syntax
WeekdayName(weekDay[,abbr[,firstDayoftheWeek]])

Parameters
weekDay Required. Numeric constant of the day of the week that should be returned in the string.

abbr   Optional. Boolean to indicate whether the returned string should be abbreviated.

firstDayoftheWeek   Optional. Numeric constant indicating the first day of the week.

Returns
String

Immediate Window Sample
```
? WeekdayName(1)
? WeekdayName(1, True)
```

SEE ALSO   Weekday, Date, Format

While...Wend

Cycles through a loop until the necessary condition is met

Description
The While...Wend structure can continue cycling while a condition is True. It is recommended that you use the Do...Loop structure.

AVAILABLE IN VB SCRIPT

Syntax
```
While condition : [statements] : Wend
```

Parameters
condition   Required. Boolean value.

Returns
N/A

Immediate Window Sample
```
i = 0

While i < 5 : ? i : i = i + 1 : Wend
```

SEE ALSO   Do...Loop, For...Next, For Each

Width

Sets a width for the output file

Description

For formatting to a file, the Width # statement will set the width between 0 and 255 for text, tabs, and spaces to be formatted. If the width is set to 0 (default), there is no set line width.

NOT AVAILABLE IN VB SCRIPT

Syntax

```
Width #fileNumber, width%
```

Parameters

fileNumber   Required. Any valid open file number.

width%   Required. Any width between 0 and 255.

Returns

N/A

Immediate Window Sample

```
Open "C:\test.txt" for Output as #1 : Width #1, 20 : _

Print #1, "Hello";Spc(15);"Hello2" : Close #1
```

SEE ALSO   Print #, Spc, Tab

With...End With

Used for a series of object references

Description

The With...End With structure enables any statement contained within it to reference the current object with a simple dot (.) command. For example, the Value property of an Excel cell may be set inside the proper With operator with the ".Value = 3" command.

AVAILABLE IN VB SCRIPT

Syntax
```
With object [statements] End With
```

Parameters
object   Required. Any valid object reference.

Returns
N/A

Immediate Window Sample
N/A

➤ Programmer's Tip

Use the With...End With structure when you want to increase the speed of your object references. When an object is accessed multiple times and is several dot (.) levels deep, use of a With keyword to create a single reference is much faster.

SEE ALSO   CreateObject, GetObject

Write

Writes data to a specified open file

Description
Unlike the Print # command, Write # can write any type of data to a file without conversion into a string.

NOT AVAILABLE IN VB SCRIPT

Syntax
```
Write #fileNumber [, var1] [, var2] [, var3] ...
```

Parameters

fileNumber   Required. Any valid open file number.

var   Optional. Variables of any valid type.

Returns

N/A

Immediate Window Sample

```
a$ = "Hello" : b = 20

Open "C:\test.txt" for Output as #1: _

Write #1, a$,b : Close #1
```

SEE ALSO   Close, Input #, Open, Print #, Write, File System
Objects (Part IV)

Exclusive Or

Description

This operator can be used to logically combine two numbers using
logical exclusion. Within the bits of the numbers, if a 1 exists in one
of the numbers but not the other, a 1 is returned in that bit. If both
bits are set to zero or 1, a zero is returned in that bit.

AVAILABLE IN VB SCRIPT

Syntax

```
a Xor b
```

Parameters

a, b   Required. Any valid numeric expression.

Returns

Variant type

Immediate Window Sample

```
? 255 Xor 8
```

SEE ALSO   And, Or, Imp, Eqv, True, False, Not

Year

Returns the Year portion of the passed Date type

Description

This function will return a Variant value between 0 and 9999 that represents the year of the date passed to it.

AVAILABLE IN VB SCRIPT

Syntax

```
Year(dateVariant)
```

Parameters

dateVariant   A valid date from which the year will be extracted.

Returns

Variant type

Immediate Window Sample

```
? Year(Now)
```

SEE ALSO   DateSerial, DateValue, Day, Month, Now, Format, Weekday

Part IV
Object Model Diagrams

IV

Programming VBA requires understanding many different facets of the programming world. Increasingly, programmers have divided large programs into a series of objects that work together. Most programs that incorporate the VBA language and development system are constructed of objects that are individually accessible. Knowing the object model (represented by an object diagram), a designer can create programs that can accomplish almost any operation available to the hands-on user. Spreadsheets can be added, text inserted into Word documents, contacts sorted in Outlook, and most other capabilities.

Part IV of this reference provides the complete object models of all of the central Office applications as well as several other popular models. For the primary Office applications and Internet Explorer, the most common object methods and properties are provided, as well as a general explanation of the object model itself. The Immediate window provides an easy way to test and understand how an object, method, or property can be used. Therefore, where possible, single-line Immediate window samples have been provided.

For Outlook and Internet Explorer, there is no Immediate window available. Therefore, the Outlook code can be placed in the Scripting window and executed from there. Internet Explorer samples have been included as simple HTML files that can be created in any text editor (such as Notepad) and saved to the disk. Internet Explorer can then be used to open the example from a file using the Browse button under the Open option.

The object model diagrams have the complete set of objects available to each application. Multiple objects are stored as a *collection*. A collection is typically named as a plural of an object. On the diagrams, each collection appears as a set of stacked cards, while the individual objects appear as single boxes. In a collection box, the collection is named first, followed by the name of the individual objects in parentheses.

The most effective way to program the object models is to use them in conjunction with the Object Browser (pressing the F2 key will show the browser in the VBA environment) that is included with all of the VB and VBA environments (it isn't included with Outlook or Internet Explorer). Use the object models to determine which objects you will need to access, and then look up the individual properties and methods within the Object Browser. Although the Object Browser itself is not available in Outlook and Internet Explorer, their object models are available for browsing through the Object Browser by using it from another Office application.

Excel

Excel was the first application to incorporate VBA and provides the most robust object implementation. Spreadsheets break down in a very hierarchical manner, so the Excel object model will appear in a way that is logical and consistent. By browsing through the object model diagram to understand the basic organization, you will be able to quickly locate the object that you need.

All open files are stored as Workbook objects in the Workbooks collection. In turn, each Worksheet in a Workbook is stored within the Worksheets collection. Cells can be accessed individually or selected as a set. All cells are accessed from a Range object. Note that there is only a single Range object, not a collection of them. Therefore if you need to access several different ranges simultaneously, they will have to be individually stored.

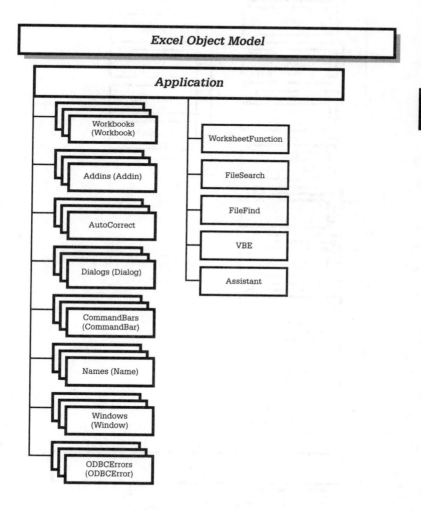

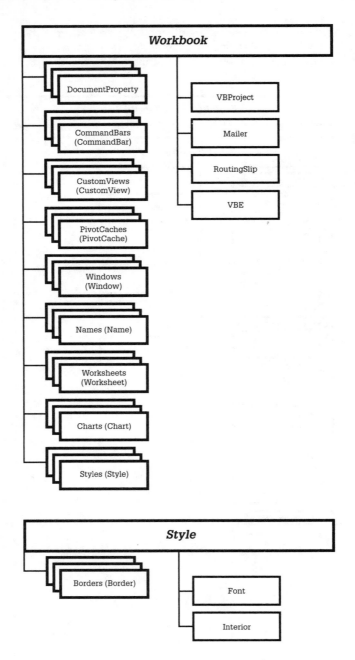

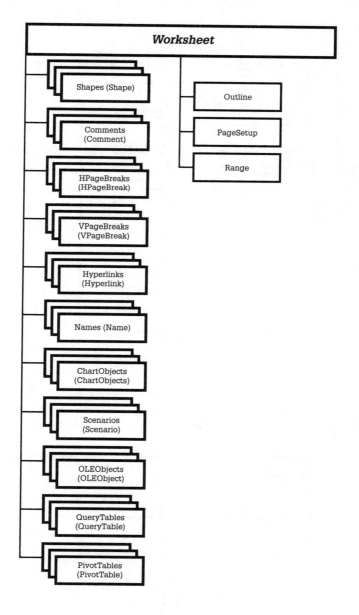

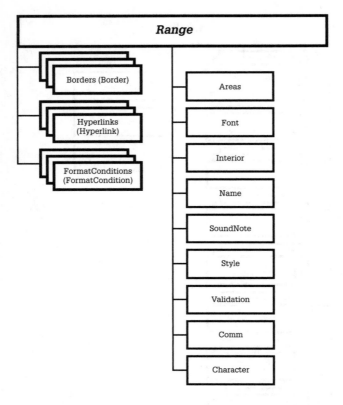

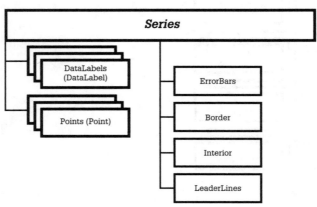

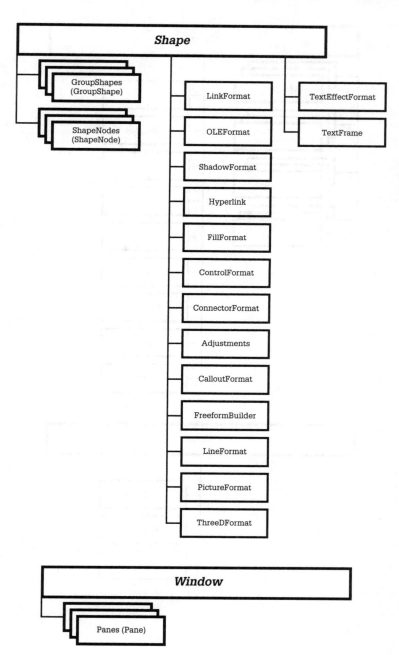

IV

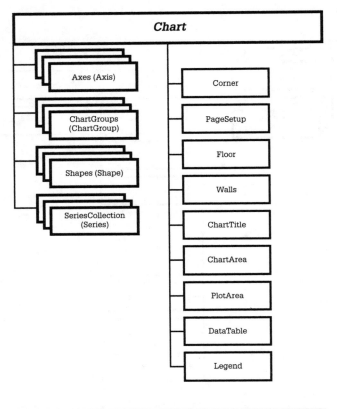

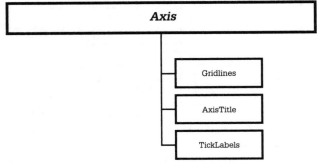

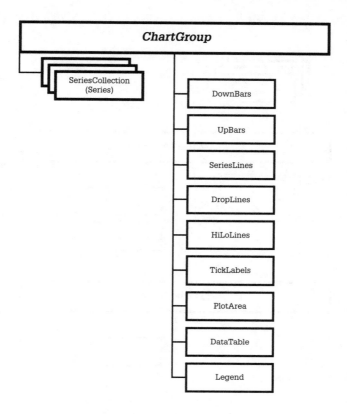

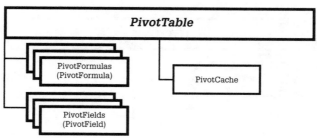

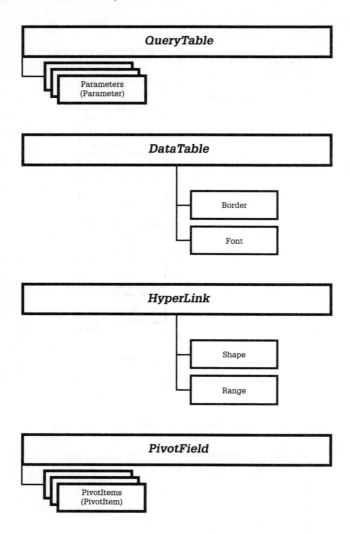

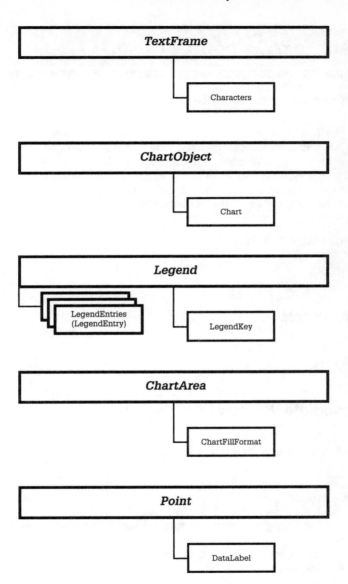

Activate Method

Activates the current specified object

Description

The Activate method can be used to activate a Workbook, Worksheet, Chart, Window, Pane, Range, or OLE object. It functions essentially like the Select method for Workbook, Worksheet, Chart, Range, and OLE objects. To activate a single cell (with the Range object), it is recommended you use this method over Select.

AVAILABLE IN VB SCRIPT

Syntax

```
[object.] Activate
```

Parameters

N/A

Returns

N/A

Immediate Window Sample

```
Sheets("Sheet2").Activate
```

SEE ALSO   ActiveSheet, ActiveWorkbook, Select

ActiveCell Property

Returns an object reference to the current active cell of the active sheet of the active workbook

Description

The ActiveCell property can be used to quickly set or determine information about the current cell. The value contained within a cell, the formula, and the formatting are all obtainable through this property.

AVAILABLE IN VB SCRIPT

Syntax
`[Application.] ActiveCell`

Parameters
N/A

Returns
Variant type

IV

Immediate Window Sample
`? ActiveCell.Value`

SEE ALSO   ActiveSheet, ActiveWorkbook

ActiveSheet Property

Returns an object reference to the current active sheet of the active workbook

Description
This property gives instant access to the currently selected sheet. It is especially useful when a button or macro is created to modify any sheet the user currently has selected. If no sheet is selected, access through the ActiveSheet object will generate an error.

AVAILABLE IN VB SCRIPT

Syntax
`[Application.] ActiveSheet`

Parameters
N/A

Returns
N/A

Immediate Window Sample
`? ActiveSheet.Name`

SEE ALSO ActiveCell, ActiveWorkbook

ActiveWorkbook Property

Returns an object reference to the current active workbook

Description
This property gives instant access to the current workbook.

AVAILABLE IN VB SCRIPT

Syntax
```
[Application.] ActiveWorkbook
```

Parameters
N/A

Returns
N/A

Immediate Window Sample
```
? ActiveWorkbook.Name
```

SEE ALSO ActiveSheet, ActiveCell

Add Method

Used to add worksheets, workbooks, and so on

Description
Use this method to add an object to the current object collection. The Immediate window example displays adding a Workbook object to the current Excel workspace and a worksheet to the current Workbook. The Add method creates instances of these objects in memory, but doesn't automatically save them. When creating an automated solution, make sure to save or close the documents you've added or modified, otherwise the program will stop execution and wait for a dialog asking for saving information that will be transparent to the user.

AVAILABLE IN VB SCRIPT

Syntax
```
Set myObject = object.Add
```

Parameters
N/A

Returns
Object type

Immediate Window Sample
```
Application.Workbooks.Add
Set a = ActiveWorkbook.Sheets.Add
```

SEE ALSO   ActiveSheet, ActiveWorkbook, DisplayAlerts

IV

AutoFilter Method

Toggles the AutoFilter setting to place the current sheet or selection in Filter mode

Description
Using the AutoFilter from a VBA program can be the quickest way to do multivariable queries. The AutoFilter may be used to select columns of information that match specific criteria. The rows that match this criteria can be copied to the Clipboard and pasted into another sheet. Use the Macro Recorder to understand how this works.

Note that one of the idiosyncrasies of the AutoFilter is the first row inclusion. If the first physical row in the sheet matches the criteria, it becomes the first logical row in the AutoFilter. However, if the first physical row does not match, the second logical row on the sheet begins the set that matches the criteria. If your program uses the AutoFilter, be sure to manually check the first row to determine where to begin copying.

AVAILABLE IN VB SCRIPT

Syntax
```
range.AutoFilter([[[[Field], Criteria1], Operator],
Criteria2])
```

Parameters

range   Range object to begin AutoFilter.

Field   Field # to conduct filter.

Criteria1, Criteria2   Values to match for the filter.

Operator   Optional. Can be set to determine how filtered results are displayed. Also allows Criteria1 and Criteria2 to have And or Or logical operators. Values may include xlAnd, xlBottom10Items, xlBottom10Percent, xlOr, xlTop10Items, or xlTop10Percent.

Returns

N/A

Immediate Window Sample

```
Selection.AutoFilter Field:=1, Criteria1:="1/1/97"
Selection.AutoFilter ' Toggles autofilter off
```

SEE ALSO   ActiveSheet, ActiveWorkbook

Calculation Property

Holds the mode of calculation for open spreadsheets

Description

This property determines when changes to a sheet will recalculate. Three modes are available: xlCalculationAutomatic, xlCalculationManual, or xlCalculationSemiautomatic. Setting the mode to manual can speed value insertion.

AVAILABLE IN VB SCRIPT

Syntax

```
[Application.] Calculation
```

Parameters

N/A

Returns

N/A

Immediate Window Sample

```
Application.Calculation = xlCalculationManual
```

SEE ALSO   Calculate

Cells Method

Allows row and column number access to information stored in a particular cell

Description
This method provides a quick way to access information stored in a cell by its ordinal index values. When creating a program to access individual cells, using this method is often much faster than selecting a range of cells and then retrieving or setting values. The Immediate window example will print the value stored in the cell in row 10, column 8.

AVAILABLE IN VB SCRIPT

Syntax
```
sheetname.Cells(row,col)
```

Parameters
row   Long value containing the row number to access.

col   Long value containing the column number to access.

Returns
Object type

Immediate Window Sample
```
? ActiveSheet.Cells(10,8).Value
```

SEE ALSO   Value

Close Method

Closes a window or a workbook

Description
The Close method is used to close a window (which requires no parameters) or to close a workbook (which can specify saving and routing information).

AVAILABLE IN VB SCRIPT

Syntax

```
[object.] Close([savechanges,filename,routeworkbook])
```

Parameters

savechanges   Boolean. Specifies whether changes should be saved to current filename or the one specified in the filename parameter. If parameter is omitted, user is prompted to save changes.

filename   Filename to save changes into.

routeworkbook   Boolean. Specifies whether changes should be routed. If parameter is omitted, user is prompted for routing instructions.

Returns

N/A

Immediate Window Sample

```
ActiveWorkbook.Close(True,"C:\Changes.xls")
ActiveWindow.Close
```

SEE ALSO   ActiveSheet, ActiveWorkbook

ColorIndex Property

Holds the color of a border, font, or interior for a cell or group of cells

Description

The ColorIndex specifies a color based on its position within the Excel palette. For a font, the constant xlColorIndexAutomatic can be used to have the font filled in the default color. An interior can use either the constant xlColorIndexAutomatic or xlColorIndexNone to specify the types of fill.

For the numbers of the other color indexes, see the Excel VBA help file under the ColorIndex entry. Several primary colors in the default Excel color palette include black = 1, white = 2, red = 3, light green = 4, blue = 5, yellow = 6, purple = 7, light blue = 8, dark red = 9, and green = 10.

AVAILABLE IN VB SCRIPT

Syntax
```
[object.] ColorIndex = indexnum
```

Parameters
indexnum   Palette index value.

Returns
N/A

Immediate Window Sample
```
Selection.Interior.ColorIndex = 6
```

SEE ALSO   Value, ActiveCell, Cells, Selection

IV

Copy Method

Copies the contents of the current object to the Clipboard or to a different part of the worksheet or workbook

Description
This method can be used to copy a selection or object to the Clipboard, to a range within a workbook, or to a worksheet within a workbook.

AVAILABLE IN VB SCRIPT

Syntax
```
object.Copy
object.Copy(destination)
object.Copy(before,after)
```

Parameters
destination   Range object to which selection will be copied.

before   Worksheet that the sheet will be copied before. If before is specified, after should remain blank.

after   Worksheet that the sheet will be copied after. If after is specified, the before parameter should remain blank.

Returns
N/A

Immediate Window Sample

```
Selection.Copy
Selection.Copy(Cells(5,5))
```

SEE ALSO   ActiveSheet, ActiveWorkbook, AutoFilter

Delete Method

Deletes an object or range

Description

Delete can be used to eliminate a specified object or information in a range of cells. When specifying a range to delete, the type of shift (up or left) to the surrounding cells may be passed.

AVAILABLE IN VB SCRIPT

Syntax

```
[object.] Delete
[object.] Delete(shift)
```

Parameters

shift   Direction to shift remaining cells after range is deleted. May be the constants xlShiftToLeft or xlShiftUp.

Returns

N/A

Immediate Window Sample

```
Cells(1,1).Delete
Cells(1,1).EntireRow.Delete
```

SEE ALSO   Cells, Select

DisplayAlerts Property

Property that determines if dialog alerts will be displayed during code execution

Description

The property can be set to False to eliminate a lengthy process from halting for user response. If set to False, the assigned default action for each dialog will be taken. This property does not automatically reset when your program's execution has completed, so be sure to reset it to the appropriate value.

AVAILABLE IN VB SCRIPT

Syntax

```
[Application.]DisplayAlerts = True|False
```

IV

Parameters

N/A

Returns

N/A

Immediate Window Sample

```
DisplayAlerts=False
```

SEE ALSO   ScreenUpdating, Close

FontStyle Property

Holds the style attributes of the Font object

Description

The style of a font can be set by using this property. Note that the Bold and Italic properties of the Font object affect and are affected by this property. Setting the Bold property to True will make the "Bold" string appear in the FontStyle string.

AVAILABLE IN VB SCRIPT

Syntax

```
font.FontStyle = styleString
```

Parameters

styleString   String of styles used separated by a space.

Returns
N/A

Immediate Window Sample
```
? Selection.Font.FontStyle
Selection.Font.FontStyle = "Bold"
Selection.Font.FontStyle = "Bold Italic"
```

SEE ALSO   Selection

Formula Property

This property allows you to set specifications or to retrieve the formula for a range

Description
Any standard formula can be entered into the Formula property. Setting the Formula property to a particular string is equivalent to typing the equal (=) sign before a formula in a cell.

AVAILABLE IN VB SCRIPT

Syntax
```
cell.Formula = formula
```

Parameters
formula   Valid standard format formula string.

Returns
N/A

Immediate Window Sample
```
ActiveCell.Formula = "=A1+10"
```

SEE ALSO   ActiveCell, FormulaR1C1

FormulaR1C1 Property

Allows you to set specifications or to retrieve the formula for a range in Row and Col format

Description

Row and column format allows formulas to be easily created that access cells relative to them. For example, the Immediate window sample demonstrates a formula that retrieves the value from one column previous to it and adds the number 10.

AVAILABLE IN VB SCRIPT

Syntax

```
range.FormulaR1C1 = formula
```

Parameters

formula   Valid formula string in row and column format.

Returns

N/A

Immediate Window Sample

```
ActiveCell.FormulaR1C1 = "=RC[-1]+10"
```

SEE ALSO   Formula, ActiveCell

HorizontalAlignment Property

Determines the horizontal alignment of an object (most often a range or style)

Description

This property can be used to set the justification of a range, style, chart title, label, and so on. The following constants determine the type of alignment: xlHAlignCenter, xlHAlignDistributed, xlHAlignJustify, xlHAlignLeft, or xlHAlignRight. For range and style objects, the following constants may also be used: xlHAlignCenterAcrossSelection, xlHAlignFill, or xlHAlignGeneral.

AVAILABLE IN VB SCRIPT

Syntax

```
object.HorizontalAlignment = alignVal
```

Parameters

alignVal   Alignment constant, including xlHAlignCenter, xlHAlignDistributed, xlHAlignJustify, xlHAlignLeft, xlHAlignRight, xlHAlignCenterAcrossSelection, xlHAlignFill, or xlHAlignGeneral.

Returns
Long type

Immediate Window Sample
```
Selection.HorizontalAlignment = xlHAlignLeft
Selection.HorizontalAlignment = xlHAlignRight
```

SEE ALSO   Selection, VerticalAlignment

Insert Method

Used to insert cells into a worksheet or characters before a string

Description
Using this method with a worksheet will shift the cells in the specified direction. On a string, the characters will be inserted preceding the current string.

AVAILABLE IN VB SCRIPT

Syntax
```
[object.] Insert(shift)
[object.] Insert(insertString)
```

Parameters
shift   Direction to shift the existing cells. Use the constants xlShiftToRight or xlShiftDown to specify the direction.

insertString   String of characters to insert preceding current string.

Returns
N/A

Immediate Window Sample
```
Selection.Insert(xlShiftDown)
ActiveCell.EntireRow.Insert
```

SEE ALSO   ActiveSheet, Selection, Delete

LineStyle Property

Sets the line style for a Border object

Description
Excel allows seven different line styles to be specified for individual parts of a border for a cell. Using this property, a subroutine could easily be created to automate the creation of a line form for reuse in Excel documents.

AVAILABLE IN VB SCRIPT

Syntax
```
border.LineStyle = borderType
```

Parameters
borderType   The type of border for the selected border sides. Use the following constants to specify the border style: xlContinuous, xlDash, xlDashDot, xlDashDotDot, xlDot, xlDouble, xlSlantDashDot, or xlLineStyleNone.

Returns
Variant type

Immediate Window Sample
```
Selection.Borders(xlEdgeBottom).LineStyle = xlDouble
```

SEE ALSO   ActiveSheet, Selection

Move Method

Moves a sheet within a workbook

Description
To move a sheet using this method, you must specify the sheet either before or after which the selected sheet is to be placed. If the before parameter is specified, the after parameter should be left empty and vice versa.

AVAILABLE IN VB SCRIPT

Syntax
```
sheet.Move(before,after)
```

Parameters
before   Object reference to a sheet that the specified sheet will be placed before.

after   Object reference to a sheet that the specified sheet will be placed after.

Returns
N/A

Immediate Window Sample
```
ActiveSheet.Move ,Sheets("Sheet3")
```

SEE ALSO   ActiveSheet, Close

Name Property

Holds the name of the object that can be used to programmatically reference it

Description
The Name property holds the string of the name used to reference an object. Instead of using an index with a collection, the name can be used to specify the object.

AVAILABLE IN VB SCRIPT

Syntax
```
object.Name = string
```

Parameters
string   Any string conforming to the standard naming conventions.

Returns
N/A

Immediate Window Sample
```
? ActiveWorkbook.Name
Sheets("Sheet1").Name = "MySheet"
ActiveSheet.Name = "MySheet"
```

SEE ALSO   Value, ActiveSheet

NumberFormat Property

Determines the display format for labels, cells, and styles

Description
This property will specify the appearance of the value in the label or cell. Formatting characters (# / , 0) and value characters (m, d, y, hh, mm, ss) are the same as those used in the format cell dialog box.

AVAILABLE IN VB SCRIPT

Syntax
```
object.NumberFormat = stringVal
```

Parameters
stringVal   Formatting string containing codes of format to display value.

Returns
N/A

Immediate Window Sample
```
ActiveCell.Value = 12
ActiveCell.NumberFormat = "General"
ActiveCell.NumberFormat = "hh:mm:ss m/d/yy"
ActiveCell.NumberFormat = _
"$###,##0.00_);[Blue]($###,##0.00)"
```

SEE ALSO   Range, ActiveCell

Range Object

Used to access one or more cells—most common object used in Excel

Description
Most programming in Excel uses the Range object to access cell values, appearance, and operation. Ranges may be specified by using cell notation or the Cells method, or by denoting them as named values.

AVAILABLE IN VB SCRIPT

Syntax
N/A

Parameters
N/A

Returns
N/A

Immediate Window Sample
```
Range("A1").Value = 10
Range("A2") = 10
Range("A3") = "Hello"
Range("A1:A8").Formula = "=Rand()"
```

SEE ALSO   DisplayAlerts, ActiveCell, Cells

ScreenUpdating Property

Toggles whether updates are displayed on the screen

Description
Displaying updates takes a great deal of processor time. If the updates are switched off for the duration of a macro execution, the execution time may be greatly diminished. Make sure that you turn updates back on when processing is complete, because Excel does not automatically return to Normal mode.

AVAILABLE IN VB SCRIPT

Syntax
```
Application.ScreenUpdating = True|False
```

Parameters
N/A

Returns
N/A

Immediate Window Sample
```
Application.ScreenUpdating = False
```

SEE ALSO   DisplayAlerts

Select Method

Selects an object such as a cell, workbook, chart, or worksheet

Description
Use the Select method to select an object, particularly a range of cells. Use the Activate method instead for a single cell. The Select method can also be used with a replace parameter to indicate the current selection will be replaced by the specified object.

AVAILABLE IN VB SCRIPT

Syntax
```
object.Select([replace])
```

Parameters
replace   Optional. Boolean. If True, current selection is replaced by specified object.

Returns
N/A

Immediate Window Sample
```
Sheets("Sheet3").Select
Range("A1:A8").Select
```

SEE ALSO   Activate, ActiveSheet, ActiveWorkbook

Value Property

Holds a value for a particular object

Description
The Value property is used extensively within the Excel object model, particularly for setting and retrieving the values of cells.

AVAILABLE IN VB SCRIPT

Syntax
`object.Value = value`

Parameters
value Dependent on the object.

Returns
N/A

Immediate Window Sample
`? ActiveCell.Value`

SEE ALSO Range, Select, Name

VerticalAlignment Property

Determines the horizontal alignment of an object (most often a range or style)

Description
This property can be used to set the justification of a range, style, chart title, label, and so on. The following constants determine the type of alignment: xlVAlignBottom, xlVAlignCenter, xlVAlignDistributed, xlVAlignJustify, or xlVAlignTop.

AVAILABLE IN VB SCRIPT

Syntax
```
object.VerticalAlignment = alignVal
```

Parameters
alignVal Alignment constant, including xlVAlignBottom, xlVAlignCenter, xlVAlignDistributed, xlVAlignJustify, or xlVAlignTop.

Returns
Long type

Immediate Window Sample
```
Selection.VerticalAlignment = xlVAlignBottom
Selection.VerticalAlignment = xlVAlignCenter
```

SEE ALSO Selection, HorizontalAlignment

Weight Property

Determines the weight or thickness of the border of a range

Description
Setting the Weight property for a Border or LineFormat object will determine how the cell or range of cells appears.

AVAILABLE IN VB SCRIPT

Syntax
```
border.Weight = lineWeight
```

Parameters
lineWeight Weight of the border should be one of these constants: xlHairline, xlThin, xlMedium, or xlThick.

Returns
Long type

Immediate Window Sample
```
Selection.Borders.Weight = xlMedium
```

SEE ALSO Pattern, Range, Selection

Word

Microsoft Word is the application that has most recently added object capabilities. Therefore, the Word object model is often not as intuitive to understand as the other applications. Some of the methods of achieving solutions may seem odd. Try frequently recording test macros of the types of tasks you will need to automate. By examining the code the recorder generates, you can better understand how Word needs to accomplish things.

Also, if objects such as paragraphs are accessed, macro execution slows dramatically when advancing through a lengthy document. What may appear to execute well on the first ten paragraphs may take substantially longer when it reaches paragraph 200. Therefore, make sure you test the macro in real-world conditions in case optimization is required.

Note that when recording with the Macro Recorder in Word, you cannot select text with the mouse. Only keyboard selections are available. Using a combination of the arrow and shift keys should allow almost any desired operation. Presumably the next version of Word will resolve this problem.

Word files are stored in the Documents collection as individual objects. The text itself can be accessed through the Paragraphs collection, but it is most often easier to make necessary changes to the document with selection functions. Some of the Immediate window examples demonstrate this type of functionality.

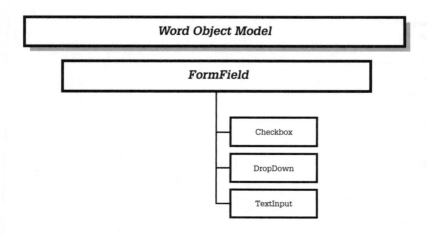

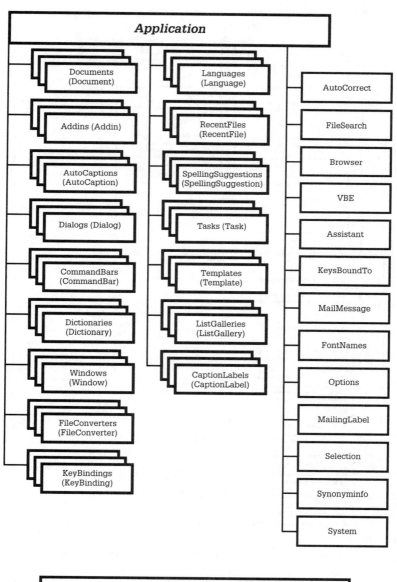

IV

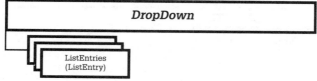

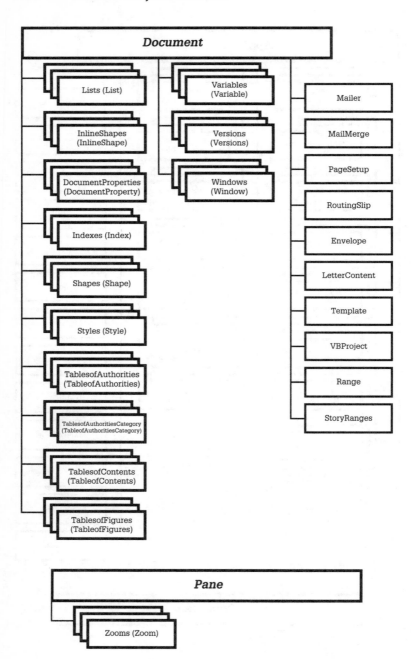

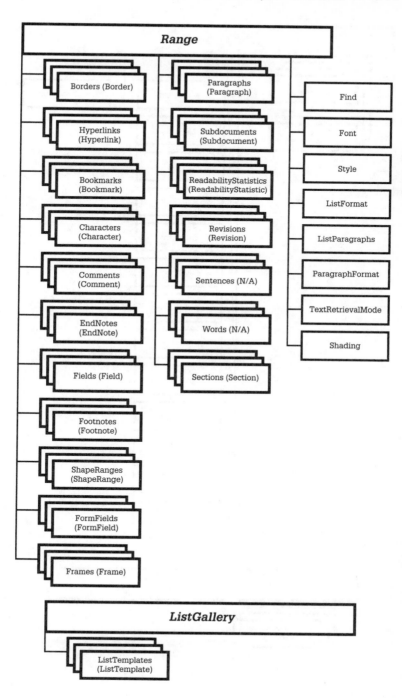

IV

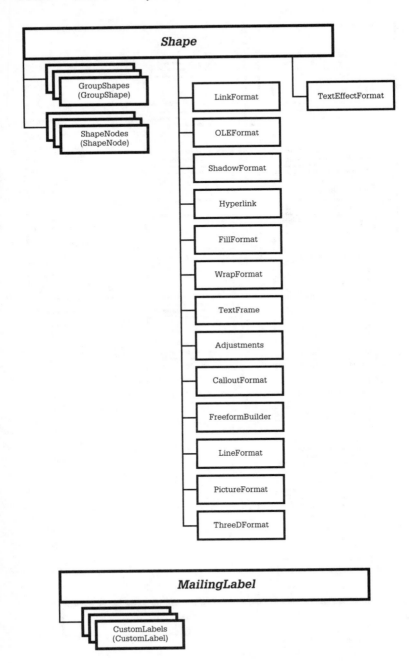

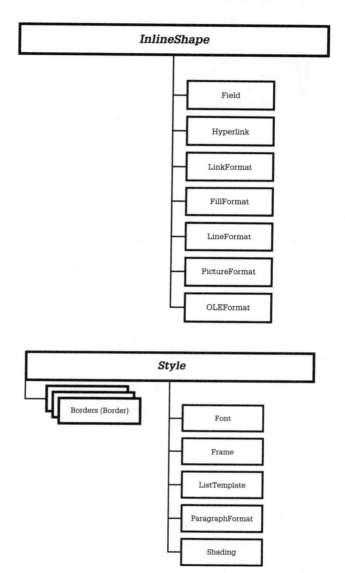

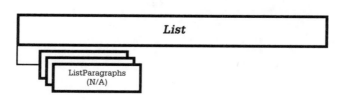

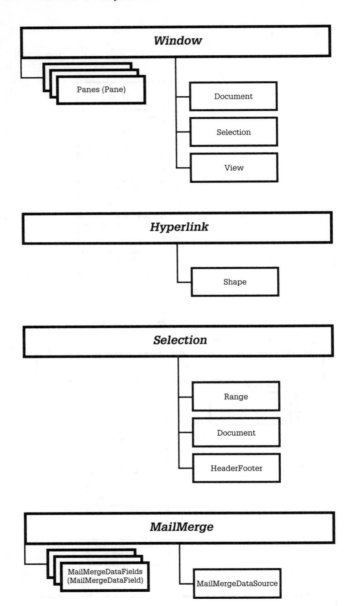

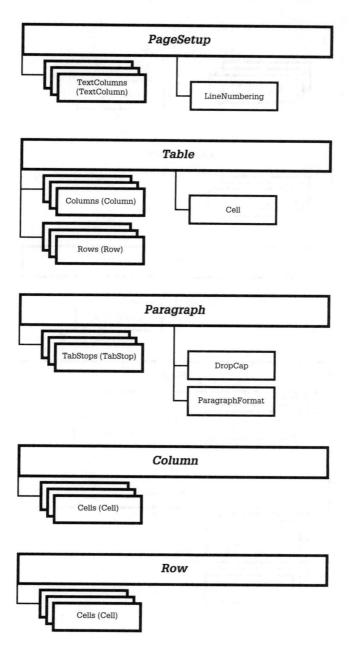

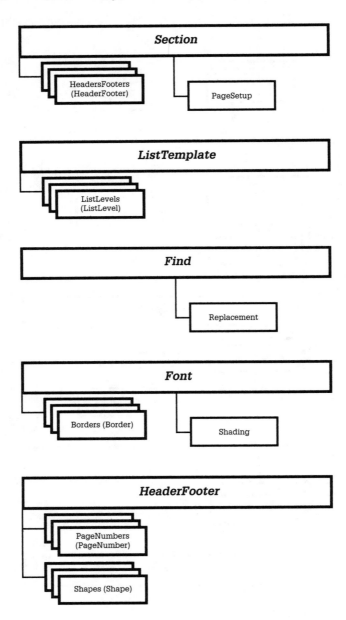

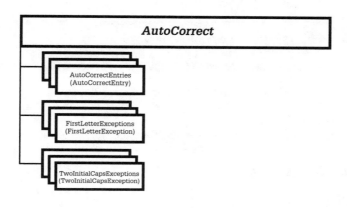

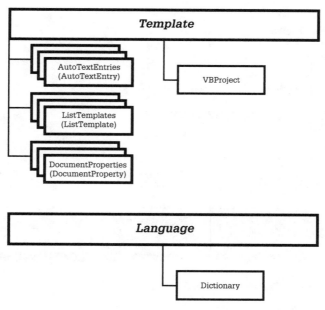

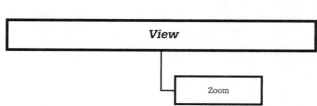

IV

ActiveDocument Property

Holds the object reference to the current active document

Description
This property can be used to easily reference the currently selected document in Word. A reference to a Document object is returned.

AVAILABLE IN VB SCRIPT

Syntax
```
[Application.] ActiveDocument
```

Parameters
N/A

Returns
Document object

Immediate Window Sample
```
? ActiveDocument.Name
Documents(1).Activate
? ActiveDocument.Name
```

SEE ALSO   Add

Add Method

Used to add an object to a particular collection

Description
The Add method can be used, as shown in the Immediate window example, to add a new document to the current Word environment.

AVAILABLE IN VB SCRIPT

Syntax
```
object.Add
```

Parameters
N/A

Returns
N/A

Immediate Window Sample
`Documents.Add`

User Tip
The parameters accepted by the Add method vary depending on the object used. For example, when adding a new document, you can specify a template that the new document should be created from. Check the Object Browser for the actual parameters that may be used.

SEE ALSO   Open, RecentFile

IV

Alignment Property

Holds the alignment of a paragraph

Description
The type of alignment specified within the Alignment property is held in a number of constants within the Word system. In the Immediate window example, the currently selected paragraph is set to a center alignment.

AVAILABLE IN VB SCRIPT

Syntax
`object.Alignment = align`

Parameters
align   A valid alignments constant, such as wdAlignParagraphCenter, wdAlignParagraphLeft, wdAlignParagraphRight, and so on.

Returns
N/A

Immediate Window Sample

```
Selection.ParagraphFormat.Alignment = _
wdAlignParagraphCenter
```

SEE ALSO   Selection

ApplyBulletDefault Method

Toggles the list formatting for a specified paragraph or range

Description

This method, when executed on a paragraph that is specified as a list, turns list formatting off. To a normal paragraph, list formatting is applied. This method must be used on a ListFormat object of a Range object.

AVAILABLE IN VB SCRIPT

Syntax

```
listformat.ApplyBulletDefault
```

Parameters

N/A

Returns

N/A

Immediate Window Sample

```
Selection.Range.ListFormat.ApplyBulletDefault
ActiveDocument.Paragraphs(2).Range.ListFormat. _
ApplyBulletDefault
```

SEE ALSO   ActiveDocument, Range

Assistant Property

Accesses the animated Assistant to allow custom help for an application

Description

The animated Assistant seems to inspire both love and hate from Office users, but programmers will find controlling the Assistant fairly easy. Animation may be set using constants such as msoAnimationSearching, msoAnimationAppear, msoAnimationGestureDown, msoAnimationIdle, msoAnimationGreeting, or msoAnimationBeginSpeaking.

AVAILABLE IN VB SCRIPT

Syntax

```
[Application.] Assistant
```

Parameters

N/A

Returns

N/A

Immediate Window Sample

```
Assistant.Visible = True
Assistant.Animation = msoAnimationSearching
Assistant.Move 100, 100
```

SEE ALSO   N/A

Compare Method

Sets up a comparison and shows comparison marks on specified document

Description

The Microsoft Word feature that allows comparison of two documents can be activated by use of this method. The filename of the document to be compared and comparison marks are automatically displayed.

AVAILABLE IN VB SCRIPT

Syntax

```
[Application.] Compare fileName
```

Parameters

fileName   Name of the file to compare to specified document.

Returns

N/A

Immediate Window Sample

```
ActiveDocument.Compare "C:\draft1.doc"
```

SEE ALSO   ActiveDocument

ComputeStatistics Method

Recalculates statistics for specified range or document

Description

This method will calculate the statistics either for the entire document or a specified range. Parameters allow the inclusion/exclusion of footnotes and endnotes and the specification of exactly the type of statistic to return.

AVAILABLE IN VB SCRIPT

Syntax

```
statValue = [object.] ComputeStatistics(statistic [,
includefootnotesandendnotes])
```

Parameters

statistic   Determines the type of statistic to be returned. Use one of these constants: wdStatisticCharacters, wdStatisticCharactersWithSpaces, wdStatisticLines, wdStatisticPages, wdStatisticParagraphs, or wdStatisticWords.

includefootnotesandendnotes   Determines whether footnotes and endnotes are included. Default is set to False.

statValue   Calculated return of type specified with statistic parameter.

Returns

Long type

Immediate Window Sample

```
? ActiveDocument.ComputeStatistics(wdStatisticPages)
```

SEE ALSO   ActiveDocument

FirstLineIndent Property

Determines the indent of the first line of the paragraph

Description

Specified in points, this property holds the first line indent value. This property may be set for individual paragraphs, styles, or a range of paragraphs.

AVAILABLE IN VB SCRIPT

Syntax

```
paragraph FirstLineIndent = indentVal
```

Parameters

indentVal   In points, the value to indent on the first line of the paragraph.

Returns

Variant type

Immediate Window Sample

```
ActiveDocument.Paragraphs(1).FirstLineIndent = 72
ActiveDocument.Paragraphs(1).FirstLineIndent= _
InchesToPoints(1)
```

SEE ALSO   ActiveDocument, Paragraphs

Font Object

Holds all of the font formatting information for a piece of text

Description

The Font object can be set to any available font, size, and style settings that are normally available in Word. The Immediate window example changes the font of the current selection in a variety of ways.

AVAILABLE IN VB SCRIPT

Syntax
```
range.Font
```

Parameters
N/A

Returns
N/A

Immediate Window Sample
```
Selection.Font.Name = "Times New Roman"
Selection.Font.Size = 10
Selection.Font.Bold = True
Selection.Font.Italic = True
```

SEE ALSO   Selection

Height Property

Holds the height of the specified object

Description
The height of most objects may be adjusted with the Height property, including shapes, rows, cols, tasks, windows, frames, custom labels, inline shapes, and so on.

AVAILABLE IN VB SCRIPT

Syntax
```
object.Height = height
```

Parameters
height   Height value within the limits of the object. Value is stored as a Single type.

Returns
N/A

Immediate Window Sample
```
ActiveWindow.WindowState = wdWindowStateNormal
ActiveWindow.Height = ActiveWindow.Height / 2
```

User Tip
Using the Width and Height properties to configure the windows allows you to create a custom macro to adjust the window settings to the sizes you most commonly use.

SEE ALSO   Width

InsertBefore Method

Inserts text before the indicated object

Description
The InsertBefore method may be used with either a Range or Selection to insert text into the document. The Immediate example demonstrates inserting the word "Hello" before the first word of the first paragraph of the document.

AVAILABLE IN VB SCRIPT

Syntax
```
object.InsertBefore(string)
```

Parameters
string   Any valid Unicode string.

Returns
N/A

Immediate Window Sample
```
ActiveDocument.Range.Paragraphs(1).Range.Words(1). _
InsertBefore "Hello"
```

SEE ALSO   Selection

LeftIndent Property

Determines the left indent of the specified paragraph, styles, or range of paragraphs

Description
This property will specify the left indent of a particular paragraph, range, or style. The indent is specified in points (1 inch = 72 points).

AVAILABLE IN VB SCRIPT

Syntax
`paragraph.LeftIndent = leftValue`

Parameters
leftValue   Amount in points to left-indent the paragraph.

Returns
Single type

Immediate Window Sample
`ActiveDocument.Paragraphs(1).LeftIndent = 72`

SEE ALSO   FirstIndent, RightIndent

LineSpacing Property

Determines the line spacing of the specified paragraph, styles, or range of paragraphs

Description
This property will specify the line spacing of a particular paragraph, range, or style. The spacing is specified in points (1 inch = 72 points).

AVAILABLE IN VB SCRIPT

Syntax
`paragraph.LineSpacing = lineValue`

Parameters

lineValue   Amount in points of the line space for the paragraph.

Returns

Single type

Immediate Window Sample

```
Selection.Paragraphs.LineSpacing = 16
Selection.Paragraphs.LineSpacing = LinesToPoints(2)
```

SEE ALSO   Paragraphs

ListParagraphs Property

Holds the object reference to all of the numbered paragraphs within a range or document

Description

All of the List Paragraphs contained within a document can be accessed individually through this property. A For...Each loop can be used to sequentially progress through each list paragraph.

AVAILABLE IN VB SCRIPT

Syntax

```
document.ListParagraphs
```

Parameters

N/A

Returns

N/A

Immediate Window Sample

```
Documents(1).ListParagraphs(1).Shading _
.BackgroundPatternColorIndex = wdBlue
```

SEE ALSO   ActiveDocument, Paragraphs

MoveDown Method

Moves the selection cursor down one unit

Description
The Move methods may be used with either a Range or Selection, and units and type of move may be defined. Move in units of lines, paragraphs, windows, or screens.

AVAILABLE IN VB SCRIPT

Syntax
```
object.MoveDown([,units,count [,extend]])
```

Parameters
units   Move down in the units specified by the constant wdLine, wdParagraph, wdWindow, or wdScreen.

count   Number of units to move selection.

extend   Determines whether selection is moved or extended. Use the constant wdMove or wdExtend.

Returns
N/A

Immediate Window Sample
```
Selection.MoveDown
Selection.MoveDown wdParagraph,1
Selection.MoveDown wdParagraph,1,wdExtend
```

SEE ALSO   MoveUp, MoveLeft, MoveRight

MoveLeft Method

Moves the selection cursor left one unit

Description
The Move methods may be used with either a Range or Selection, and units and type of move may be defined. Move in units of lines, paragraphs, windows, or screens.

AVAILABLE IN VB SCRIPT

Syntax
```
object.MoveLeft([,units,count [,extend]])
```

Parameters
units   Move left in the units specified by the constant wdCell, wdCharacter, wdWord, or wdSentence.

count   Number of units to move selection.

extend   Determines whether selection is moved or extended. Use the constant wdMove or wdExtend.

Returns
N/A

Immediate Window Sample
```
Selection.MoveLeft
Selection.MoveLeft wdCharacter,1
Selection.MoveLeft wdCharacter,1,wdExtend
```

SEE ALSO   MoveDown, MoveUp, MoveRight

MoveRight Method

Moves the selection cursor right one unit

Description
The Move methods may be used with either a Range or Selection, and units and type of move may be defined. Move in units of lines, paragraphs, windows, or screens.

AVAILABLE IN VB SCRIPT

Syntax
```
object.MoveRight([,unit,count [,extend]])
```

Parameters

units   Move right in the units specified by the constant wdCell, wdCharacter, wdWord, or wdSentence.

count   Number of units to move selection.

extend   Determines whether selection is moved or extended. Use the constant wdMove or wdExtend.

Returns

N/A

Immediate Window Sample

```
Selection.MoveRight
Selection.MoveRight wdCharacter,1
Selection.MoveRight wdCharacter,1,wdExtend
```

SEE ALSO   MoveDown, MoveUp, MoveLeft

MoveUp Method

Moves the current selection up one unit

Description

The Move methods may be used with either a Range or Selection, and units and type of move may be defined. Move in units of lines, paragraphs, windows, or screens.

AVAILABLE IN VB SCRIPT

Syntax

```
object.MoveUp([,units,count [,extend]])
```

Parameters

units   Move up in the units specified by the constant wdLine, wdParagraph, wdWindow, or wdScreen.

count   Number of units to move selection.

extend   Determines whether selection is moved or extended. Use the constant wdMove or wdExtend.

Returns

N/A

Immediate Window Sample

```
Selection.MoveUp
Selection.MoveUp wdParagraph,1
Selection.MoveUp wdParagraph,1,wdExtend
```

SEE ALSO   MoveDown, MoveLeft, MoveRight

Name Property

Holds the name of the object that can be used to programmatically reference it

Description

The Name property holds the string of the name used to reference an object. Instead of using an index with a collection, the name can be used to specify the object.

AVAILABLE IN VB SCRIPT

Syntax

```
object.Name = string
```

Parameters

string   Any string conforming to the standard naming conventions.

Returns

N/A

Immediate Window Sample

```
? ActiveDocument.Name
```

User Tip

The Name property of a document is read-only. To change the name, you must use the SaveAs method.

SEE ALSO   ActiveDocument

Open Method

Opens the specified object

Description

This method can be used to open files through a number of objects (such as Documents or RecentFiles).

AVAILABLE IN VB SCRIPT

Syntax

`object.Open(filename$)`

Parameters

filename$ May specify the path and filename of any file Word can open.

Returns

Object type

Immediate Window Sample

`Documents.Open "c:\mydoc.doc"`

SEE ALSO   Add

Paragraphs Collection

Holds all of the paragraphs for a particular document

Description

All of the actual text, styles, and other information for each paragraph of a document are held by the individual objects stored in the Paragraphs collection. Note that accessing long documents by paragraph can be a slow process.

AVAILABLE IN VB SCRIPT

Syntax

`object.Paragraphs(index)`

Parameters

index   Paragraph number to be accessed.

Returns

N/A

Immediate Window Sample

```
? ActiveDocument.Range.Paragraphs.Count
ActiveDocument.Range.Paragraphs(1).Range.Words(1) _
= "Hello"
```

SEE ALSO   Add

IV

RightIndent Property

Determines the right indent of the specified paragraph, styles, or range of paragraphs

Description

This property will specify the right indent of a particular paragraph, range, or style. The indent is specified in points (1 inch = 72 points).

AVAILABLE IN VB SCRIPT

Syntax

```
paragraph.RightIndent = rightValue
```

Parameters

rightValue   Amount in points to right-indent the paragraph.

Returns

Single type

Immediate Window Sample

```
Selection.Paragraphs.RightIndent = 72
```

SEE ALSO   LeftIndent

Selection Object

Holds the range of the current selection

Description
The Selection object provides access to the current user selection. Manipulating the Selection object also allows a document to be quickly and easily modified.

AVAILABLE IN VB SCRIPT

Syntax
```
[Application].Selection
```

Parameters
N/A

Returns
N/A

Immediate Window Sample
```
Selection.TypeText "Replace"
```

SEE ALSO   InsertBefore

Shading Property

Holds the reference to the Shading object used by other objects, such as paragraphs

Description
Setting properties of the Shading object can render the background, foreground, and shading texture of objects.

AVAILABLE IN VB SCRIPT

Syntax
```
object.Shading
```

Parameters

N/A

Returns

N/A

Immediate Window Sample

```
Selection.Paragraphs.Shading.Texture =
wdTexture12Pt5Percent
Selection.Paragraphs.Shading. _
BackgroundPatternColorIndex = wdRed
```

SEE ALSO   Selection

IV

SpaceAfter Property

Determines the amount of space after a specified paragraph, styles, or range of paragraphs

Description

This property will specify the amount of space after a particular paragraph, range, or style. The spacing is specified in points (1 inch = 72 points).

AVAILABLE IN VB SCRIPT

Syntax

```
paragraph.SpaceAfter = afterValue
```

Parameters

afterValue   Amount in points of space after the paragraph.

Returns

Single type

Immediate Window Sample

```
Selection.Paragraphs.SpaceAfter = 12
```

SEE ALSO   LineSpacing, SpaceBefore

SpaceBefore Property

Determines the amount of space before a specified paragraph, styles, or range of paragraphs

Description
This property will specify the amount of space before a particular paragraph, range, or style. The spacing is specified in points (1 inch = 72 points).

AVAILABLE IN VB SCRIPT

Syntax
```
paragraph.SpaceBefore = beforeValue
```

Parameters
beforeValue   Amount in points of space before the paragraph.

Returns
Single type

Immediate Window Sample
```
Selection.Paragraphs.SpaceBefore = 12
```

SEE ALSO   LineSpacing, SpaceAfter

TypeBackspace Method

Backspaces at the current selection

Description
The method will provide the same functionality (including across multiple selected characters) as the user pressing the BACKSPACE key.

AVAILABLE IN VB SCRIPT

Syntax
```
object.TypeBackspace
```

Parameters

N/A

Returns

N/A

Immediate Window Sample

`Selection.TypeBackspace`

SEE ALSO   Selection, Paragraphs

TypeText Method

Enters text at the current selection

Description

Text is entered as if from the keyboard. This means that any currently selected text will be automatically deleted.

AVAILABLE IN VB SCRIPT

Syntax

`object.TypeText string`

Parameters

string   Any valid character string.

Returns

N/A

Immediate Window Sample

`Selection.TypeText "Hello World"`

SEE ALSO   Selection, TypeBackspace, Paragraphs

Width Property

Holds the width of the specified object

Description

The width of most objects may be adjusted with the Width property, including shapes, rows, cols, tasks, windows, frames, custom labels, inline shapes, and so on.

AVAILABLE IN VB SCRIPT

Syntax

```
object.Width = width
```

Parameters

width Width value within the limits of the object. Value is stored as a Single type.

Returns

N/A

Immediate Window Sample

```
ActiveWindow.WindowState = wdWindowStateNormal
ActiveWindow.Width = ActiveWindow.Width / 2
```

SEE ALSO Height

PowerPoint

The PowerPoint object model is very straightforward. The primary objects are the Presentation objects in the Presentations collection. Individual Slide objects are stored within the Slides collection. The Shape objects, while they appear standard across the Office applications, have slight variations in the context of each application. The PowerPoint implementation of the Shape object varies slightly, so examine code that is being moved from another VBA application carefully.

IV

Many of the Immediate window examples assume that there is an open presentation that contains at least a single slide. The slide is duplicated in some commands, new objects are inserted, and so on. When running the examples, simply keep an open disposable presentation for correct execution.

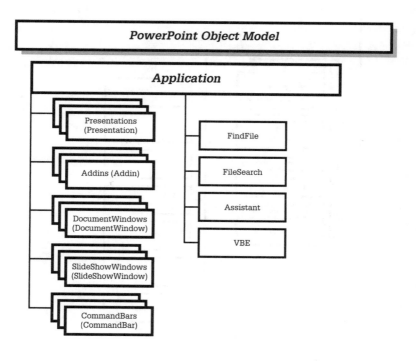

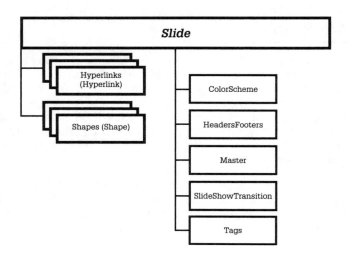

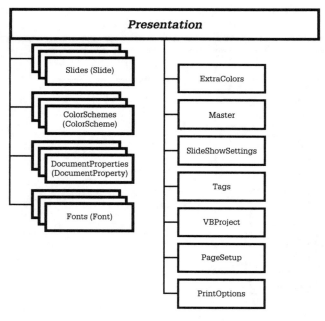

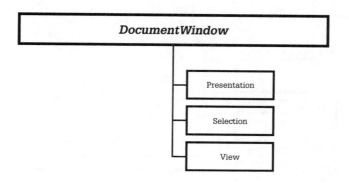

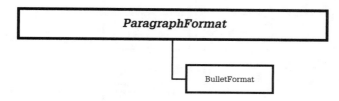

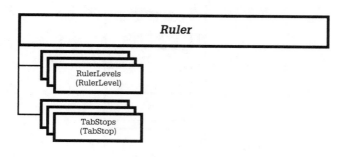

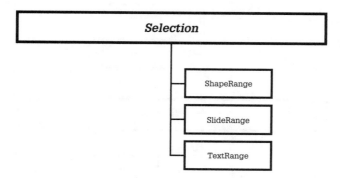

IV

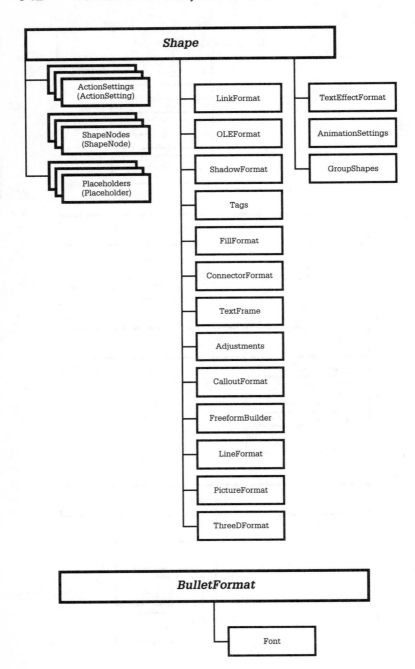

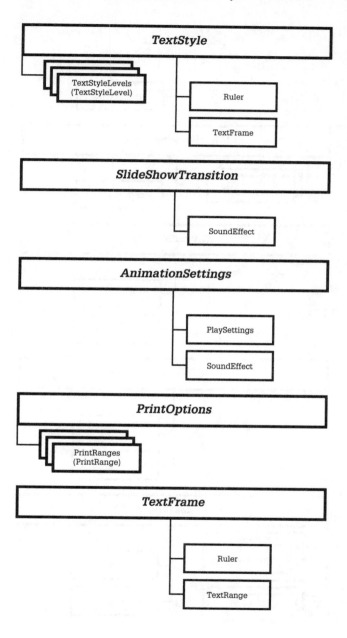

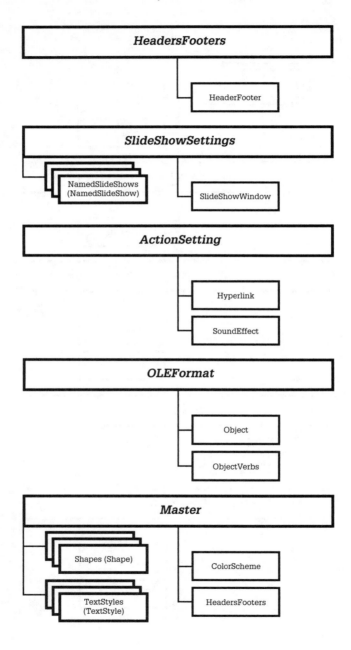

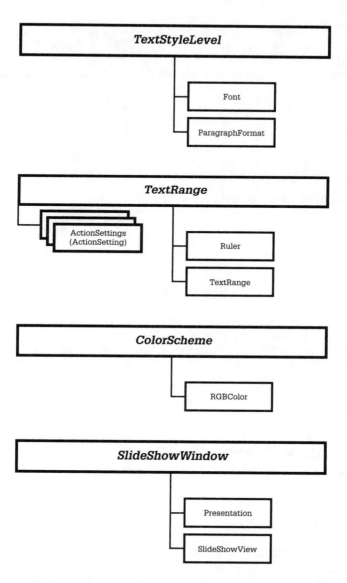

IV

Action Property

Determines the action that will be taken when an event occurs

Description

The ActionSetting object holds the complete specifications of an event, including the Action property to specify what will occur when the event happens.

AVAILABLE IN VB SCRIPT

Syntax

```
actionSetting.Action = actionType
```

Parameters

actionType   Specifies action that should take place. Use one of the following constants to specify the action: ppActionEndShow, ppActionFirstSlide, ppActionHyperlink, ppActionLastSlide, ppActionLastSlideViewed, ppActionMixed, ppActionNamedSlideShow, ppActionNextSlide, ppActionNone, ppActionOLEVerb, ppActionPreviousSlide, ppActionRunMacro, or ppActionRunProgram.

Returns

Long type

Immediate Window Sample

```
ActivePresentation.Slides(1).Shapes(1) _
.ActionSettings(ppMouseOver).Action = _
ppActionNextSlide
```

SEE ALSO   ActionVerb

ActionVerb Property

Determines the verb of the action to take place when an action event occurs

Description
The ActionVerb property works in conjunction with the Action property by specifying the verb for the action. Possible values include those shown in the Object action combo box on the Play Settings tab in the Custom Animation dialog box.

AVAILABLE IN VB SCRIPT

Syntax
```
actionSetting.ActionVerb = actionVerbType
```

Parameters
actionVerbType   String containing a verb setting such as "Play" or "Edit".

Returns
String type

Immediate Window Sample
```
ActivePresentation.Slides(1).Shapes(1) _
.ActionSettings(ppMouseOver).ActionVerb = "Play"
```

SEE ALSO   Action

AddLabel Method

Adds a Label object to the current Shapes collection

Description
This method adds a new Label shape to the Shapes collection. Other methods such as AddCallout, AddConnector, and so on, can create other shapes. The Immediate window example adds a shape and then sets the text that is displayed.

AVAILABLE IN VB SCRIPT

Syntax
```
object.AddLabel(orient,x,y,width,height)
```

Parameters
orient   Orientation available as a set of constants within PowerPoint

x, y Single values in points for the top and left corners of the label

width, height Single values in points for the width and height of the label

Returns
Object type

Immediate Window Sample
```
set b = ActivePresentation.Slides(1).Shapes.AddLabel( _
msoTextOrientationHorizontal,50,100,100,100) _
b.textframe.textrange.text = "Yeah"
```

SEE ALSO Duplicate

AdvanceOnTime Property

Determines whether the slide automatically advances after AdvanceTime has been exceeded

Description
This property determines whether the slide will automatically advance to the next slide using the time stored in the AdvanceTime property.

AVAILABLE IN VB SCRIPT

Syntax
```
slide.AdvanceOnTime = onTimeFlag
```

Parameters
onTimeFlag Boolean. Indicates whether slide should advance automatically.

Returns
Long type

Immediate Window Sample
```
ActivePresentation.Slides(1).SlideShowTransition _
.AdvanceTime = 10 ' seconds
```

```
ActivePresentation.Slides(1).SlideShowTransition _
.AdvanceOnTime = true
```

SEE ALSO   AdvanceTime

AdvanceTime Property

Number of seconds until automatic advance to the next slide

IV

Description
After the AdvanceOnTime property has been set to True, this property determines the amount of time to pause before moving to the next slide.

AVAILABLE IN VB SCRIPT

Syntax
```
slide.AdvanceTime = onTimeValue
```

Parameters
onTimeValue   Amount in seconds to wait before continuing to the next slide

Returns
Single type

Immediate Window Sample
```
ActivePresentation.Slides(1).SlideShowTransition _
.AdvanceTime = 10 ' seconds
ActivePresentation.Slides(1).SlideShowTransition _
.AdvanceOnTime = true
```

SEE ALSO   AdvanceOnTime

AfterEffect Property

Determines the appearance of a particular shape after it's been built

Description

Shapes can be added to a slide with animation settings. After they have been "built," this property determines their appearance. This property may be used to dim items after they are originally presented.

AVAILABLE IN VB SCRIPT

Syntax

```
animationsettings.AfterEffect = effectType
```

Parameters

effectType   The type of after effect specified by one of the following constants: ppAfterEffectDim, ppAfterEffectHide, ppAfterEffectHideOnClick, ppAfterEffectMixed, or ppAfterEffectNothing.

Returns

Long type

Immediate Window Sample

```
ActivePresentation.Slides(1).Shapes.Title. _
AnimationSettings_
.AfterEffect = ppAfterEffectHide
```

AnimateAction Property

Determines whether color of shape is inverted when mouse event occurs

Description

The ActionSettings object determines what reaction occurs after an event. The AnimateAction property determines if the shape will be inverted when this action occurs. Using the function will make the shape invert when the action takes place, as if it was a command button. You can use this capability to add graphic buttons to your presentation.

AVAILABLE IN VB SCRIPT

Syntax
```
actionsettings.AnimateAction = actionFlag
```

Parameters
actionFlag   Boolean. Set to True if shape is inverted after action.

Returns
Long type

Immediate Window Sample
```
ActivePresentation.Slides(1).Shapes(1) _
.ActionSettings(ppMouseOver).AnimateAction = True
```

SEE ALSO   Action, ActionVerb

IV

BeginConnect Method

Sets the beginning of the connector between two shapes

Description
PowerPoint allows a connector to be created between two shapes that automatically adjusts when the size or position of the shapes changes. This method sets the beginning of the connector to a shape. The Immediate window example requires two shapes to exist on slide 1.

AVAILABLE IN VB SCRIPT

Syntax
```
object.BeginConnect(connectedShape, connectionSite)
```

Parameters
connectedShape   Object reference to shape to begin connection.

connectionSite   Site on shape to begin connection.

Returns
Variant type

Immediate Window Sample

```
Set firstShape = ActivePresentation. _
Slides(1).Shapes(1)
Set secondShape = ActivePresentation. _
Slides(1).Shapes(2)
Set connect = ActivePresentation.Slides(1).Shapes _
.AddConnector(msoConnectorCurve, 0, 0, 100, 100)_
connect.connectorformat.BeginConnect firstShape, 1
connect.connectorformat.EndConnect secondShape, 1
```

SEE ALSO   Shape

ChartUnitEffects Property

Determines the animation effects for graphs

Description

As a graph is built with animation, this property allows the selection of animation by series, category, or element. For the animation to display, the Animate property must be set to True.

AVAILABLE IN VB SCRIPT

Syntax

```
animationsettings.ChartUnitEffects = effectType
```

Parameters

effectType   This parameter determines how the chart will be animated. Use one of the following constants: ppAnimateByCategory, ppAnimateByCategoryElements, ppAnimateBySeries, ppAnimateBySeriesElements, or ppAnimateChartMixed.

Returns

Long type

Immediate Window Sample

```
ActivePresentation.Slides(1).Shapes.Title. _
AnimationSettings _
.ChartUnitEffects = True
```

Color Object

Holds the color formatting for a foreground, background, gradient, or patterned color

Description
The Color object is used with AnimationSettings, FillFormat, Font, LineFormat, ShadowFormat, SlideShowView, and ThreeDFormat objects. Colors stored in the object can be individual RGB colors or color schemes created with the SchemeColor property.

AVAILABLE IN VB SCRIPT

Syntax
`object.Color`

Parameters
N/A

Returns
N/A

Immediate Window Sample
```
ActivePresentation.Slides(1).Shapes(1).TextFrame _
.TextRange.Font.Color.SchemeColor = ppForeground
```

Count Property

Used to determine how many objects are in a collection

Description
The Count property can be used with a For...Next loop to cycle through all of the objects held in a collection.

AVAILABLE IN VB SCRIPT

Syntax
```
object.Count
```

Parameters
N/A

Returns
Long type

Immediate Window Sample
```
? ActivePresentation.Slides.Count
```

SEE ALSO AddLabel

DeleteText Method

Deletes all of the text in a Shape object

Description
This method will eliminate all of the text stored in a TextFrame object.

AVAILABLE IN VB SCRIPT

Syntax
```
textframe.DeleteText
```

Parameters
N/A

Returns
N/A

Immediate Window Sample
```
ActivePresentation.Slides(1).Shapes(1) _
.TextFrame.DeleteText
```

SEE ALSO AddLabel

DisplayMasterShapes Property

Determines whether slide displays shapes on slide master

Description

This property will determine if the shapes and text stored on the slide master will be displayed in the background of the current slide. The default when a new slide is created is to set this property to True. Note that setting the DisplayMasterShapes does not automatically set the slide to the master color scheme. Use the FollowMasterBackground and ColorScheme properties to ensure the slide matches.

AVAILABLE IN VB SCRIPT

Syntax

```
slide.DisplayMasterShapes = msFlag
```

Parameters

msFlag   Setting this property to True will display the slide master shapes in the background.

Returns

Long type

Immediate Window Sample

```
ActivePresentation.Slides(1) .DisplayMasterShapes = True
```

SEE ALSO   RGB

Duplicate Method

Duplicates specified object

Description

The Duplicate method can be used within PowerPoint to make a duplicate of an object and all of the objects stored within the object. The Immediate window example demonstrates duplicating the first slide and any objects contained in it.

AVAILABLE IN VB SCRIPT

IV

Syntax
`object.Duplicate`

Parameters
N/A

Returns
N/A

Immediate Window Sample
`ActivePresentation.Slides(1).Duplicate`

SEE ALSO AddLabel

EntryEffect Property

Determines the animation effect upon entry to the current slide

Description
This property specifies the animation effect that will be used when this slide is entered. The transition effect may be set to any of the numerous constants supplied with PowerPoint.

AVAILABLE IN VB SCRIPT

Syntax
`EntryEffect = effectType`

Parameters
effectType The effects available for entry are numerous. Use any of the following constants: ppEffectAppear, ppEffectBlindsHorizontal, ppEffectBlindsVertical, ppEffectBoxIn, ppEffectBoxOut, ppEffectCheckerboardAcross, ppEffectCheckerboardDown, ppEffectCoverDown, ppEffectCoverLeft, ppEffectCoverLeftDown, ppEffectCoverLeftUp, ppEffectCoverRight, ppEffectCoverRightDown, ppEffectCoverRightUp, ppEffectCoverUp, ppEffectCrawlFromDown, ppEffectCrawlFromLeft, ppEffectCrawlFromRight, ppEffectCrawlFromUp, ppEffectCut, ppEffectCutThroughBlack, ppEffectDissolve, ppEffectFade, ppEffectFlashOnceFast, ppEffectFlashOnceMedium, ppEffectFlashOnceSlow, ppEffectFlyFromBottom, ppEffectFlyFromBottomLeft, ppEffectFlyFromBottomRight,

ppEffectFlyFromLeft, ppEffectFlyFromRight, ppEffectFlyFromTop, ppEffectFlyFromTopLeft, ppEffectFlyFromTopRight, ppEffectMixed, ppEffectNone, ppEffectPeekFromDown, ppEffectPeekFromLeft, ppEffectPeekFromRight, ppEffectPeekFromUp, ppEffectRandom, ppEffectRandomBarsHorizontal, ppEffectRandomBarsVertical, ppEffectSplitHorizontalIn, ppEffectSplitHorizontalOut, ppEffectSplitVerticalIn, ppEffectSplitVerticalOut, ppEffectStripsDownLeft, ppEffectStripsDownRight, ppEffectStripsLeftDown, ppEffectStripsLeftUp, ppEffectStripsRightDown, ppEffectStripsRightUp, ppEffectStripsUpLeft, ppEffectStripsUpRight, ppEffectUncoverDown, ppEffectUncoverLeft, ppEffectUncoverLeftDown, ppEffectUncoverLeftUp, ppEffectUncoverRight, ppEffectUncoverRightDown, ppEffectUncoverRightUp, ppEffectUncoverUp, ppEffectWipeDown, ppEffectWipeLeft, ppEffectWipeRight, ppEffectWipeUp.

Returns
Variant type

Immediate Window Sample
```
ActivePresentation.Slides(2).Shapes.Title. _
AnimationSettings _
.EntryEffect = ppEffectWipeLeft
```

SEE ALSO   Animate

GotoSlide Method

Changes the View to the specified slide number

Description
This method will change the slide currently displayed to the one specified. The specified slide also becomes the current active slide.

AVAILABLE IN VB SCRIPT

Syntax
```
view.GotoSlide(index)
```

Parameters
index   Long type. Number of current slide to display.

Returns
N/A

Immediate Window Sample
`Windows(1).View.GotoSlide 2`

SEE ALSO EntryEffect

GradientColorType Property

Determines the gradient type of a Fill object

Description
The GradientColorType property can be used to determine the gradient type of a Fill object. Use individual methods such as PresetGradient or TwoColorGradient to set this parameter.

AVAILABLE IN VB SCRIPT

Syntax
`fill.GradientColorType = gradType`

Parameters
gradType Long type. Values can be compared with the following constants: msoGradientColorMixed, msoGradientOneColor, msoGradientPresetColors, or msoGradientTwoColors.

Returns
Long type

Immediate Window Sample
`? ActivePresentation.Slides(1).Shapes(1) _`
`.Fill.GradientColorType`

SEE ALSO PresetGradient, TwoColorGradient

GradientDegree Property

Determines the darkness or lightness of a one-color gradient in a Fill object

Description

This property varies in value from 0 (black mixed with foreground color) to 1 (white mixed with foreground color). Decimals determine the degree of mixing.

AVAILABLE IN VB SCRIPT

Syntax

```
fill.GradientDegree
```

Parameters

N/A

Returns

Single type

Immediate Window Sample

```
? ActivePresentation.Slides(1).Shapes(1) _
.Fill.GradientDegree
```

SEE ALSO   PresetGradient

GradientStyle Property

Determines the style/direction of the gradient fill of a Fill object

Description

The GradientStyle property is read-only and can be set by use of one of the gradient fill methods. The style affects the direction and appearance of the gradient. An error will be generated by the Fill object if this property is accessed when the fill does not contain a gradient.

AVAILABLE IN VB SCRIPT

Syntax

```
fill.GradientStyle = gradStyle
```

Parameters

gradStyle   This property may be compared against one of the following constants: msoGradientDiagonalDown,

msoGradientDiagonalUp, msoGradientFromCenter,
msoGradientFromCorner, msoGradientFromTitle,
msoGradientHorizontal, msoGradientMixed, or
msoGradientVertical.

Returns
Long type

Immediate Window Sample
```
? ActivePresentation.Slides(1).Shapes(1) _
.Fill.GradientStyle
```

SEE ALSO   PresetGradient, TwoColorGradient

HideWhileNotPlaying Property

Determines whether a multimedia clip is hidden when not playing

Description
The HideWhileNotPlaying property determines whether the media
clip is hidden when not playing. The Immediate window example
requires the first object on the first slide to be a media clip.

AVAILABLE IN VB SCRIPT

Syntax
```
playsettings.HideWhileNotPlaying = hpFlag
```

Parameters
hpFlag   Boolean. Set to True if media clip should be hidden while
not playing.

Returns
Long type

Immediate Window Sample
```
ActivePresentation.Slides(1).Shapes(1). _
AnimationSettings _
.PlaySettings.HideWhileNotPlaying = True
```

SEE ALSO   Animate, LoopUntilStopped

Hyperlink Property

Provides reference to the Hyperlink object for hyperlink connections

Description
A Hyperlink can be used to jump to an HTTP site, to a file, or to another presentation. By use of this property, a shape can be configured to act as a hyperlink when a specific event occurs.

AVAILABLE IN VB SCRIPT

Syntax
```
object.Hyperlink
```

Parameters
N/A

Returns
Hyperlink object type

Immediate Window Sample
```
ActivePresentation.Slides(1).Shapes(1) _
.ActionSettings(ppMouseClick).Action = _
ppActionHyperlink
ActivePresentation.Slides(1).Shapes(1) _
.ActionSettings(ppMouseClick) _
.Hyperlink.Address = "http://www.cvisual.com"
```

SEE ALSO   ActionVerb

LoopUntilStopped Property

Determines whether a media clip or slide show will repeat until stopped

IV

Description

This property can be used to make a slide show or a sound or video clip repeat. The Immediate window example expects the first shape on the first slide to be a media clip.

AVAILABLE IN VB SCRIPT

Syntax

```
playsettings.LoopUntilStopped = luFlag
```

Parameters

luFlag Boolean. Set to True to continue cycling until a slide transition, mouse click, or another media clip begins.

Returns

Long type

Immediate Window Sample

```
ActivePresentation.Slides(1).Shapes(1). _
AnimationSettings.PlaySettings.LoopUntilStopped =
True
```

SEE ALSO   Animate

Name Property

Holds the name of the object that can be used to programmatically reference it

Description

The Name property holds the string of the name used to reference an object. Instead of using an index with a collection, the name can be used to specify the object.

AVAILABLE IN VB SCRIPT

Syntax

```
object.Name = string
```

Parameters

string Any string conforming to the standard naming conventions.

Returns
N/A

Immediate Window Sample
```
? ActivePresentation.Name
? ActivePresentation.Slides(1).Name
```

SEE ALSO   ActivePresentation

PresetGradient Method

IV

Creates a gradient for the specified Fill object

Description
Use of this method creates a preset gradient in the Fill object. The style of the gradient designates its general appearance, while the gradType can be set to one of 24 different constants.

AVAILABLE IN VB SCRIPT

Syntax
```
fill.PresetGradient(style,variant, gradType)
```

Parameters
style   Use one of the following: msoGradientDiagonalDown, msoGradientDiagonalUp, msoGradientFromCenter, msoGradientFromCorner, msoGradientFromTitle, msoGradientHorizontal, or msoGradientVertical.

variant   The gradient variant that can have a value of 1 to 4.

gradType   Type of gradient. Use one of the following constants: msoGradientBrass, msoGradientCalmWater, msoGradientChrome, msoGradientChromeII, msoGradientDaybreak, msoGradientDesert, msoGradientEarlySunset, msoGradientFire, msoGradientFog, msoGradientGold, msoGradientGoldII, msoGradientHorizon, msoGradientLateSunset, msoGradientMahogany, msoGradientMoss, msoGradientNightfall, msoGradientOcean, msoGradientParchment, msoGradientPeacock, msoGradientRainbow, msoGradientRainbowII, msoGradientSapphire, msoGradientSilver, or msoGradientWheat.

Returns

N/A

Immediate Window Sample

```
ActivePresentation.Slides(1).Shapes(1).Fill _
.PresetGradient msoGradientVertical, _
1, msoGradientChrome
```

PresetTextured Method

Creates a gradient for the specified Fill object

Description

Use of this method creates a preset texture in the Fill object. The style of the texture designates its general appearance.

AVAILABLE IN VB SCRIPT

Syntax

```
fill.PresetTextured(texture)
```

Parameters

texture   Specifies the type of texture to create for the Fill object. Use one of the following constants: msoTextureBlueTissuePaper, msoTextureBouquet, msoTextureBrownMarble, msoTextureCanvas, msoTextureCork, msoTextureDenim, msoTextureFishFossil, msoTextureGranite, msoTextureGreenMarble, msoTextureMediumWood, msoTextureNewsprint, msoTextureOak, msoTexturePaperBag, msoTexturePapyrus, msoTextureParchment, msoTexturePinkTissuePaper, msoTexturePurpleMesh, msoTextureRecycledPaper, msoTextureSand, msoTextureStationery, msoTextureWalnut, msoTextureWaterDroplets, msoTextureWhiteMarble, or msoTextureWovenMat.

Returns

Variant type

Immediate Window Sample

```
ActivePresentation.Slides(1).Shapes(1).Fill _
.PresetTextured msoTextureGreenMarble
```

SEE ALSO   PresetGradient

RGB Property

Stores the color value to be displayed by an object

Description

The RGB property is available in any of the ColorScheme objects used in PowerPoint. Change of a particular color is accomplished by setting the property to a Long RGB color value. The Immediate window example shows setting the background color of the first slide to red.

AVAILABLE IN VB SCRIPT

Syntax

```
object.RGB = color
```

Parameters

color   Long data type representing an RGB value.

Returns

N/A

Immediate Window Sample

```
ActivePresentation.Slides(1). _
ColorScheme(ppBackground).RGB = RGB(255,0,0)
```

SEE ALSO   Color

Rotation Property

Contains the degrees rotation of a Shape object

Description

The Rotation property may be set in degrees to the desired angle for the object. The Immediate window example creates a label on the first slide and rotates it 45 degrees.

IV

AVAILABLE IN VB SCRIPT

Syntax
```
object.Rotation = rotate
```

Parameters
rotate   Single value of degrees rotation.

Returns
N/A

Immediate Window Sample
```
set b = ActivePresentation.Slides(1).Shapes.AddLabel _
(msoTextOrientationHorizontal,50,100,100,100) _
b.textframe.textrange.text = "Yeah"
b.rotation = 45
```

SEE ALSO   AddLabel

Run Property

Determines which macro or presentation is executed when an event occurs

Description
The Run property holds a string containing the name of the macro or presentation that is automatically executed when a particular action occurs.

AVAILABLE IN VB SCRIPT

Syntax
```
actionsetting.Run = actionName
```

Parameters
actionName   String. Name of macro or presentation to execute when event occurs.

Returns
String type

Immediate Window Sample

```
ActivePresentation.Slides(1).Shapes(1) _
.ActionSettings(ppMouseOver) _
.Action = ppActionRunMacro
ActivePresentation.Slides(1).Shapes(1) _
.ActionSettings(ppMouseOver) _
.AnimateAction = True
ActivePresentation.Slides(1).Shapes(1) _
.ActionSettings(ppMouseOver) _
.Run = "myMacro"
```

SEE ALSO Animate

IV

SlideRange Object

Contains references to selected slides

Description

The SlideRange object allows macro changes to be made to a series of selected slides. By making changes to the SlideRange object, changes are automatically effected in all specified slides.

AVAILABLE IN VB SCRIPT

Syntax

```
selection.SlideRange
```

Parameters

N/A

Returns

N/A

Immediate Window Sample

```
Windows(1).Selection.SlideRange _
.ColorScheme.Colors(ppBackground).RGB = RGB(255, 0, 0)
```

SEE ALSO RGB

Speed Property

Determines the speed of transition to the specified slide

Description
This property governs the speed of the transition to the specified slide. Pick a transition effect that works best with the particular speed.

AVAILABLE IN VB SCRIPT

Syntax
```
slideshowtransition.Speed = transSpeed
```

Parameters
transSpeed Long. Determines the speed of transition to the specified slide. Use one of the following constant values: ppTransitionSpeedFast, ppTransitionSpeedMedium, ppTransitionSpeedMixed, or ppTransitionSpeedSlow.

Returns
Long type

Immediate Window Sample
```
ActivePresentation.Slides(1).SlideShowTransition _
.Speed = ppTransitionSpeedSlow
```

SEE ALSO EntryEffect

TextRange Object

Contains all of the text attached to a Shape object

Description
The TextRange object is the object that contains the Font, ParagraphFormat, and ActionSettings objects for a particular shape. The Text property of the TextRange object holds the actual text of the shape.

AVAILABLE IN VB SCRIPT

Syntax
```
shape.TextRange
```

Parameters
N/A

Returns
N/A

Immediate Window Sample
```
ActiveWindow.Selection.TextRange.Copy
```

SEE ALSO   AddLabel

ThreeD Object

Adds the 3-D appearance to Shape objects

Description
The new 3-D capabilities added to PowerPoint can be controlled through the ThreeD object. Extrusions, rotations, and perspectives can be added by varying the settings of this object.

AVAILABLE IN VB SCRIPT

Syntax
```
shape.ThreeD
```

Parameters
N/A

Returns
N/A

Immediate Window Sample
```
With ActivePresentation.Slides(1).Shapes(1).ThreeD _
.Visible = True : .Depth = 50 : _
.ExtrusionColor.RGB = RGB(255, 0, 0) : End With
```

SEE ALSO   RGB, Color

ToggleVerticalText Method

Toggles the vertical text appearance on a WordArt object

Description
This method will cause the text shown in a WordArt object to be displayed vertically. Text flow is toggled every time this method is executed. The Immediate window example requires that the third shape on the first slide is a WordArt object. If it isn't, an error will occur when executing the code.

AVAILABLE IN VB SCRIPT

Syntax
```
texteffect.ToggleVerticalText
```

Parameters
N/A

Returns
N/A

Immediate Window Sample
```
ActivePresentation.Slides(1).Shapes(3) _
.TextEffect.ToggleVerticalText
```

SEE ALSO   PresetTextEffect

TwoColorGradient Method

Creates a two-color gradient for the Fill object

Description
This method creates a two-color gradient from the Forecolor and Backcolor RGB values stored in the Fill object.

AVAILABLE IN VB SCRIPT

Syntax

```
fill.TwoColorGradient(style,variant)
```

Parameters

style The direction/type of gradient is specified using one of the following constants: msoGradientDiagonalDown, msoGradientDiagonalUp, msoGradientFromCenter, msoGradientFromCorner, msoGradientFromTitle, msoGradientHorizontal, or msoGradientVertical.

variant Gradient variant that can be a value of 1 to 4.

IV

Returns

N/A

Immediate Window Sample

```
ActivePresentation.Slides(1).Shapes(1).Fill _
    .ForeColor.RGB = RGB(255, 0, 0)
ActivePresentation.Slides(1).Shapes(1).Fill _
    .BackColor.RGB = RGB(0, 0, 0)
ActivePresentation.Slides(1).Shapes(1).Fill _
    .TwoColorGradient msoGradientHorizontal, 1
```

SEE ALSO PresetGradient

Words Method

Returns a TextRange object that contains the specified words

Description

This method allows the extraction of particular words into a TextRange object. Use of the TextRange object will allow the manipulation of the text, style, and so on, of the specified words.

AVAILABLE IN VB SCRIPT

Syntax

```
paragraph.Words([start] [, length])
```

Parameters

start Beginning word to be returned.

length Number of words to be returned.

Returns

TextRange object

Immediate Window Sample

```
ActivePresentation.Slides(1).Shapes(1).TextFrame. _
TextRange.Paragraphs(1).Words(1, 2).Font.Bold = True
```

SEE ALSO ActivePresentation, Shape

Access

Microsoft Access has only recently made the transition from the Access Basic language to including the entire VBA system. Most of the Access system can only be partially accessed. You might notice when looking at the object model that it is quite sparse. Only forms, reports, and modules are considered within the Access system. All database access occurs through the Data Access Object model.

Data Access Objects (DAO) are the general objects provided for all of the Office applications (and Visual Basic itself) to access database information. The native file format of the DAO is Microsoft Access file format, so any VBA-enabled application can read access files. The section that follows the Access section details the DAO Jet engine.

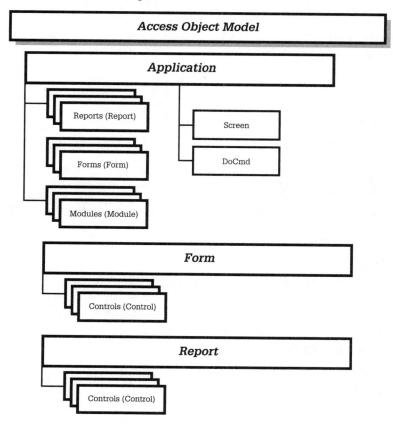

Count Property

Returns the number of objects held in the collection

Description

Use the Count property within Access to determine how many forms, reports, and so on, are held in a specific collection. The Immediate window example demonstrates how many Module objects exist in the current project.

AVAILABLE IN VB SCRIPT

Syntax
```
object.Count
```

Parameters
Long type

Returns
N/A

Immediate Window Sample
```
? Modules.Count
```

DoCmd Object

Executes specific Access commands

Description

Because the Access object model is not yet complete, there are still functions that cannot be performed through it. The DoCmd object provides a number of capabilities to send commands to the Access program.

AVAILABLE IN VB SCRIPT

Syntax
```
DoCmd.method
```

Parameters
N/A

Returns
N/A

Immediate Window Sample
`DoCmd.Beep`

HourGlass Method

Changes the cursor to an hourglass or back to normal

Description
Calling the HourGlass method on the DoCmd object will change
the mouse pointer to an hourglass icon showing the user that work
is in progress.

AVAILABLE IN VB SCRIPT

Syntax
`DoCmd.HourGlass flag`

Parameters
flag   Indicates whether to set the hourglass (1) or return to the
default cursor (0).

Returns
N/A

Immediate Window Sample
```
DoCmd.HourGlass 1
DoCmd.HourGlass 0
```

User Tip
Make sure to set the hourglass when an operation will take some
time. It often confuses the user when the computer is processing
but the cursor remains active. A general rule of thumb is that more
than three seconds of processing should show the hourglass. More
than 30 seconds of processing should implement some type of
status display or progress bar.

Name Property

Holds the name of the object that can be used to programmatically reference it

Description

The Name property holds the string of the name used to reference an object. Instead of using an index with a collection, the name can be used to specify the object.

AVAILABLE IN VB SCRIPT

Syntax

```
object.Name = string
```

Parameters

string   Any string conforming to the standard naming conventions.

Returns

N/A

Immediate Window Sample

```
? Modules(0).Name
```

ActiveX Data Objects (ADO)

Visual Basic began including database access in Version 3 with the addition of the JET database engine. Through each revision, database access has become more robust with each new version. From DAO, RDO, and ODBC Direct, the new ActiveX Data Objects (ADO) are set to replace all other Microsoft data objects.

The ADO model provides simplified access to the underlying C++-based OLE DB database access middleware. OLE DB provides independent data source object interaction by using interchangeable drives much like ODBC. Unlike ODBC, ADO/OLE DB supports more than just traditional data sources such as SQL-based data systems. The object basis of the new data object model lets a driver support returned data types for anything from row-based database information to geographic spatial information.

There are two ADO object models: ActiveX Data Objects Library and ActiveX Data Objects Recordset Library. The Recordset Library is a condensed version mostly used for client-side ADO access. The full library, known as ADODB, will need to be used by most programmers.

IV

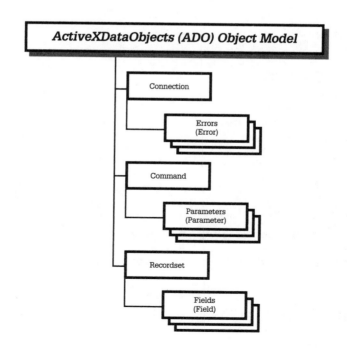

AddNew Method

Adds a new record to the data source

Description
This method, when used with a Recordset object, creates a new record in the current data source. Once the AddNew method has been used, the current record points to this new record. Therefore, any modification to the fields will be saved in this new record.

AVAILABLE IN VB SCRIPT

Syntax
```
recordsetObject.AddNew([fieldList],[values])
```

Parameters
fieldList   List of fields to add automatically to the new record. Must have corresponding value for each field listed.

values   Value for each field in the fieldList parameter for adding to the new record.

Returns
N/A

Code Sample
```
myRS.AddNew
myRS!firstName = "Royal"
myRS!lastName = "Shaw"
myRS.Update
```

SEE ALSO   EditMode, MoveLast, MoveNext, Requery

Clone Method

Creates a clone of the specified Recordset object

Description

This method is used to duplicate a recordset from the current recordset. It can save a great deal of processing time if a duplicate recordset is needed, because a clone does not execute an entirely new query.

AVAILABLE IN VB SCRIPT

Syntax

```
recordsetObject.Clone
```

Parameters

N/A

Returns

Recordset object

Code Sample

```
Dim oldRS As ADO.Recordset
Dim newRS As ADO.Recordset

Set newRS = oldRS.Clone
```

> ### Programmer's Tip
> The Clone method can be especially useful when you're working with Data Controls. If a subquery is required with the recordset displayed by the control, cloning the set can be the best solution to querying the data set without disturbing the user display of the data.

SEE ALSO   CommandText, CommandType, EditMode, NextRecordset, Open

CommandText Property

Holds the string sent to the OLE DB driver when the Execute method is activated

Description

This property contains the text of the command to be sent when the Execute method is activated. This property is usually set to equal a SQL command.

AVAILABLE IN VB SCRIPT

Syntax

```
commandObject.CommandText = myStr
```

Parameters

myStr String type containing the text to send the OLE DB Data Provider, most often in the form of a SQL command.

Returns

N/A

Code Sample

```
Command myCommand = New ADODB.Command
myCommand.CommandText = "SELECT * from authors"
```

SEE ALSO Clone, CommandType, Execute, Open

CommandType Property

Specifies the type of Command object

Description

This property indicates the type of Command object. Constant values contained in this property include adCmdText (1), adCmdTable (2), adCmdStoredProc (4), and adCmdUnknown (8). The default is adCmdUnknown.

AVAILABLE IN VB SCRIPT

Syntax

```
commandObject.CommandType = myCommandT
```

Parameters

myCommandT Integer value of one of the constants of the command type.

Returns
N/A

Code Sample
```
Command myCommand = New ADODB.Command
myCommand.CommandType = 1 ' cmdText
myCommand.CommandText = "SELECT * from authors"
```

SEE ALSO   Execute, Open

ConnectionString Property

Holds the string that indicates the data provider

Description
The text of the ConnectionString can also contain the data provider, the filename of the connection data, as well as the user name and password for transmission when the Connection is opened. If the user name and password are not supplied to the source through the ConnectionString, they are passed through the userID and password parameters to identify the user for login.

AVAILABLE IN VB SCRIPT

Syntax
```
connectionObject.ConnectionString = myStr
```

Parameters
myStr   String that holds the connection parameters.

Returns
N/A

Code Sample
```
Dim myConnect As ADODB.Connection
Set myConnect = New ADODB.Connection
myConnect.ConnectionString = "driver={SQL Server};" & _
    "server=MarinerServ;uid=sa;pwd=;database=pubs"
myConnect.Open
```

SEE ALSO   Provider, Source

EditMode Property

Indicates the edit mode of the current record

Description
This property indicates the status of the current record. If the record has been edited but not saved, the value is set to 1. If a new record has been added by use of the AddNew method, the value is set to 2. If no editing is in progress, the property is set to zero.

The modes contained in this property can include adEditNone(0), adEditInProgress (1), adEditAdd (2), and adEditDelete (4).

AVAILABLE IN VB SCRIPT

Syntax
```
recordsetObject.EditMode = modeNum
```

Parameters
modeNum   Integer type.

Returns
N/A

Code Sample
```
MsgBox myRS.EditMode
```

SEE ALSO   AddNew, Clone

Execute Method

This method executes SQL code against a data source

Description
This method is used to send SQL to the data source. The method is used in the same way on either a Command object or a Connection object. After the execution has occurred, it will return the number of records affected by the command.

If the source is an ODBC data source, the SQL command will be interpreted through ODBC to access the data. If the source is a direct OLE DB driver and the source can accept SQL commands, the driver merely passes the execution statement through to the source for processing.

When the Execute statement has completed its operation, it will return the number of records that were affected by the operation. If the operation has no records that it directly affects (such as the creation of a stored procedure), the number zero is returned.

AVAILABLE IN VB SCRIPT

IV

Syntax

```
connectionObject.Execute([recordsAffected],
[parameters], [options])
```

Parameters

recordsAffected   The records that will be affected by the Execute operation.

parameters   Any parameters to be passed to stored procedures or other code executed by this method.

options   Options specifying how the Execute method should address the Data Provider.

Returns

Recordset object

Code Sample

```
' Create an ADO object
Set Conn = Server.CreateObject("ADODB.Connection")
' Connect to an ODBC data source called myODBC
Conn.Open "myODBC"
' Select all of the fields and records from the table
sql="SELECT * FROM myTable"
' Execute the query
Set myRS = Conn.Execute(sql)
```

SEE ALSO   ConnectionString, Open, Source, Provider

GetRows Method

Returns the specified number of rows in an Array object

Description

This method is used to copy rows from the recordset into an array.
Rather than using a loop to provide the copying, this command will
instantly move the information contained within a recordset into an
array object. Note that the method will expand the array
automatically to accommodate the size of the recordset.

AVAILABLE IN VB SCRIPT

Syntax

```
recordsetObject.GetRows([rows], [start], [fields])
```

Parameters

rows   Number of rows to included in the array.

start   First record to return.

fields   Fields or columns to be returned in the array.

Returns

Long type

Code Sample

```
' Create an ADO object
Set Conn = Server.CreateObject("ADODB.Connection")
' Connect to an ODBC data source called myODBC
Conn.Open "myODBC"
' Select all of the fields and records from the table
sql="SELECT * FROM myTable"
' Execute the query
Set myRS = Conn.Execute(sql)
' Get 20 records into the array
myArray=myRS.GetRows(20)
```

SEE ALSO   Clone, Open

MoveLast Method

Moves the recordset cursor to the last record in the set

Description
Executing this method will move the cursor to the last record in the recordset and make it the current record.

AVAILABLE IN VB SCRIPT

IV

Syntax
```
recordsetObject.MoveLast
```

Parameters
N/A

Returns
N/A

Code Sample
```
myRS.MoveLast
```

SEE ALSO   AddNew, MoveNext

MoveNext Method

Moves the recordset cursor to the next record in the set

Description
Executing this method will move the cursor to the next record in the recordset and make it the current record. If the current record is in edit mode and this method is executed, the changes will be lost.

AVAILABLE IN VB SCRIPT

Syntax
```
recordsetObject.MoveNext
```

Parameters
N/A

Returns

N/A

Code Sample

```
myRS.MoveNext
```

SEE ALSO   AddNew, MoveLast

NextRecordset Method

In a compound Recordset object, activates the next Recordset in the list

Description

If the recordset is based on a compound command set, the NextRecordset method will clear the current recordset and execute the next command. A *compound recordset* is one created with a command string that contains multiple queries.

For example, the query string of a Command object might be set to:

```
select * from table1; select * from table2
```

If there are no more recordsets to use, the recordset returned will be empty, which means that both the BOF and the EOF properties are set to True.

AVAILABLE IN VB SCRIPT

Syntax

```
recordsetObject.NextRecordset([records])
```

Parameters

records   Determines the records affected.

Returns

Recordset object

Code Sample
```
Dim myRSS As ADODB.Recordset
myConnect = "Provider=sqloledb;" & _
   "Data Source=srv;Initial Catalog=pubs;User Id=sa;"_
   &"Password=; "
Set rstCompound = New ADODB.Recordset
myRSS.ConnectionString = myConnect
multiStr = "SELECT * FROM authors; "SELECT * FROM jobs"
myRSS.Open multiStr

Do Until myRSS Is Nothing
    Set myRSS = myRSS.NextRecordset
Loop
```

SEE ALSO   Clone, ConnectionString, Open, Provider

IV

Open Method

Opens the specified connection, command, or recordset

Description
A connection may be opened with the Open method. This method requires three parameters: ConnectionString, userID, and password. The ConnectionString indicates the data source that will be used, such as a JET database or ODBC data source.

The ConnectionString stores the string used to connect to the data source. The Open method allows an optional ConnectionString parameter. If none is passed in the Open method, the string is retrieved from this property. When a parameter is passed to the Open method, it overrides what is stored in the property and stores the new string in the property.

AVAILABLE IN VB SCRIPT

Syntax
```
connectionObject.Open([connectStr],[userID],[pass-
word],[options])
```

Parameters
connectStr   The connection string sent to the Data Provider.

userID   User ID to log on to the data source.

password   Password to log on to the data source.

options   Options for the Data Provider.

Returns
N/A

Code Sample
```
myConnect = "Provider=sqloledb;" & _
    "Data Source=srv;Initial Catalog=pubs;"_
    User&"Id=sa;Password=; "
myRS.Open "SELECT * FROM authors", myConnect, _
    , , adCmdText
```

SEE ALSO   Clone, ConnectionString, Provider, Source

Provider Property

In the Connection object, holds the name of the OLE DB Data Provider

Description
The Provider property holds the name of the provider for the particular data source. If the Provider will be an ODBC driver or there is no Provider set, the MSDASQL provider will be used as the default. As more products have OLE DB native interfaces, more providers will be available.

AVAILABLE IN VB SCRIPT

Syntax
```
connectionObject.Provider = myStr
```

Parameters
myStr   String type that references the data provider.

Returns
N/A

Code Sample

```
Dim myConnectObj As New ADODB.Connection
MsgBox myConnectObj.Provider
```

SEE ALSO   ConnectionString, Open, Source

Requery Method

Reexecutes a query of a Recordset object for any record updates

Description

This method is used to requery the data source and retrieve any changes that may have occurred or any new records that meet the criteria in the original query. Requery is often necessary if a great deal of time has passed since the data was originally acquired.

The Requery method may also be necessary if changes were made to the database using direct SQL commands rather than interfacing through the ADO methods such as Update.

When changes occur to the recordset, such as remote users adding or modifying records, these changes are not automatically reflected in the data set stored in memory. The Requery( ) method can be used to refresh the current recordset to show any updates. Accessing a recordset from the Data Control through the Recordset property, you may requery the data displayed in the bound control.

AVAILABLE IN VB SCRIPT

Syntax

```
recordsetObject.Requery(options)
```

Parameters

options   Long data type.

Returns

N/A

Code Sample

```
myRS.Requery()
```

SEE ALSO   AddNew, Clone, Open

Source Property

String that defines which data source will be accessed

Description

This property contains the name of the data source where the Recordset object retrieves its data. This property string might contain the name of a table, a query, a Command object, or a stored procedure. If the Source indicates a Command object, the ActiveConnection of the Recordset object will be set to match the equivalent property stored in the Command object.

AVAILABLE IN VB SCRIPT

Syntax

```
recordsetObject.Source = myVar
```

Parameters

myVar   Variant data type that holds the name or query string on the database object.

Returns

N/A

Code Sample

```
MsgBox myRS.Source
```

SEE ALSO   ConnectionString, Open, Provider

Data Access Objects (DAO)

Data Access Objects (DAO) are the general objects provided for all of the Office applications (and Visual Basic itself) to access database information. The native file format of the DAO is Microsoft Access file format, so any VBA-enabled application can read Access files. The actual database engine used by DAO is known as the Jet engine. You will often see information addressing optimization of the Jet engine.

The DAO format consists of a series of Workspace objects. Each Workspace is a separate security user login zone. Within the Workspace, Databases collections hold the individual Database objects that are currently open. Each Database object can contain several objects, most important of which is the Tabledefs collection. Each Tabledef object held in the collection defines the structure of individual tables stored in the database.

All of the Immediate window examples in this section were designed for use from within Microsoft Access. Some of the examples access a table named "myNames" that has two fields, ID and Name. It is necessary to create this database to run the examples without modification. If you use a different database file, be aware that some of the examples try to access these structures and will need to be modified appropriately.

There is also a Data Access Objects for ODBC. You will find the object model in the "Other Models" section. Most of the functionality is the same as the Jet model, with the primary exception of security, which is handled through the ODBC Connection object.

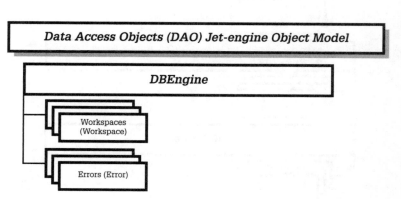

Data Access Objects (DAO) Jet-engine Object Model

DBEngine

Workspaces
(Workspace)

Errors (Error)

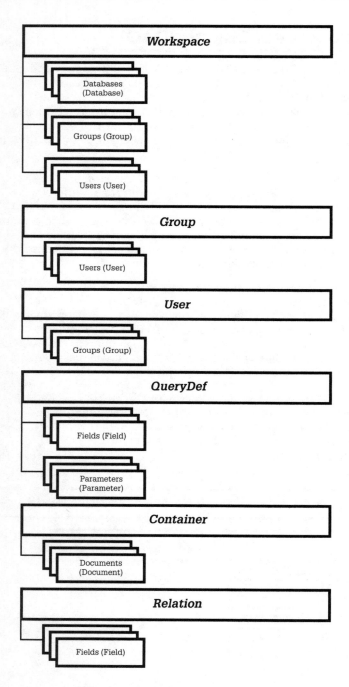

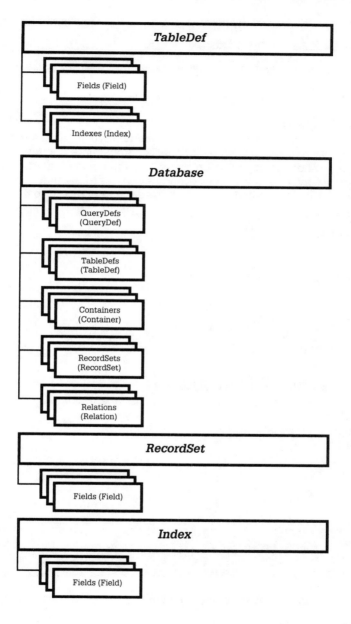

AddNew Method

Creates a new record in the specified table

Description

To create a new record, the AddNew method will append a record to the end of the specified recordset. The Immediate window example shows a record being added to a table named myNames that contains two fields. The second field is set to the name "Joe," and the Update method is called to store the new record to the table.

AVAILABLE IN VB SCRIPT

Syntax

```
object.AddNew
```

Parameters

N/A

Returns

N/A

Immediate Window Sample

```
Set a = dbEngine.Workspaces(0).Databases(0). _
Tabledefs("myNames")
a.OpenRecordset
a.AddNew
a.Field(1) = "Joe"
a.Update
```

SEE ALSO   CommitTrans

CommitTrans

Commits any records currently held in the current transaction

Description

A transaction can contain one or more changes to one or more records. When the CommitTrans method is called, either all of the current operations stored in the transaction are written, or a single failure means none is written. A transaction begins with calling the BeginTrans method; a transaction can complete with either the CommitTrans or RollBack methods.

AVAILABLE IN VB SCRIPT

Syntax
dbEngine.CommitTrans

Parameters
N/A

Returns
N/A

Immediate Window Sample
N/A

SEE ALSO   BeginTrans, RollBack

Database Object

Contains all of the tables and queries for a database

Description
The Database object is held in a collection of Databases that are all of the open databases within a workspace. The Immediate window example displays the name of the first Database object in the collection. If the object is an Access file, the name displayed is a complete path and filename.

AVAILABLE IN VB SCRIPT

Syntax
N/A

Parameters
N/A

Returns
N/A

IV

Immediate Window Sample

```
? dbEngine.Workspaces(0).Databases.Count
? dbEngine.Workspaces(0).Databases(0).Name
```

SEE ALSO Workspace, Tabledef

Delete Method

Deletes an object from a collection

Description

The Delete method on many of the Access objects allows you to remove an object (such as a database, table, query, field, and so on) from a collection. The Immediate window example removes one of the fields from the myNames table.

AVAILABLE IN VB SCRIPT

Syntax

```
object.Delete(object)
```

Parameters

object May be either the ordinal index number or the name of the object to be removed.

Returns

N/A

Immediate Window Sample

```
Set a = dbEngine.Workspaces(0).Databases(0). _
Tabledefs("myNames")
a.Fields.Delete("name")
```

SEE ALSO Database object

Field Object

Holds the actual structure information for a particular field within a table

Description

The Field object can be used to reference either the field within the Table object that it represents, or the data stored within the data field itself. The Immediate window example displays all of the fields contained in the myName table.

AVAILABLE IN VB SCRIPT

Syntax

N/A

Parameters

N/A

Returns

N/A

Immediate Window Sample

```
Set a = dbEngine.Workspaces(0).Databases(0). _
Tabledefs("myNames")
? a.Fields.count
for i = 0 to a.Fields.Count -1 : ? a.Fields(i).Name :
Next i
```

SEE ALSO   AddNew, Database object

Refresh Method

Requeries the specified structure for updated information

Description

The Refresh method can be used on databases to locate new tables, on tables to locate new fields, or on recordsets to access new records that have been added.

AVAILABLE IN VB SCRIPT

Syntax

object.Refresh

Parameters

N/A

Returns
N/A

Immediate Window Sample
```
Set a = dbEngine.Workspaces(0).Databases(0). _
Tabledefs("myNames")
a.Fields.Refresh
```

SEE ALSO   Database object

RollBack Method

Aborts any operations currently held in the transaction

Description
A transaction begun with the BeginTrans method can be revoked with the RollBack method. This may be caused by an error while writing one of the records or by any other abort reason.

Syntax
```
dbEngine.RollBack
```

Parameters
N/A

Returns
N/A

Immediate Window Sample
N/A

SEE ALSO   BeginTrans, CommitTrans

Tabledef Object

Holds the structure and data of a table

Description
The Tabledef object is stored within the Tabledefs collection for all of the tables within a particular database. The Immediate window example shows obtaining the count and name of the Tabledefs of

the collection. Also demonstrated is the display of the DateCreated property of a table named myNames.

AVAILABLE IN VB SCRIPT

Syntax
N/A

Parameters
N/A

Returns
N/A

Immediate Window Sample
```
? dbEngine.Workspaces(0).Databases(0).Tabledefs.count
? DbEngine.Workspaces(0).Databases(0). _
Tabledefs(0).Name
? DbEngine.Workspaces(0).Databases(0). _
Tabledefs("myNames").DateCreated
```

SEE ALSO   Database

Workspace Object

Object that holds the current database workspaces

Description
Each Workspace has particular security privileges for access to a Database held within the Databases collection.

AVAILABLE IN VB SCRIPT

Syntax
N/A

Parameters
N/A

Returns
N/A

Immediate Window Sample
```
? dbEngine.Workspaces.Count
```

SEE ALSO   Database, Tabledef

Outlook

Microsoft Outlook includes the VB Script language instead of VBA. Therefore, it uses a custom VB Script environment that is not as robust as those included with the other Office applications. All code is placed within the tabbed pages of an Item form, so accessing objects is done through the hierarchical chain from that form.

The Immediate window examples provided in this section are most easily tested by adding the code to a button that you've placed on a modified tab page. In the Scripting window, place code that begins with "Sub myButton_Click()", where myButton is the name of the button. End the subroutine definition with the traditional "End Sub". If you simply place this code in the script window and select the Run menu command, many of the samples will work. However, all of the samples work when included in a button Click event.

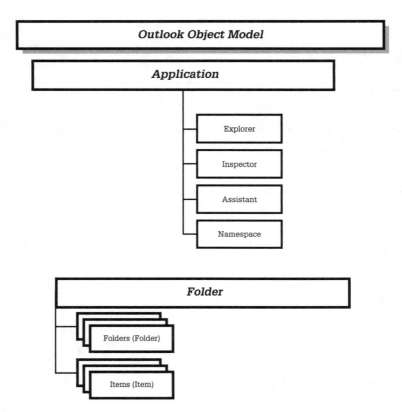

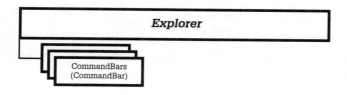

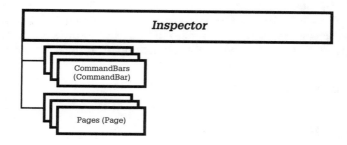

IV

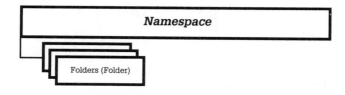

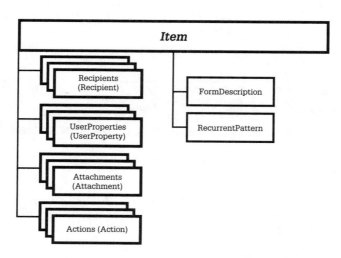

Address Property

Holds the e-mail address of the specified recipient

Description

This property holds the e-mail address after a recipient has been added. The e-mail address is retrieved from the Address book. Use this property to determine or change the e-mail address for the mail item.

AVAILABLE IN VB SCRIPT

Syntax

```
recipient.Address = email
```

Parameters

email   String. Holds specified mail item e-mail address.

Returns

Variant type

Immediate Window Sample

```
Set myItem = Application.CreateItem(0) ' olMailItem
Set myRecipient = myItem.Recipients.Add "Dan Rahmel"
MsgBox myRecipient.Address
```

SEE ALSO   CreateItem

Body Property

Contains the body text of an item

Description

This property contains the plain text (or clear text) of an item such as a mail message or a post. Change the body of the item by changing the value of this property.

AVAILABLE IN VB SCRIPT

Syntax

```
item.Body = text
```

Parameters

text   String. Body text of message.

Returns

String type

Immediate Window Sample

```
Set myItem = Application.CreateItem(0) ' olMailItem
myItem.Body = "Welcome to VB Script!"
```

SEE ALSO   CreateItem, Address

IV

ClearRecurrencePattern Method

Clears the recurrence pattern for an appointment or task

Description

Calling this method sets the single occurrence state of a task or appointment.

AVAILABLE IN VB SCRIPT

Syntax

```
appointment.ClearRecurrencePattern
```

Parameters

N/A

Returns

N/A

Immediate Window Sample

```
myApptment.ClearRecurrencePattern
```

SEE ALSO   AllDayEvent

Controls Property

Provides access to controls stored on a modified tab

Description

Each tab that is visible can have controls such as Text Box, List Box, Check Box, Options, and so on. The Controls property provides access to the Controls collection for a tab.

AVAILABLE IN VB SCRIPT

Syntax

```
object.Controls
```

Parameters

N/A

Returns

N/A

Immediate Window Sample

```
Set myCtls = Item.GetInspector. _
ModifiedFormPages("(P.1)").Controls
If myCtls("chkMyBox") Then MsgBox "Checked"
```

SEE ALSO GetInspector

Count Property

Returns the number of items in collection

Description

To determine the number of objects in a collection, access the Count property. Although the For...Next loop can be used with the Count property, instead use the For...Each loop to move through an object collection.

AVAILABLE IN VB SCRIPT

Syntax

```
collection.Count
```

Parameters

N/A

Returns

Long type

Immediate Window Sample

```
MsgBox Folders.Count
```

SEE ALSO   GetDefaultFolder

CreateItem Method

Creates a new Outlook item

Description

To create a new contact, note, or other Outlook item, the CreateItem method will add it to the current file.

AVAILABLE IN VB SCRIPT

Syntax

```
Set object = Application.CreateItem(itmType)
```

Parameters

itmType   Type of new item to insert.

Returns

Object type

Immediate Window Sample

```
Set newContact = Application.CreateItem(4) ' Contact
Set newNote = Application.CreateItem(5) ' Note
```

SEE ALSO   Controls

CreateObject Method

Creates an object reference based on the class or class ID specified

Description

This method instantiates an OLE Automation object from the specified class or class ID.

AVAILABLE IN VB SCRIPT

Syntax

```
Set object = CreateObject(class)
```

Parameters
class Class identified by string that contains either the class name or the class ID.

Returns
Object type

Immediate Window Sample
```
Set myObject = CreateObject("Outlook.Application")
Set nms = myObject.GetNameSpace("MAPI")
```

SEE ALSO CreateItem

CurrentFolder Property

Determines the current folder shown in the Explorer

Description
The CurrentFolder property holds the category of folder that is selected for the user to view.

AVAILABLE IN VB SCRIPT

Syntax
```
explorer.CurrentFolder = folderRef
```

Parameters
folderRef Reference to the folder that is shown in the Explorer view.

Returns
MAPIFolder type

Immediate Window Sample
```
Set Application.ActiveExplorer.CurrentFolder = _
    olNameSpace.GetDefaultFolder(olFolderCalendar)
```

SEE ALSO GetNameSpace

CurrentUser Property

Holds the identification of the user currently logged into Outlook

Description
Accessing the CurrentUser property will provide the name of the currently logged-in user. Using the property can allow recording of who is accessing the item.

IV

AVAILABLE IN VB SCRIPT

Syntax
namespace.CurrentUser

Parameters
N/A

Returns
N/A

Immediate Window Sample
```
Set nms = Application.GetNameSpace("MAPI")
MsgBox nms.CurrentUser
```

SEE ALSO   GetNameSpace

Display Method

Displays the specified item

Description
Calling the Display method will make an item visible. When a new item is created, the item is invisible by default. An item can be a Contact sheet, a Meeting, an Email entry, or any other Outlook form-based object.

AVAILABLE IN VB SCRIPT

Syntax
```
object.Display
```

Parameters
N/A

Returns
N/A

Immediate Window Sample
```
Set newContact = Application.CreateItem(4)
newContact.Display
```

SEE ALSO   CreateItem, DisplayName

DisplayName Property

Determines the caption below the attachment

Description
For an attachment to a piece of mail, the DisplayName property
may be used to set it to something other than the actual filename.
Therefore, even if you're sending to a system using the
eight-character DOS file convention, the name on the attachment
can be descriptive.

AVAILABLE IN VB SCRIPT

Syntax
```
attach.DisplayName = name
```

Parameters
name   String. Contains the name that will be displayed on the
attachment when item is viewed.

Returns
String type

Immediate Window Sample
```
Set myItem = Application.CreateItem(0) ' olMailItem
Set myAttachments = myItem.Attachments
Set myAttach = myAttachments.Add "C:\test.xls"
myAttach.DisplayName = "This is a test"
```

SEE ALSO   CreateItem, Body

Duration Property

Determines the duration in minutes of the appointment

Description
Sets the duration of an appointment or journal entry in minutes. This property is also used within appointments for the recurrence pattern.

AVAILABLE IN VB SCRIPT

Syntax
```
item.Duration = minutes
```

Parameters
minutes   Long. Duration in minutes.

Returns
Long type

Immediate Window Sample
```
Set myItem = Application.CreateItem(1) _
' olAppointmentItem
myItem.Duration = 48 * 60 ' 2 days = 48 hrs * 60 min
```

SEE ALSO   AllDayEvent, ClearRecurrencePattern

FileAs Property

Contains the keyword string when a contact is filed

Description
This property is automatically initialized when contact is first created. Use the property to set or retrieve the default keyword string.

AVAILABLE IN VB SCRIPT

Syntax
```
item.FileAs = fileStr
```

Parameters
fileStr   String. Default keyword string assigned to contact.

Returns
String type

Immediate Window Sample
```
Set myItem = Application.CreateItem(2) _
' olContactItem
myItem.FileAs = "DP artist"
```

SEE ALSO   CreateItem, DisplayName

GetDefaultFolder Method

Provides a reference to one of the default folders

Description
Complete access to the items within a folder is possible once an object reference to the folder itself has been obtained.

AVAILABLE IN VB SCRIPT

Syntax
```
Set myObject = object.GetDefaultFolder(fnum)
```

Parameters
fnum   Contains the index number of the desired folder.

Returns
Object type

Immediate Window Sample
```
Set myContacts = Application. _
GetNameSpace("MAPI").GetDefaultFolder(10)
```

SEE ALSO   GetNameSpace

GetInspector Property

Provides the top-level Inspector object

Description
The Inspector is required for access to many parts of the Outlook system. Using the GetInspector property, code on an Item form can obtain a reference.

AVAILABLE IN VB SCRIPT

IV

Syntax
```
Set myObject = object.GetInspector
```

Parameters
object   Valid Item object.

Returns
Object type

Immediate Window Sample
```
Set a = myItem.GetInspector
```

SEE ALSO   CreateItem

GetNameSpace Method

Returns the object reference to the NameSpace object of the type specified

Description
This method returns the reference from the root data source. The object can be used to retrieve information from the folders, to get user information, and to access other data sources. Currently, only the "MAPI" name space type is supported.

AVAILABLE IN VB SCRIPT

Syntax

```
Set object = GetNameSpace(type)
```

Parameters

type String. Name space type to return object reference.

Returns

String type

Immediate Window Sample

```
Set nms = Application.GetNameSpace("MAPI")
```

SEE ALSO CreateItem, GetDefaultFolder

Importance Property

Determines the importance of an Outlook item

Description

This property contains the importance level (low, normal, or high) of an item. This property is available to every item type.

AVAILABLE IN VB SCRIPT

Syntax

```
item.Importance = level
```

Parameters

level Long. The level can be set to one of three values: olImportanceLow (0), olImportanceNormal (1), and olImportanceHigh (2).

Returns

Long type

Immediate Window Sample

```
Set myItem = Application.CreateItem(1) _
' olAppointmentItem
myItem.Importance = 2 ' olImportanceHigh
```

SEE ALSO   AllDayEvent, ClearRecurrencePattern, CreateItem, Duration

MeetingStatus Property

Determines the meeting status of an Appointment item

Description
The MeetingStatus property can determine the status of a meeting and make the MeetingRequestItem available to the appointment.

AVAILABLE IN VB SCRIPT

Syntax
```
item.MeetingStatus = meetType
```

Parameters
meetType   Long. The type can be set to one of three values: olMeeting (1), olMeetingCanceled (5), olMeetingReceived (3), or olNonMeeting (0).

Returns
Long type

Immediate Window Sample
```
Set myItem = Application.CreateItem(1) _
' olAppointmentItem
myItem.MeetingStatus = 1 ' olMeeting
```

SEE ALSO   AllDayEvent, ClearRecurrencePattern, CreateItem, Duration

ModifiedFormPages Property

Holds reference to any of the user-modifiable tabs collection

Description
In Outlook, all form construction occurs on the additional hidden tabs of an Item object. This property provides a reference to enable access to items on the modified pages.

AVAILABLE IN VB SCRIPT

Syntax
```
object.ModifiedFormPages
```

Parameters
N/A

Returns
N/A

Immediate Window Sample
```
Set myPages = Item.GetInspector.ModifiedFormPages
```

SEE ALSO   CreateItem, GetInspector

ResponseState Property

Determines the status of a task request

Description
This property can be used to quickly set or determine information on the overall status of a task request. Using this property with an automated routine can presort incoming tasks.

AVAILABLE IN VB SCRIPT

Syntax
```
item.ResponseState = state
```

Parameters
state   Long. Holds the current state of the task that is one of these values: olTaskAccept (2), olTaskAssign (1), olTaskDecline (3), or olTaskSimple (0).

Returns
Long type

Immediate Window Sample
```
Set myItem = Application.CreateItem(3) ' olTaskItem
myItem.ResponseState = 1 ' TaskAssign
```

SEE ALSO   CreateItem, Save

Save Method

Stores any changes in the form fields to the Outlook database

Description

Programmatically or through user interaction, changes that occur to the Outlook fields are not automatically stored to the file. Calling the Save method will update any changes.

AVAILABLE IN VB SCRIPT

Syntax

```
object.Save
```

Parameters

object   Any valid Item object.

Returns

N/A

Immediate Window Sample

```
Item.Save
```

SEE ALSO   CreateItem, Duration, ResponseState

Sensitivity Property

Determines the sensitivity or confidentiality of an item

Description

The Sensitivity property can be set to make an item Normal, Personal, Private, or Confidential.

AVAILABLE IN VB SCRIPT

Syntax

```
item.Sensitivity = value
```

Parameters

value   Long. The sensitivity is determined by one of the following values: olConfidential (3), olNormal (0), olPersonal (1), or olPrivate (2).

Returns

Long type

Immediate Window Sample

```
Set myItem = Application.CreateItem(1) _
' olAppointmentItem
myItem.Sensitivity = 3 ' olConfidential
```

SEE ALSO   CreateItem, ResponseState

ShowFormPage Method

Shows a specified form page

Description

This method sets the form page to be shown by the Inspector. The Immediate window example requires a page named MyPage to exist in the item.

AVAILABLE IN VB SCRIPT

Syntax

```
inspector.ShowFormPage(pageName)
```

Parameters

pageName   String. Name of page to be hidden.

Returns

String type

Immediate Window Sample

```
Application.GetInspector.ShowFormPage("MyPage")
```

SEE ALSO   GetInspector, HideFormPage

UserProperties Collection

Holds all of the fields or properties added by a user

Description

All of the normal fields are referenced by simply using the dot (.)
command. However, properties/fields added by the user are stored
in the UserProperties collection and must be referenced through it.

IV

AVAILABLE IN VB SCRIPT

Syntax

```
item.UserProperties(propName)
```

Parameters

propName   String. Valid property name.

Returns

Variant type

Immediate Window Sample

```
MsgBox Item.UserProperties("Custom1").Value
```

SEE ALSO   Controls, CreateItem

Internet Explorer

The Internet Explorer object model has a more important use than the potential VB Script code that can be embedded into an HTML page. Microsoft has integrated Internet Explorer into the Windows 98 operating system. Internet Explorer can be used by programs like any other ActiveX plug-in or OLE Control. Therefore, not only can you embed a browser within your own programs, but other software developers also are likely to provide this same capability. When the IE browser object is added to a VBA environment, you will need to use the object model to control the actions of the embedded browser.

Currently, the Internet Explorer object model will be used primarily by Web page developers. VB Script to control the objects is contained in a <SCRIPT> tag. For this section, examples have been included as simple HTML source files to demonstrate the capabilities. These can be entered into any text editor, such as Notepad, and loaded into Internet Explorer.

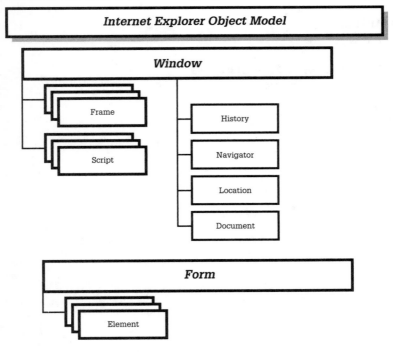

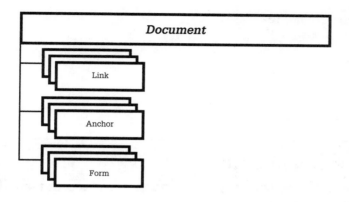

Back Method

Moves the browser back one link

Description
Use the Back method (there is also a Forward method available) to move within the History list of the current browser.

Syntax
```
History.Back
```

Parameters
N/A

Returns
N/A

HTML Code Sample
```
<HTML>
<BODY>
<FORM NAME="myForm">
        String: <INPUT NAME="myString" VALUE=""
        MAXLENGTH="50" SIZE=50>
        <INPUT TYPE="BUTTON" VALUE="Go"
        NAME="cmdGo">
</FORM>

<SCRIPT LANGUAGE="VBScript">
```

```
Sub cmdGo_OnClick
    History.Back
End Sub
</SCRIPT>
</BODY>
</HTML>
```

SEE ALSO   Document

Document Object

This object is the central HTML document

Description
The Document object holds all of the HTML, form, ActiveX, Java, and other objects for the current page. The sample code is a simple HTML page that uses VB Script and the Write method of the Document object to write text to the page text.

Syntax
N/A

Parameters
N/A

Returns
N/A

HTML Code Sample
```
<HTML>
<SCRIPT LANGUAGE="VBScript">
<!--
    myGreeting = "Hello World<P>"
    Document.Write myGreeting
-->
</SCRIPT>
</HTML><BR>
```

SEE ALSO   Back, HRef

HRef Property

The HRef property holds the currently browsed URL location

Description
Examining this property will allow a program to determine the current URL. Setting the property will change the viewed site to the new URL.

IV

Syntax
```
Location.HRef = string
```

Parameters
string   Required. Complete URL to a location.

Returns
N/A

HTML Code Sample
```
<HTML>
<BODY>
<FORM NAME="myForm">
        String: <INPUT NAME="myString" VALUE=""
        MAXLENGTH="50" SIZE=50>
        <INPUT TYPE="BUTTON" VALUE="Go"
        NAME="cmdGo">
</FORM>

<SCRIPT LANGUAGE="VBScript">
Sub cmdGo_OnClick
    Dim curForm
    Set curForm=Document.Forms.item(0)
    Location.HRef = curForm.myString.Value
End Sub
</SCRIPT>
</BODY>
</HTML>
```

User Tip

Make sure the HRef property is set to a complete URL (that is, http://...). If the URL is incomplete, an error won't be generated. The browser will simply not move to the new location.

SEE ALSO Document, Back

Item Method

Returns a reference to an item stored on the HTML page

Description

Use the Item method to gain references to objects that are active on the current page. The sample code demonstrates referencing a Form object on the page and retrieving the value from the input text box.

Syntax

```
Set myObject = object.Item(refNum)
```

Parameters

refNum The reference number of the object within the HTML page.

Returns

Object type

HTML Code Sample

```
<HTML>
<BODY>
<FORM NAME="myForm">
        String: <INPUT NAME="myString" VALUE=""
        MAXLENGTH="50" SIZE=50>
        <INPUT TYPE="BUTTON" VALUE="Go"
        NAME="cmdGo">
</FORM>

<SCRIPT LANGUAGE="VBScript">
Sub cmdGo_OnClick
    Dim curForm
```

```
    Set curForm=Document.Forms.item(0)
    MsgBox "You entered: " + curForm.myString.Value
End Sub
</SCRIPT>
</BODY>
</HTML><BR>
```

SEE ALSO   Document, Submit

Submit Method

Sends the data entered into the user form

Description
By trapping the Submit method, as shown in the sample code, the contents of submitted information can be checked. If the data is valid, calling the Submit method manually will actually activate the Submit operation.

Syntax
```
object.Submit
```

Parameters
N/A

Returns
N/A

HTML Code Sample
```
<HTML>
<BODY>
<FORM NAME="myForm">
        String: <INPUT NAME="myString" VALUE=""
        MAXLENGTH="50" SIZE=50>
        <INPUT TYPE="BUTTON" VALUE="Go"
        NAME="cmdGo">
</FORM>

<SCRIPT LANGUAGE="VBScript">
Sub cmdGo_OnClick
    Dim curForm
    Set curForm=Document.Forms.item(0)
```

IV

```
    If RTrim(curForm.myString.Value)="" then
        MsgBox "Empty.", 16, "Bad."
    Else
        MsgBox "Full", 32, "OK."
        curForm.Submit
    End if
End Sub
</SCRIPT>
</BODY>
</HTML><BR>
```

SEE ALSO   Document, Item

Active Server Pages (ASP)

Active Server Pages (ASP) is the programming environment that executes on Microsoft's web server, known as the Internet Information Server (IIS). ASP includes a number of objects that must be understood to create effective web-based applications. These objects include access to user input form data, session variables, user browser cookies, and even HTTP response output streams.

Be aware that many of the most commonly used routines and data sources should be placed in the global.asa file for global access from all the pages of that application. Additionally, objects created in global.asa can remain instantiated for the duration of the user session.

IV

Active Server Pages (ASP) Object Model

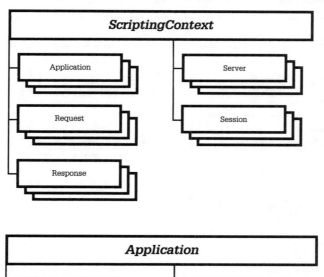

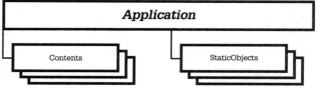

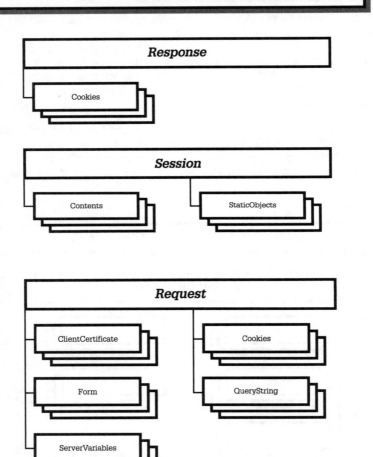

Cookies Property

Holds the values of client browser cookies in the Request or
Response objects

Description

Cookies can store values in the client browser. In a *Request* object,
the properties stored on the browser can be read, and these
properties are read-only. In a *Response* object, a cookie can be
written into the browser, and these Cookies properties are
write-only.

IV

AVAILABLE IN VB SCRIPT

Syntax

```
object.Cookies[myName] = myStr
```

Parameters

object   Either a Response or Request object.

myName   Name string of the cookie.

myStr   String value of the specified cookie.

Returns

N/A

Code Sample

```
Response.Cookies("mySingleCookie").Value = "Apple"
Response.Cookies("myMultiCookie")( "Inventor").Value _
    = "Ben Franklin"
Response.Cookies("myMultiCookie")( "Inventor").Value _
    = "Thomas Edison"
```

SEE ALSO   Form, QueryString

ContentType Property

Determines the MIME type to be sent to the browser

Description

Each HTTP document sent to the browser has a document type that tells the browser how to display the incoming file. For example, the ContentType for a JPEG file would be the "image/JPEG" string. Other common types are "text/plain" and "text/HTML." The sample code writes a 3D VRML format file into the browser.

AVAILABLE IN VB SCRIPT

Syntax

```
responseObject.ContentType = myStr
```

Parameters

myStr   String type that defines the MIME type of the document.

Returns

N/A

Code Sample

```
Response.ContentType = "x-world/x-vrml"
Response.Write "#VRML V2.0 utf8"
Response.Write "Shape { geometry Box {size 1 1 1} "
Response.Write "  appearance Appearance {"
Response.Write "  # Make the box the color blue"
Response.Write "  material Material " & _
     { diffuseColor 0 0 1 }"
Response.Write "  } "
Response.Write "}"
```

SEE ALSO   Write, WriteBlankLines

Expires Property

Sets the amount of time before the page expires on the client browser

Description

This property tells the browser when to eliminate the page that is being sent from the client cache. The Expires property sets the time in minutes before the page expires. Setting the property to 0 makes the page expire from the cache as soon as it is received.

AVAILABLE IN VB SCRIPT

Syntax
```
responseObject.Expires = myNum
```

Parameters
myNum Number of minutes before page expires in user cache.

Returns
N/A

Code Sample
```
Response.Expires=7*24*60 ' 7 days worth of minutes
```

SEE ALSO WriteBlankLines

Form Property

A property of the Request object that returns submitted form data

Description
Form properties contain all of the values that have been passed to the ASP file from a submitted form. By addressing the properties by name, the values submitted by the user can be retrieved.

AVAILABLE IN VB SCRIPT

Syntax
```
requestObject.Form[myRef] = myStr
```

Parameters
myRef Name string or index number of the specified value.

myStr The string value of the specified form parameter.

Returns
N/A

Code Sample

```
Response.Write Request.Form("singleFormParam") _
    & "<P>"
Response.Write Request.Form("multiFormParam")(1) _
    & "<P>"
Response.Write Request.Form("multiFormParam")(2) _
    & "<P>"
```

SEE ALSO   Cookies, QueryString

QueryString Property

Returns the values of the parameters passed in the URL

Description

When a URL is passed through the HTTP protocol, it can contain encoded parameters following the question mark (?) character. For example, the following URL would pass three parameters in the QueryString property:

```
http://www.cvisual.com/
search.asp?parm1=My&parm2=3&parm3=parameters
```

The QueryString property allows access to all these parameters. The strings in this property are read-only.

AVAILABLE IN VB SCRIPT

Syntax

```
requestObject.QueryString[myRef] = myStr
```

Parameters

myRef   Name string or index number of the specified value.

myStr   String value of the specified query.

Returns

N/A

Code Sample

```
For I = 1 To Request.QueryString.Count
    Response.Write Request.QueryString(I) & "<BR>"
Next
```

SEE ALSO   Cookies, Form

ScriptTimeout Property

Amount of time before a script is aborted

Description

This property, specified in minutes, can be used to limit the time
that it takes to execute the script before the script is aborted. This
property occurs in the Server object. This can prevent a long query
or endless loop from stalling the user indefinitely.

AVAILABLE IN VB SCRIPT

Syntax

```
serverObject.ScriptTimeout = myVal
```

Parameters

myVal   Long value type specifying the maximum duration
before timeout.

Returns

N/A

Code Sample

```
Server.ScriptTimeout = 4
```

SEE ALSO   ServerVariables

ServerVariables Property

Variables that store the state of the current server and client
systems

Description

The ServerVariables properties contain the variables stored by the
server about the current client and the state of the server. Some of
these variables are recorded in the server log file with each HTTP
event.

The following are common server variable names: AUTH_TYPE, CONTENT_LENGTH, CONTENT_TYPE, GATEWAY_INTERFACE, HTTP_<HeaderName>, LOGON_USER, PATH_INFO, PATH_TRANSLATED, QUERY_STRING, REMOTE_ADDR, REMOTE_HOST, REQUEST_METHOD, SCRIPT_MAP, SCRIPT_NAME, SERVER_NAME, SERVER_PORT, SERVER_PORT_SECURE, SERVER_PROTOCOL , SERVER_SOFTWARE, and URL. These strings are read-only.

AVAILABLE IN VB SCRIPT

Syntax
```
requestObject.ServerVariables[myRef] = myVar
```

Parameters
myRef   Name string or index number of the specified value.

myVar   Variant value type of the specified server variable.

Returns
N/A

Code Sample
```
Response.Write Request _
.ServerVariables("QUERY_STRING") _
    & "<P>"
```

SEE ALSO   Cookies, Form, QueryString, SessionID

SessionID Property

Holds the SessionID number of the current visitor

Description
When the user accesses a web page initially, a Session is created and assigned a SessionID. This SessionID value is sent to the client's browser as a cookie and stored in the SessionID property. Programs can use the SessionID to track the user and to record visit preferences. This property contains a read-only string.

AVAILABLE IN VB SCRIPT

Syntax
```
requestObject.SessionID = myStr
```

Parameters
myStr   The string value of the ID of the Session.

Returns
String type

Code Sample
```
Response.Write "SessionID:" & Request.SessionID
```

SEE ALSO   ServerVariables

URLEndcode Method

Applies URL encoding to passed string

Description
This method provides URL encoding for characters such as spaces, control, or escape characters. Once converted, the resultant string can be passed as a parameter in a URL.

AVAILABLE IN VB SCRIPT

Syntax
```
serverObject.URLEncode(myStr)
```

Parameters
myStr   The string value to be encoded into the URL format.

Returns
String type

Code Sample
```
myURLStr = Server.URLEncode( _
    "This is a test!! Test the & character, too.")
```

SEE ALSO   Write

Write Method

Sends characters to the browser

Description

This method of the Response object sends text to the browser. Note that the text sent is actual HTML, so any paragraph, table, or other tags can be included in the Write string.

AVAILABLE IN VB SCRIPT

Syntax

```
responseObject.Write(myStr)
```

Parameters

myStr   The string value to send to browser.

Returns

N/A

Code Sample

```
Response.Write "Hello VBR" & "<P>"
```

SEE ALSO   WriteBlankLines

File System Object (FSO)

The File System Object first appeared in the release of the Internet Information Server. Since then, Microsoft has been moving to unify all of the development environments under this open system to provide a common way to access disk files. Visual Basic 6 and all of the other development environments included in Visual Studio 6.0 support the File System Object.

Although Visual Basic includes built-in commands to support many of these functions, using these objects enables all of your code for file access to be standardized—even the VB Script code in your applications can access these objects with the proper permissions.

IV

Because the File System Object is available in so many different programming environments, the code presented can be placed in a Visual Basic procedure, between VB Script tags in an ASP file, or anywhere else that the File System Object is available. The File System Object is located in the Microsoft Scripting Runtime object model in the References dialog box.

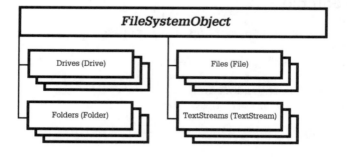

File System Objects (FSO) Object Model

FileSystemObject

Drives (Drive)

Folders (Folder)

Files (File)

TextStreams (TextStream)

AtEndofLine Property

For the TextStream object, flag is True if end of line is reached

Description
This property for the TextStream object indicates whether the end of the line has been reached for the current file that is open for reading. This property is read-only.

AVAILABLE IN VB SCRIPT

Syntax
```
textStreamObject.AtEndofLine = myFlag
```

Parameters
myFlag   Boolean value. True indicates end of line has been reached.

Returns
N/A

Code Sample
```
Dim fso, myFile
Set fso = CreateObject("Scripting.FileSystemObject")
' 1 = Read file
Set myFile = fso.OpenTextFile("c:\test.txt", 1, True)
tempStr = ""
Do While myFile.AtEndOfLine <> True
     tempStr = tempStr + myFile.Read(1)
Loop
MsgBox tempStr
myFile.Close
```

SEE ALSO   AtEndofStream

AtEndofStream Property

Flags if end of TextStream has been reached

Description
This property for the TextStream object indicates the end of the TextStream for files that are open for reading has been reached. This property is read-only.

AVAILABLE IN VB SCRIPT

Syntax
```
textStreamObject.AtEndofStream = myFlag
```

Parameters
myFlag   Boolean value. True indicates end of file has been reached.

Returns
N/A

Code Sample
```
Dim fso, myFile
Set fso = CreateObject("Scripting.FileSystemObject")
' 1 = Read file
Set myFile = fso.OpenTextFile("c:\test.txt", 1, True)
Do Until myFile.AtEndOfStream
     MsgBox myFile.ReadLine()
Loop
myFile.Close
```

SEE ALSO   AtEndOfFile

CreateTextFile Method

Creates a text file that can be used for writing or reading

Description
This method creates a text file of the given name and returns an open TextStream object that references it. The TextStream is open for both reading and writing modes.

AVAILABLE IN VB SCRIPT

Syntax
```
fso.CreateTextFile(fileName, [overwrite], [unicode])
```

IV

Parameters

fileName   String value of file to be created.

overwrite   Boolean value that specifies whether existing file of the same name should be overwritten. Default is True.

unicode   Boolean value that specifies whether to use Unicode (True) or ASCII (False). Default is False.

Returns

TextStream object

Code Sample

```
Dim fso, myFile
Set fso = CreateObject("Scripting.FileSystemObject")
Set myFile = fso.CreateTextFile("c:\test.txt", True)
myFile.WriteLine "Hello VBR"
myFile.Close
```

SEE ALSO   OpenTextFile

OpenTextFile Method

Opens a text file into the specified TextStream object

Description

This method opens a text file for reading, writing, or appending. The ioMode parameter passed to the method can have one of the following three constants: ForReading (1), ForWriting (2), or ForAppending (8).

AVAILABLE IN VB SCRIPT

Syntax

```
fso.OpenTextFile(fileName, [ioMode], [create], [format])
```

Parameters

fileName   String value of the file to be opened.

ioMode   Integer type. Specifies the mode the file is to be opened using.

create Boolean value that specifies whether a new file should be created if the specified filename is not found. Default is False.

format Tristate value. Indicates whether to use Unicode (-1), ASCII (0), or the System Default (-2). Default is ASCII.

Returns
TextStream object

Code Sample
```
Dim fso, myFile
Set fso = CreateObject("Scripting.FileSystemObject")
' 1 = Read file
Set myFile = fso.OpenTextFile("c:\test.txt", 1, True)
MsgBox myFile.ReadLine()
myFile.Close
```

SEE ALSO CreateTextFile

IV

Read Method

Reads characters from a TextStream

Description
This method in the TextStream object reads the specified number of characters into a string. Note that this method supports both ASCII and Unicode type files.

AVAILABLE IN VB SCRIPT

Syntax
```
textStreamObject.Read(myVal)
```

Parameters
myVal Long data type specifying the number of characters to be read.

Returns
String type

Code Sample

```
Dim fso, myFile
Set fso = CreateObject("Scripting.FileSystemObject")
' 1 = Read file
Set myFile = fso.OpenTextFile("c:\test.txt", 1, True)
MsgBox myFile.Read(9)
myFile.Close
```

SEE ALSO   OpenTextFile, SkipLine, WriteBlankLines

SkipLine Method

Skips all of the characters on the current line of file

Description

This method for the TextStream object skips all of the characters up to and including the newline character of the current file. The code example uses the file created in the WriteBlankLines code example.

AVAILABLE IN VB SCRIPT

Syntax

```
textStreamObject.SkipLine()
```

Parameters

N/A

Returns

N/A

Code Sample

```
Dim fso, myFile
Set fso = CreateObject("Scripting.FileSystemObject")
' 1 = Read file
Set myFile = fso.OpenTextFile("c:\test.txt", 1, True)
For i = 1 to 6
     myFile.SkipLine
Next
```

```
MsgBox myFile.Read(9)
myFile.Close
```

SEE ALSO   OpenTextFile, Read, SkipLine

WriteBlankLines Method

Writes a number of blank lines into a text stream

IV

Description

One of the methods of the TextStream object, WriteBlankLines will write the appropriate newline character codes for the specified number of lines.

AVAILABLE IN VB SCRIPT

Syntax

```
textStreamObject.WriteBlankLines(numLines)
```

Parameters

numLines   Long data type containing the number of blank lines to be written.

Returns

N/A

Code Sample

```
Dim fso, myFile
Set fso = CreateObject("Scripting.FileSystemObject")
' 2 = Write file
Set myFile = fso.OpenTextFile("c:\test.txt", 2, True)
myFile.WriteLine "Hello VBR"
myFile.WriteBlankLines 5
myFile.WriteLine "Hello VBR"
myFile.Close
```

SEE ALSO   SkipLine, Write

Other Object Models

The following object models are handy to have for reference, but you may not need them every day. Remember to use the Object Browser (F2 from the VBA environment) to examine the exact methods and properties available for any object or collection. If you have the proper help file installed (the system will tell you), you can select a property or method and press the F1 key to show the help related to that item that is selected in the Object Browser.

If the object set you need does not appear in the Object Browser (for example, you need access to the Word object model while in the Excel environment), you probably haven't added it to the available references. Select the References option to select the desired object models. The References option appears under different menus in different applications, but appears under the Tools menu in VBA. Simply place a check box to the left of any object model you need to examine. The objects will now appear in the Object Browser.

If you cannot locate the object set you need in the list, it may not be registered on your system. Make sure you have the application installed. If you still cannot locate it, you may just be overlooking it in the list. Some companies, like Microsoft, usually place the company name before the entry (for example, Microsoft Outlook Object Library), but not always. Initials are often used as well ("IE" stands for "Internet Explorer"). Carefully check the list for the item that you need.

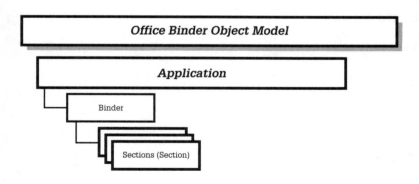

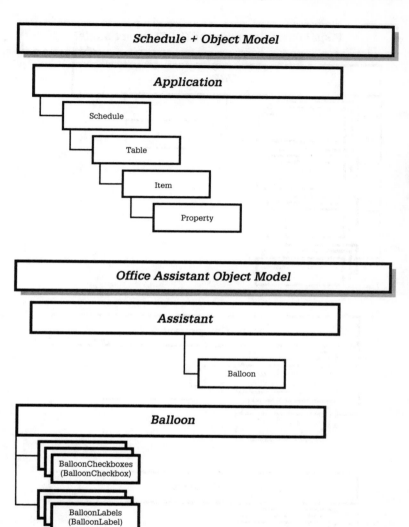

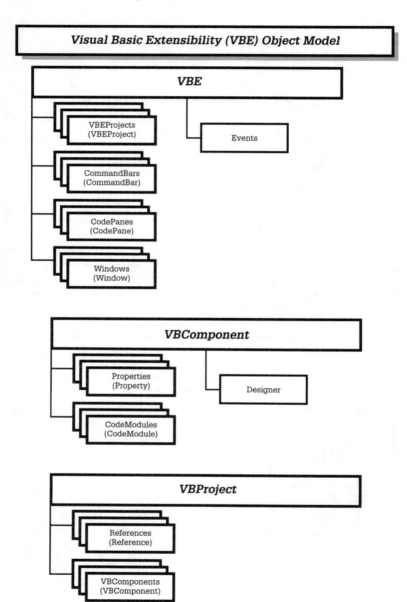

Microsoft Project Object Model

Application

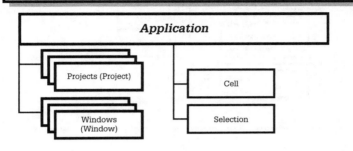

- Projects (Project)
- Windows (Window)
- Cell
- Selection

Project

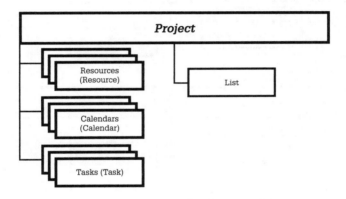

- Resources (Resource)
- Calendars (Calendar)
- Tasks (Task)
- List

Resource

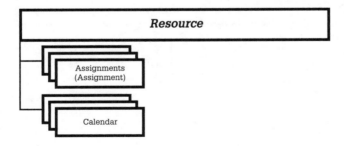

- Assignments (Assignment)
- Calendar

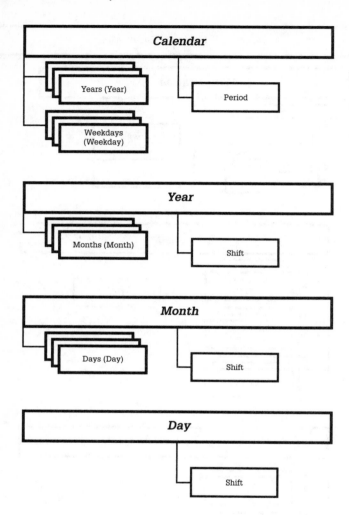

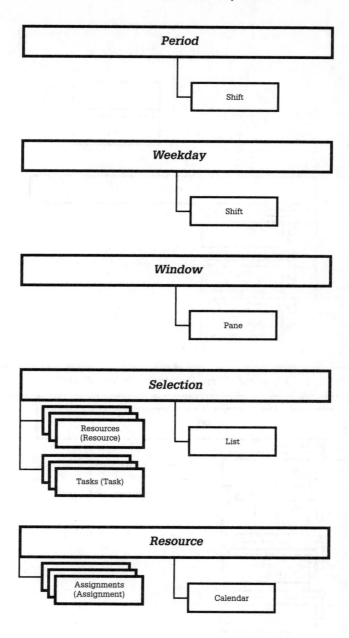

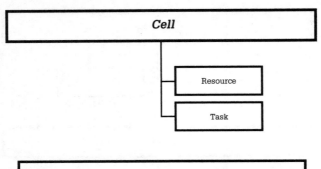

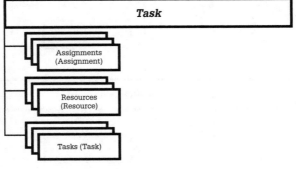

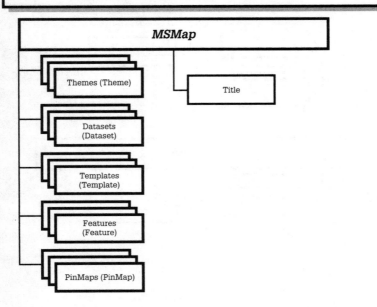

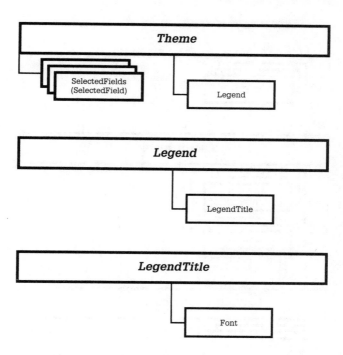

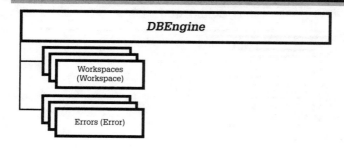

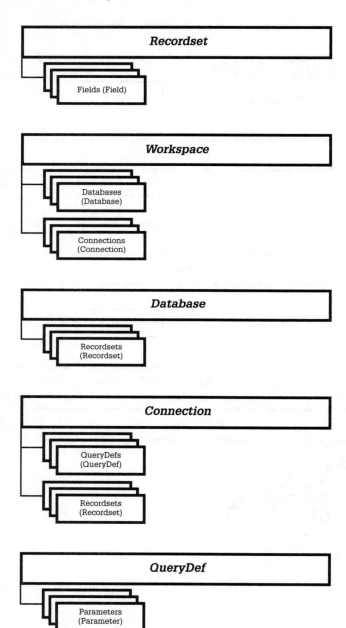